Diffusion of Distances

Diffusion of Distances

*Dialogues between Chinese
and Western Poetics*

WAI-LIM YIP

University of California Press

BERKELEY   LOS ANGELES   OXFORD

University of California Press
Berkeley and Los Angeles, California

University of California Press, Ltd.
Oxford, England

© 1993 by
The Regents of the University of California

Library of Congress Cataloging-in-Publication Data

Yip, Wai-lim.
    Diffusion of distances : dialogues between Chinese and
    Western poetics / Wai-lim Yip.
        p.   cm.
    Includes index.
    ISBN 0-520-07736-9 (alk. paper)
    1. Chinese language — Versification. 2. Chinese
    poetry — History and criticism. 3. Poetics. I. Title.
    PL1279.Y56   1993
    895.1´1009 — dc20   92-15325
                                                        CIP

For   Tzu-mei
     June
     David
     &
     Jonas

Contents

Acknowledgments

A slightly different form of chapter 1 first appeared as a conference paper, "The Use of 'Models' in East–West Comparative Literature," in *Tamkang Review* 6, no. 2, and 7, no. 1 (October 1975–April 1976). An earlier, much shorter version of chapter 2 was published as the Introduction to my *Chinese Poetry: Major Modes and Genres* (Berkeley: University of California Press, 1976). Portions of chapter 3 appeared in *New Asia Academic Bulletin* 1 (1978) and as "A New Line, A New Mind: Language and the Original World" in *Literary Theory Today*, ed. M. A. Abbas and T. W. Wong (Hong Kong: University of Hong Kong Press, 1981). Parts of chapters 2 and 4 appeared as "Classical Chinese and Modern Anglo-American Poetry: Convergence of Languages and Poetry" in *Comparative Literature Studies* 40, no. 1 (March 1974), and "Aesthetic Consciousness of Landscape in Chinese and Anglo-American Poetry" originally appeared in *Comparative Literature Studies* 15, no. 2 (June 1978). (Copyright 1974 and 1978 by The Pennsylvania State University; reproduced by permission of the Pennsylvania State University Press.) Chapter 6 was included as "Reflections on Historical Totality and the Study of Modern Chinese Literature" in the Comparative Literature Conference Proceedings in *Tamkang Review* 10, no. 1 and no. 2 (Fall–Winter 1979). A fragment of the Epilogue appeared in an article entitled "The Framing of Critical Theories: A Reconsideration" in *Asian Culture Quarterly* 14, no. 3 (Autumn 1968). I am grateful to the editors and publishers for permission to reprint.

The book was conceived as early as the academic year 1969–70 under an ACLS grant, although some of the essays written then were channeled into other contexts. In the next stage of the book's metamorphosis, the Committee on Research of the University of California came to my aid. To both the ACLS and the Committee on Research I would like to acknowledge my debt. While I was writing these essays, many colleagues and friends afforded inspiration and stimulation. I would like to single out for special thanks Professor Claudio Guillén (University of California, San Diego, and Harvard University), Professor Roy Harvey Pearce (University of California, San Diego), and

Professor Fredric Jameson (University of California, San Diego, and Duke University) for their continual trust in my ability to bridge the gap between Chinese and Western poetics, giving me courage to break into new terrains. A special friend, Professor William Rogers of San Diego State University, read my entire manuscript with fine discernments that made me reconsider some parts of my argument. He also made many stylistic suggestions. So did Professor Dan McLeod, who likes most of the poets I studied in this book. I am also grateful to Professor Stanley Chodorow, Dean of Humanities and Arts in the University of California, San Diego, for spending many hours in converting my manuscript from its more complicated computer format to a PC format that I could work with. It would have been a total nightmare if I had to retype everything from beginning to end. Finally, all my heartfelt thanks and love must go to my wife, Tzu-mei, who has been doing everything she can to keep me fit and sane so that I could embark on this rugged journey with comfort and satisfaction.

A Note on Transliteration

This book employs the Wade-Giles system of transliteration because to use the pinyin system would alter too many names, phrases, and titles long established in the English world. However, I have prepared a conversion chart at the end of the book for those who are familiar only with the pinyin system.

Prologue

Our ideal of vital being rises not in our identification in a
hierarchy of higher forms but in our identification with the
universe. To compose such a symposium of the whole, such
a totality, all the old excluded orders must be included. The
female, the proletariat, the foreign, the animal and
vegetative; the unconscious and the unknown.
> —Robert Duncan, "Rites of Participation"

In a sense, East–West studies are or could become the
climax for which all these years of comparative study
would have been a preparation. The great theoretical issues
regarding literature in general will only be fully faced, I
think, when two great bodies of poetry, the Chinese and the
European and Anglo-American, are jointly known and
reflected upon!
> —Claudio Guillén, letter to author

These are transparent words; both Duncan and Guillén propose to
widen the circumference of consciousness, a point that needs no ex-
planation and speaks quite eloquently for itself. And yet, both in the
classroom and in the published world, neither "the symposium of the
whole" nor "mutual reflection" between the East and the West (nor,
for that matter, between the "written" and the "oral" traditions) has
been given much serious attention. Despite a good deal of earnest
protest about cultural exchange, ethnocentrism (open or subterra-
nean) remains stubbornly entrenched in Western academia. One may
argue here that Oriental departments and other programs of ethnic
studies have been established (some are nearly a century old) and
that many translations have been made, some in as many as eighty to
ninety versions. But what is at stake here is not a question of "inclu-
sion" *only* (though, clearly, most current humanities sequences are
Eurocentric and many remain Euro-exclusive) but *also* a question of
representation. Simply put, it is a question of whether the indigenous
aesthetic horizon is allowed to represent itself *as it is* and *not as it is
framed* within the hermeneutical habits and the poetic economy of

1

the West. The essays collected in this volume, written for the most part between 1973 and 1988, compose a series of responses and challenges to, and dialogues with, the dominant mode of interpretation, which has not been particularly hospitable to literatures founded on non-Western aesthetic values or expectations.

I became aware of the problems of representation in cross-cultural contexts very early, although I did not really get a handle on this until I began to write on Pound's translations of Chinese poetry. Because I was a bilingual poet and translator, long before I began my graduate work, I read poetry across national boundaries as a matter of course. Of the translations I was reading at that time, English translations of Chinese poetry disturbed me the most. I found, to my dismay, formidable distortions of the Chinese indigenous aesthetic horizon in treacherous modes of representation. I was so enraged that when I published my first outcry against this distress,[1] I could not resist using Ezra Pound's judgmental phrase: "Wrong from the start." Translation is a "pass·port" between two cultures in which they face each other and through which they pass from one state to the other. It involves the confrontation, negotiation, and modification of cultural codes and systems. It requires a "double consciousness" that includes the state of mind of the original author (source horizon), as it was constituted by what Pound once called "the power of tradition, of centuries of race consciousness, of agreement, of association," and that of the expressive potentials of the target language (target horizon), which has its own "power of tradition, of centuries of race consciousness, of agreement, of association." Most English translations of Chinese poetry simply let the target horizon mask and master the source horizon. The translators seemed unaware that classical Chinese poetry possesses a whole different set of cultural-aesthetic assumptions, that its syntax is in many ways inseparable from perception, and that by imposing Indo-European linguistic habits upon the classical Chinese without any adjustment they were significantly changing the source horizon, a situation I tried to rectify in my *Ezra Pound's "Cathay"* (1969) and in the Introduction to my *Chinese Poetry: Major Modes and Genres* (1976). Unforgivable distortions and misfits are many, some of which are given a philosophical and aesthetic probing in chapter 2. Just to illustrate the kind and extent of these kinds of distortion, let me offer an example here that is not discussed in my book, although it is still a widely circulated misconception: that the Tao (Way) of the Taoists can be rendered as (the Christian) God or as (the Platonic) Logos!

Clearly, the case of treacherous representation of the OTHER in these translations calls for simultaneous investigations into both the source horizon and the target horizon, with equal attention and respect to the specific ways each of these horizons is constituted. When I became a graduate student in the early 1960s, I had hoped to be enlightened with methodologies and guidelines for such an investigation. As it turned out, the problems and questions I raise in chapter 1—"The Use of 'Models' in East–West Comparative Literature"—and have implied in the rest of this book were hardly taken up back then. There was (and I believe still is) a vague trust in some fundamental "universalism," as if one could judge all literatures on a single scale, as if there were one master narrative to which we can resort for all our evaluative activities, as if what had been valid literary standards for all Europe must also be valid for the rest of the world! Awareness of differences in models, the kind that I call for and outline in chapters 1 and 6 and the Epilogue, was totally absent, let alone the much-needed "self-reflection" on the various problems resulting from the unconscious internalization of certain models as primary norms and absolutes. For East–West students, there were no books to follow. Students were (and, unfortunately, still are in many universities in the West) often sent to take courses in separate departments— English, French, German, Spanish, Chinese, and so forth—as if, after sufficient exposure to different literatures, they would naturally come up with some truly universal "common poetics." But the fact is that most Western students and critics of Chinese literature are still being guided, unconsciously, by the critical assumptions of Western literature. I must hasten to add that there is nothing wrong with Western critical methods. As a matter of fact, with proper telescoping, they can be very stimulating and enriching to the study of Chinese literature, but the lack of awareness of differences in models will, at certain crucial moments, lead the scholar to judge the wrong things for the wrong cultural-aesthetic reasons.

What happened in the classroom also happened in published studies. Until quite recently, when a small number of scholars began to produce studies with concerns similar to mine, most articles and books on East-West literary relations have focused mainly on surface resemblances between two genetically unrelated works, the so-called parallel studies, without questioning the aesthetic grounding of each work separately, through comparison and contrast, so that the deeper, differing working dynamics of each system can be revealed.[2]

The distress I encountered as a graduate student and as a teacher,

both in the classroom and in the published world, has larger impli-
cations for university education. For example, if we are to have a
"symposium of the whole," how are we to reorganize the humanities
sequence, the so-called great books or major writers sequence, the
history of critical theories, the history of world literature, and the his-
tory of ideas? How are we to rewrite history in its totality? Central in
the answers to these questions is that the word "international" should
mean, literally, *inter*national, *inter*perception, and *inter*reflection; it
should mean that we must not see other cultures from one master
code or one hegemonic center of concern but from several differing
codes or several centers of concerns. The goal of cultural exchange,
like economic exchange, should not be to conquer one mode with
another but to provide a truly open forum for dialogue through
interreflection and "double perception" — that is, a gap or rift created
by the copresence of two sets of provisional responses to two cultural
"worlds." This gap or double perception allows us to mark the coding
activities of either system by those of the other so as to understand
more fully the making and the unmaking of discourses and hier-
archies of aesthetics and power. As I say in the Epilogue, different
critical and aesthetic positions will have a chance to look at each
other frankly, to recognize among themselves potential areas of con-
vergence and divergence as well as their possibilities and limitations
both as isolated theories and as cooperative projects to extend each
other. Here, I find that Fredric Jameson's recent reading of Gadamer
complements my views quite cogently:

> Each hermeneutical confrontation, between an interpreter and
> a "text," between an interpreter of one culture and the text of
> another culture, always mobilizes, at each pole of the interpre-
> tive encounter, a whole deployment of prejudice and ideology:
> one in terms of which the text, as an act, is to be understood, the
> other which motivates the interpreter in his attempt to appropri-
> ate this alien act. Such false problems as that of the "suspension
> of disbelief" imply that historical distance of this kind . . . is the
> fundamental barrier to understanding and needs in one way or
> another to be lifted, abolished or "suspended" in order for any
> adequate "historical" understanding or reading to take place. . . .
> Not only is this ideal of some abolition of the content of prej-
> udices of either or both sides of the hermeneutic encounter
> impossible, but such a suppression would in any case be
> undesirable, since what is wanted is very precisely just this
> encounter between ideological fields of text and interpreter.
> "Fusion" is not to be understood as the abolition of difference,

as the "formation of one horizon" . . . but a preservation of
tension, a coexistence within radical difference, a relationship
by way of radical difference.[3]

Thus, this orientation would not condone mapping a course for modern world culture or history solely through the coding interests of the West, namely the appropriation of the non-Western world in terms of the interests of globalization (or multinational trade) as charted out by the consumer-oriented, goal-directed, instrumental reason of the post-Enlightenment West. In place of the principle of domination, I would like to see a cartography that allows students to follow two or several courses at the same time. Likewise, in the mapping of a department of literature, a humanities sequence, or a book of the major texts of critical theory, I would like to see a truly open dialogue that preserves the tension between cultural differences and that remains open to rethinking the ways in which various trajectories of theories have been constituted. The margin must be brought back onto the stage as an equal partner to play out the differences.

My essays, both by raising metacritical questions concerning the application of theories and by probing into actual cases of convergences and divergences—in syntax, perception, consciousness of the world, aesthetic consciousness of landscape, the framing of hermeneutical-aesthetical paradigms, and so on—intend to seek out, through comparison and contrast, possible guidelines that can perhaps lead to a more reasonable mapping of cultural phenomena in their multiplicities. For, as I argue in the Epilogue, no theory can claim to be final. All theories of culture must be considered exploratory, looking toward a true convergence in the future.

I would like to take up this opportunity to raise another problem. To many readers, these are separate essays; they are not integrated and do not form a matrixed presentation. The fact is that, even though they were written over a number of years, they were conceived as interrelated, interreferential, and interdefining. One essay grows or branches from another. One essay complements the other. I am not unfamiliar with the conventions of constructing a so-called integrated, unified presentation. Indeed, I have studied and followed the rhetorical topoi of *exordium, narratio argumentatio* or *probatio, refutatio,* and *peroratio* or *epilogue,* but I have never been very comfortable with this rhetorical tradition, for several reasons. This way of constructing a "narrative," in spite of its dominance in the Western tradition, suffers from an inescapable reductionism; namely, one is forced to isolate and privilege one element among many and, through a process of selection, discrimination, and closure, to differentiate the so-called relevant from the irrelevant before connecting them according to some predetermined set of relationships. But is the so-called irrelevant really irrelevant? Let us take a real dialogic situation. Full communication in a real-life conversation seldom involves a clean, straight line argument but a lot of backtracking, reiterating, drifting, moving back and forth, and "digression." When recorded in writing, it will be "straightened out," euphemistically called "formalized," but we also know that in this process many nuances may have been suppressed and sacrificed, some of which, now cut off from the umbilical cord of the original moment, are waiting to be retrieved to be put into another context. Here we are reminded of William James's discussion of the role of the subjective will in breaking the total order in order to control it:[4]

> The conceiving or theorizing faculty . . . functions *exclusively for the sake of ends* that do not exist at all in the world of impressions we receive by way of our senses. . . . The world's contents are *given* to each of us in an order so foreign to our subjective interests that we can hardly . . . picture to ourselves what it is like. We have to break that order altogether — and by picking out from it the items which concern us, and connecting them with others far away, which we say "belong" with them, we are able to make out definite threads of sequence and tendency.[5]

I felt uncomfortable precisely because of this "breaking" and because, as I argue in great detail in chapter 3 and in the Epilogue, there is another mode by which we can minimize this breaking, namely, the Taoist project. The Taoist project began with full awareness of the restrictive and distortive activities of names and words and their power-wielding violence, opening up reconsiderations of language on both the aesthetic and political levels. On the level of aesthetics, by questioning the limits of language the Taoists suggest a de-creative–creative dialectic to repossess the prepredicative concrete world, which is immanent and needs no human supervision. This is achieved by employing a series of language strategies — asyntactical structures that leave the reader-viewer in an "engaging–disengaging" relationship with the world, the diffusion of distances to make revolving perspective possible, negative space to become a departure point for retrieval of the undifferentiated, the use of paradox and other off-norm words, phrases, or events to reinscribe the off-norms as norms and the so-called norms as off-norms. On the political level, the Taoist project becomes a counterdiscourse to the territorialization of power, an act to disarm the tyranny of language so as to reawaken the memories of the suppressed or repressed part of the natural self.[6]

It is no accident that a lot of critical and theoretical formulations in classical Chinese did not always follow the progression from *exordium* to *epilogue,* although such a progression is not exactly alien to the Chinese.[7] Instead, they chose a poetic form, as in the case of Lu Chi's "Wen-fu," or used the form called *shih-hua,* or "poetry talks," which are "fragments" on the art of poetry or anecdotes on poets and poetry rather than long-winded arguments and explanations. These "poetry talks" are like Arnoldian "touchstone" passages that remain stuck in our minds after all the Platonic-Aristotelian argumentations are forgotten. Or take *Ars Poetica (The Twenty-four Orders of Poetry)* by Ssu-k'ung T'u (837–908), a poem from which appears in the first section of chapter 5. The poems from this work are poems of *ars poetica*: They operate with a kind of hexagrammatic structure, rather than with linear argumentation, and use intercorrespondences and interwebbing to form a dynamic, multivocalic, thick-textured musical composition.[8]

Writing in English and in an academic context, I try to strike a balance between the two modes. Within each essay, I basically follow the strategies of a matrixed presentation, but I want to bring back to the larger structure an interwebbing, interdialogic activity among the essays. As such, I have indulged myself in a bit of musical play (thesis, antithesis, repetition, and variation of leitmotifs), a bit of wandering, and a bit of poetic structure to tease the reader into playing with the text instead of reading for a predetermined conclusion.

Here is a story about two walkers. They were told to get to the central library from the far end of the campus. One person was so intent upon the idea of getting there that he went straight to the library without paying any attention to the activities on the square, the art objects that were placed somewhat off the path leading to the library, the blooming flowers, the people along the way. The other person took a leisurely walk, stopping at times to watch someone playing a simple wooden flute, branching off from the main, straighter road to take a longer, roundabout route so that he could enjoy the flowers, dream about them, meditate on them for a few moments, and look at buildings and other human constructions, appreciating their co-extensive relationships with the trees around them, before finally arriving at the library perhaps an hour later.

Do we really have to hurry to the end?

1   The Use of "Models" in East–West Comparative Literature

To begin, listen to this fable:

> Once upon a time, there lived under the water a frog and a fish.
> They often played together and became fast friends. One day,
> the frog jumped out of the water and roamed for a whole day
> on earth. He saw many new and fresh things such as people,
> birds, cars, etc. He was totally fascinated by them and hurried
> back into the water to recount his new discoveries to the fish.
> Seeing the fish, he said, "The world on land was simply
> marvelous. There are people, wearing hats and clothes, with
> sticks in their hands and shoes on their feet." As he was so
> describing, there appeared in the fish's mind a fish, wearing a
> hat and clothes, with a stick under its fins and shoes dangling
> from its tail. The frog continued, "There are birds spreading out
> wings flying across the sky." In the fish's mind now appeared a
> fish spreading out its fins flying in the air. "Then there are cars
> rolling upon four wheels." In the fish's mind emerged a fish
> rolling on with four round wheels.

What does this fable tell us? It informs us about several related ques-
tions concerning models and the function of models in all mental
constructions. All conceptions, whether they be literary creations or
pedagogical investigations, proceed, consciously or unconsciously,
from some kind of model upon which most formal and judgmental
decisions depend. The fish, without having seen people, has to rely
on his own model, the model that is most familiar to him, to structure
his conception of human beings. A model is, therefore, a structuring
activity through which materials at hand can be fitted into a form.

Such activity can be best seen in the way in which a genre works upon the poet and the critic. When negotiating with existential experiences, the poet must seek out a form that presents them, perhaps a sonnet or a *lü-shih* (regulated poem), and a set of aesthetic strategies and techniques that capture the essence of these experiences to concretize some abstract ideas, and arrive at a luminous perspective from a variety of aspects in an ordered revelation. If and when the adopted model cannot accommodate the materials from existential experiences, the poet will modify or transform the model by adding, subtracting, and even reversing the strategies and viewpoints of the original form to create a new model for aesthetic purpose. When dealing with a work of art, the critic must also enter into the process of this structuring activity and must first know the adopted model and understand the manner of selection and combination the poet employs in modifying and transforming the model in question before fully commanding the working dynamics of the poem. Hence, Claudio Guillén says:

> A genre is an invitation to form. Now, the concept of genre looks forward and backward at the same time. Backward, toward literary works that already exist. . . . Looking toward the future, then, the conception of a particular genre may not only incite or make possible the writing of a new work; it may provoke, later on, the critics' search for the total form of the same work. . . . The genre is a structural model, an invitation to the actual construction of the work of art.[1]

But the selection of a model can give rise to very restrictive and sometimes erroneous results. In the fable, the fish's image of human beings was distorted, and we know where it went wrong: The fish confined his image of humans within the limits of his own model, but he was unaware that the human model is totally different; hence, he could not picture, structure, and understand human beings from the human perspective. It is needless for me to emphasize here the importance of getting outside the limitations of one's own model and point of view.

To move from the fable to literary investigations, the first possible response to the above argument could be this: Literary works are written by human beings, not by other species of animals. The work in front of us is derived from a human model, and, as the hypothesis could go, all human beings have the same fundamental organic and expressive needs. Thus, there can be no difficulty of the kind the fish encountered. Many critics, proceeding from this hypothesis, pronounce, therefore, that as soon as we grasp a fundamental unchanged model and the essentials therein, we can apply it to literary works of other peoples and other cultures. Such an assumption has been very popular with monoculturally oriented critics and scholars. But facts defy such a naive position. To begin with, we do not know how to establish such a fundamental model that can subsume other models without doing an injustice to them. Over the centuries people have employed many models — all of which are historically derived and determined, many of which are radically different from one another, and a few of which are mutually exclusive — to structure, combine, and judge. Perhaps we can assume that something like a fundamental model was possible with prehistoric people of "the first harmony" and that there was such an innocent state in which people, like young children unbiased by cultural specifications, were able to respond freely to the undistorted fullness and freshness of all objects and events in an essentially similar manner. But the word "culture" implies human-imposed structuring activities in our process of ordering things into some manageable form. It seems an unequivocal historical fact that the embryonic forms of these structuring activities or cultural models often differ with different people in different geographical environments. We must first have this historical awareness of differences in models in order to come to a more just perspective in East–West comparative studies.

We certainly do not want to believe that people could be subject to the same kind of erroneous image making that plagued the fish, but witness these passages:

> The Chinese, which, in its long duration, hath brought this picture down, through hieroglyphics, to a simple mark, or character, hath not yet (from the poverty of its inventive genius and its aversion to foreign commerce) been able to find out an abridgement of those marks, by letters.[2]

> BOSWELL: What do you say to the written character of their [Chinese] language?
>
> JOHNSON: Sir, they have not an alphabet. They have not been able to form what other nations have formed![3]

As if the letter — the abstract, arbitrary sign — is the most fundamental sign! These writers do not ask *why* there are ideograms and what aesthetic horizon, what thinking mechanics have conditioned such structural acts? They are not simply frogs inside the well (who see only a limited sky); they hold in their minds a model to which they are predisposed to regard as more excellent and more ultimate! I am not implying that the Chinese ideograms are better—to say this would be equally erroneous—but simply that the use of ideograms represents a system of thought (quite distinct from that represented by abstract alphabets) in which it is important that individuals communicate concretely in images and objects, to arrest things in their simultaneous multiple spatial relationships, and to suggest and represent an abstract idea by keeping close to the total environment captured in a composite image.[4] In contrast, thinking based on alphabet languages tends toward the elaboration of abstract ideas, analytical discursiveness, and syllogistic progression. Both linguistic systems have their advantages; both have their unique charms. It is the lack of a root understanding of these differences in systems of communication that has led to distorted perceptions.

Perhaps we should say that both Warbuton and Johnson were innocent, having, like the fish, no access to the other model. But what about the translators of Chinese poetry over the past one hundred years? A translator is at once a reader, critic, and poet who not only appreciates but also conceives, structures, and *decides*. When translators first came into contact with Chinese poetry, what assumptions took place in their consciousnesses, and how did such assumptions condition (in fact obstruct in some cases) their access to the original aesthetic implications of the Chinese model? I have dealt with this phenomenon in great detail in several articles.[5] I will repeat here only the parts that are most relevant to the discussion of models:

> For over ten decades, translators of Chinese poetry have been out of key with the original texts, proceeding from the assumption implicit in their practice that the essentials of the Chinese poem were to be grasped through interpretation and then recast into conventional Western linguistic structures. . . . They all ignore the special mode of presentation of reality constituted or made possible by certain syntactical structures in the Chinese lines.[6]

> All the translators, starting with Giles, must have been led by the sparseness of syntax in the original to believe that the Chinese characters were telegraphic—shorthand signs for a longhand message—and they thus took it as their task to translate the shorthand into longhand, poetry into prose, and to add

commentary all along to aid understanding. They did not know that the Chinese characters in the poem point toward a finer shade of suggestive beauty, a beauty which discursive, analytical, longhand "unfolding" destroys completely. The fact is that [the images in the Chinese poem], often co-existing in spatial relationship, form an atmosphere or environment, an ambience, in which the reader may move and be directly present, poised for a moment before he himself becomes part of that atmosphere, an atmosphere that evokes (but does not state) an aura of feeling . . . a situation [in which] he may participate in completing the aesthetic experience of an intense moment, the primary form of which the poet had arrested in concrete data.[7]

It is obvious that the Chinese aesthetic horizon here is intimately bound up with the embryonic perceptual procedures represented by the structures of the Chinese characters. The neglect of the Chinese model and the resulting distortions due to externally imposed Western models must be carefully rectified by East–West comparatists by probing into the root essentials of both cultural-literary horizons.

Similar distortions are found in other disciplines. Although most scholars would deny it, they assume that the model they use for one area of experience can be applied to other areas of experience. For example, when the early anthropologists investigated "primitive" tribal cultures, many of them depended upon the concepts and values of culture deduced statistically from Western history and concluded that certain tribes were uncivilized, backward, and barbaric. They did not know that the cultural values they were seeking (industrial progress, material superiority, logical thinking, etc.) are perhaps limited; they did not know or perhaps care that these tribes possessed *another* world view or another source and form of spiritual value that the West lacks and perhaps needs most urgently. Only recently have anthropologists and sociologists come to realize the limitations of their model of investigation, and slowly they are beginning to modify their attitudes. Again, we can look at some of the problems raised in minorities studies in the United States. Why did most black leaders so vehemently demand that Afro-American studies departments be headed by blacks, in particular, blacks from Africa? Because they have discovered that over the past centuries the image of black culture has been filtered through the colored spectacles of whites; its original form has been continually reshaped through the ideas of white people. They found that even some blacks themselves, having been immersed in white cultural consciousness for too long, have not been able to liberate themselves from it so as to see their own image from an indigenous point of view.

The importance of root understanding of models being fundamental, how are we to proceed to command them, particularly when models take so many forms? There are what we may call conceptual models (world views, concepts of nature, etc.), aesthetic and linguistic models, and functional models (genre, form, prototypes of characters, etc.). Since each model has its own potentialities and limitations, how are we to trace them out for use? We all know that what accounts for model A may not work for model B. Where are we to obtain the essentials shared by both models, the so-called universality, the "ideal forms" of Platonism, the "universal structures" of Aristotle? Can "universality" be established, can a set of structuring behavior patterns be found among three or four different cultural systems? Are we to proceed to discover such universals from the logical systems handed down to us since the Greek philosophers? Without denying the greatness of the Greek philosophers, their findings and concepts have their limitations and are perhaps not comprehensive enough for us to depend on. Let us look at a few recent critiques of the Greek system. First, from Jean Dubuffet's *Anticultural Positions*:

> One of the principal characteristics of Western culture is the belief that the nature of man is very different from the nature of other beings in the world. . . . The Western man has, at least, a great contempt for trees and rivers, and hates to be like them . . . the so-called primitive man loves and admires trees and rivers. . . . He has a very strong sense of continuity of all things . . . [and has] a feeling that man is not the owner of the beings, but only one of them among the others. . . . Western man believes . . . that the shape of the world is the same shape of his reason. . . . Occidental culture is very fond of analysis . . . [and] thinks everything can be known by way of dismantling it or dissecting it into all its parts, and studying separately each of these parts. . . . I have a very strong feeling that the sum of the parts does not equal the whole.[8]

Now Charles Olson's "Human Universe":

> The Greeks went on to declare all speculation as enclosed in the "UNIVERSE of discourse." It is their word and the refuge of all metaphysicians since — as though language, too, was an absolute instead of (as even man is) instrument, and not to be extended, however much the urge, to cover what each, man and language, is in the hands of: what we share, and which is

enough, of power and beauty, not to need an exaggeration of words, especially that spreading one, "universe." For discourse is hardly such, or at least only arbitrarily a universe. In any case, so extended (logos given so much more of its part than live speech), discourse has arrogated to itself a good deal of experience which needed to stay put. . . . We stay unaware how two means of discourse the Greeks appear to have invented *hugely* intermit our participation in our experience, and so prevent discovery. . . . With Aristotle, the two great means appear: logic and classification. And it is they that have so fastened themselves on habits of thought that action is interfered with, absolutely interfered with.[9]

Robert Duncan goes so far as to denounce Plato with these vehement words: "It was not only the Poet, but Mother and Father also, that Plato would exclude from his Republic. In the extreme of the rationalist presumption, the nursery is not the nursery of an eternal child but a grown-up, a rational man."[10]

These antirationalist criticisms are perhaps a little overreactive, but it is also true that Plato and Aristotle attempted to promote only a segment of our total experience (which must include both intuitive, direct experience as well as rational activity) as the model of discourse. And as such, the reliability of what develops from this prototype of discourse has to be called into question. When one of the structuralists, Lévi-Strauss, searches for common structure underlying different institutions and customs in different cultures, the method he postulates is likewise to be doubted. Lévi-Strauss says:

In anthropology as in linguistics, therefore, it is not comparison that supports generalization, but the other way around. If . . . the unconscious activity of man consists in imposing forms upon content, and if these forms are fundamentally the same for all minds — ancient and modern, primitive and civilized . . . it is necessary and sufficient to grasp the unconscious structure underlying each institution and each custom, in order to obtain a principle of interpretation valid for other institutions and other customs.[11]

"Unconscious structure" must mean a structuring method that rises above conscious and logical activity, but what method does Lévi-Strauss offer? The computer binary system, which postulates that all thought processes can be explained from the positive/negative binary relationships: animality/humanity, raw/cooked, and so forth. But such a system, as Dr. Leach once criticized, is applicable to only certain limited phenomena.[12] Lévi-Strauss's method is rationalistic and scientific in spirit, with roots reaching back to the Greek system, and is basically at variance with the unconscious activity he proposes to uncover. The difficulty confronting Lévi-Strauss can be understood in the words of Martin Heidegger, who in an imagined dialogue with a Japanese says,

INQUIRER: The danger of our dialogues was hidden in language itself, not in what we discussed, not in the way in which we tried to do so.

JAPANESE: But Count Kuki had uncommonly good command of German, and of French and English, did he not?

I: Of course, he could say in European languages whatever was under discussion. But we were discussing *Iki*; and here it was I to whom the spirit of the Japanese language remained closed — as it is to this day.

J: The languages of the dialogue shifted everything into European.

I: Yet the dialogue tried to say the essential nature of Eastasian art and poetry.

J: Now I am beginning to understand better where you smell the danger. The language of the dialogue constantly destroyed the possibility of saying what the dialogue was about.

I: Sometime ago I called language, clumsily enough, the house of Being. If man by virtue of his language dwells within the claim and call of Being, then we Europeans presumably dwell in an entirely different house than Eastasian man.

J: Assuming that the languages of the two are not merely different but are other in nature, and radically so.

I: And so, a dialogue from house to house remains nearly impossible.[13]

Linguistic models and thought systems are intimately related, insep-arable. The "houses" that Lévi-Strauss charts out scientifically from his myth studies pose the similar threat of incomplete communication between or among them. Most important of all, the computer can analyze works of intellectual, rationalist activity; it cannot easily handle the whole span of sense impressions and intuitive flashes of experience like those we find in poetic creativity, for example. (It is obvious that the so-called computer poem, computer music, and computer painting differ from human-created works in that the latter often contain sudden and unexpected elements not contained in works generated by the computer.) Therefore, we find that the most successful literary investigations done by structuralists are analyses of narrative literature (narrative poetry, myth, fable, and drama), in which the central task is to frame levels of meanings within the narrative. There is hardly any satisfactory structuralist treatment of lyrical poetry, part of the reason being what we might call the *chance* elements that defy the predictive range of binary thinking. One must recognize that although computers also possess the ability to make choices, such choices are made within the range of probability, the programming of which is performed by a person using logic, classification, and a range of choices conditioned by cultural upbringing. It is doubtful whether this programmer can achieve the miraculous predictive power that can subsume the operative dynamics of other cultural models.[14] Here lies the danger of the method of Lévi-Strauss.

Structural linguists like to talk about "deep structure" constructed out of "universals." They often begin with a "grammar tree" established from, say, English and apply it to other non-Indo-European languages. I had the chance to raise some of the following questions with my colleagues: There is no tense conjugation in Chinese; there is a different concept of time in the Hopi language; and there are no number distinctions in the Wintu and Tilopia languages; what roles do they play in the "deep structure" based on the Western model, which emphasizes these essentials? These linguistic differences were often pushed aside as anomalies and exceptions. I need not recount the specific aesthetic perception the tenseless Chinese has helped to promote, a fact I have written about on several occasions,[15] but let us listen to a linguist, Benjamin Lee Whorf, who tends to think that the implications of the so-called Hopi "anomalies" reflect a different world view. In his "An American Indian Model of the Universe," he links the grammatical "peculiarities" to the Hopi concept of cosmic order:

> I find it gratituous to assume that a Hopi who knows only the
> Hopi language and the cultural ideas of his own society has the
> same notions, often supposed to be intuitions, of time and space
> that we have, and that are generally assumed to be universal. In
> particular, he has no general notion or intuition of TIME as a
> smooth flowing continuum in which everything in the universe
> proceeds at an equal rate out of a future, through a present, into
> the past; or, in which, to reverse the picture, the observer is
> being carried in the stream of duration away from a past and

into a future. . . . The Hopi language is seen to contain no
words, grammatical forms, constructions or expressions that
refer directly to what we call "time," or to past, present, or
future, or to enduring or lasting . . . [or] that even refer to space
in such a way as to exclude that element of existence that we
call "time."[16]

Whorf thinks that we cannot even find adequate words in the
Western languages to clearly define the Hopi metaphysics. The "two
utterly separated and unconnected aspects of reality," space and time,
and "the threefold division, past, present and future," cannot contain
the Hopi cosmology. We can only approximate the Hopi cosmic
forms with tentative Western terminology. For instance, we can say,
the Hopi universe consists of what we may call the manifested and
manifesting (or unmanifest) or perhaps objective and subjective.

The objective or manifested comprises all that is or has been
accessible to the senses, the historical physical universe, in fact,
with no attempt to distinguish between present and past but
excluding everything that we call future. The subjective or
manifesting comprises all that we call future BUT NOT
MERELY THIS; it includes equally and indistinguishably all
that we call mental — everything that appears or exists in the
mind or, as the Hopi would prefer to say, in the HEART,[17] not
only the heart of men but the heart of animals, plants, and
things, and behind and within all the forms and appearances of
nature in the heart of nature, and by an implication and
extension . . . so charged is the idea with religious and magical
awareness, in the heart of the COSMOS, itself. The subjective
realm (subjective from our viewpoint, but intensely real and
quivering with life, power, and potency to the Hopi) . . . is in a
dynamic state, yet not a state of motion — it is not advancing us
out of a future, but ALREADY WITH US in vital and mental
form, and its dynamism is at work in the field of eventuating or
manifesting, i.e. evolving without motion from the subjective
by degrees to a result which is objective.[18]

This eventuating process cannot be translated into "will come" or
"will come to" but perhaps "eventuates to here" (*pewi*) or "eventuates
from it" (*angqö*).

Whorf has demonstrated excellently that to arrive at a universal
basis for discussion and understanding it is dangerous to proceed
from only one model; we must begin simultaneously with two or
three models, comparing and contrasting them with full respect and
attention to the indigenous "peculiarities" and cultural "anomalies."

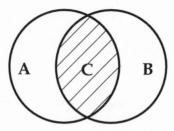

Figure 1. Cultural convergences and divergences

If we use two circles to illustrate this (Fig. 1), circle A representing one model and circle B another model and C, the shaded overlapping part of the two circles representing resemblances between the two models, then C is perhaps the basis for establishing a fundamental model. We must not apply all the structuring characteristics of circle A onto circle B or vice versa. Quite often, the parts that do not overlap (i.e., the divergences) can bring us closer than the resemblances to the root understanding of the two models. We must try, first and foremost, to command the working dynamics from the basic differences of the two models, defining these dynamics from within their indigenous sources and from without, by comparison and contrast, before setting up any fundamental universals. We do not for one moment doubt Jakobson's two basic operating axes in language — selection and combination — but we must admit also that different cultures would yield different modes of selection and combination. For example, one central function in Western poetry has been the metaphoric structure, but for many Chinese poems it is only secondary and sometimes even absent, such as in the poems of Wang Wei, Meng Hao-jan, Wei Ying-wu, Liu Tsung-yüan, and the Sung landscapists; these poems are, in essence, nonmetaphoric and nonsymbolic, poems in which the vehicle contains the tenor. Such poetry, coming from a Taoist thing-oriented ("to view things as things view themselves") aesthetic horizon,[19] naturally selects and combines according to a method quite different from that of human-oriented metaphoric poetry.

In our search for a root understanding of models, we must not take it for granted that once a model is established it remains unchanged. The model, stimulating poets to look for new forms and critics to make new summaries, constantly grows, changes, and stretches to fit new experiential demands. Sometimes a poet may begin with a model and, through modification and transformation, end up with a countermodel. Hence, when we proceed to define a model, we should also be aware of the historical formation of the model; the so-called extrinsic part of literature and literary history must be reintroduced to form a clear contour from which illuminating points can be made.

The use of models was hardly a problem in the early stage of Europe-centered comparative literary studies. One possible reason is the fact that, despite all the surface differences among the national literatures in Europe, their systems of thought, linguistic structures, and rhetorical procedures all derived from one common intellectual source, a source that emphasized the Platonic dichotomy of reality and appearance, the absolute status of space and time, and the value of logical elaboration and discursive syntax. These concepts continued from classical Greek antiquity through the medieval Latin and to the modern European national literatures. This has been most convincingly demonstrated by E. R. Curtius in his famous book *European Literature and the Latin Middle Ages*. While it is true that each of these national literatures possesses a strong local character and a color of its own, all of them share a common heritage on the level of perceptual and structuring activities.

Only in the past hundred years or so, when two genetically unrelated cultures, the Oriental and the Occidental, and their literatures have come into direct confrontation, has the problem of models become critical. Only then did Westerners begin to doubt the reliability of established models when applied to works of other cultures.

While the substantial differences would become an insurmountable challenge to the comparatists, it is exciting and gratifying to anticipate in such studies the possibility of arriving at a perspective that is manageably dependable and the possibility of widening the intellectual horizon of both cultures. In the midst of this enthusiasm, we must also become aware of the warnings of Ulrich Weisstein, C. T. Hsia, and Charles Witke:

> I do not deny . . . the relevance of Étiemble's call for a comparative study of such aspects as metrics, iconology, iconography, stylistics, but hesitate nevertheless to extend the study of parallels to phenomena pertaining to two different civilizations. For it seems to me that only within a single civilization can one find those common elements of a consciously or unconsciously upheld tradition in thought, feeling and imagination which may, in cases of a fairly simultaneous emergence, be regarded as signifying common trends, and which even beyond the confines of time and space, often constitute an astounding

> bound of unity. . . . Thus, studies of the kind represented by
> comparisons between Rainer Maria Rilke and Antonio Machado
> or Rilke and Wallace Stevens . . . are more easily defensible
> from the point of view of comparative literature than is the
> attempt to discover a likeness of pattern in Western and Mid- or
> Far-Eastern Poetry.[20]

These words of Ulrich Weisstein are depressing; he sounds as if we should not go beyond cultural limits to seek for wider horizons, and his tone implies a certain degree of closedness. The real issue that plagues him is obviously the problem of model.

C. T. Hsia warns us not to approach the classic Chinese novel with the yardsticks of Flaubert and James, who demand "a consistent point-of-view, a unified impression of life as conceived and planned by a master intelligence, an individual style fully consonant with the author's emotional attitude toward his subject-matter" and who abhor "didacticism [and] authorial digression"[21] — none of which seems to be diligently observed by the Chinese novel. Again, this calls for a root study of the aesthetic *raison d'être* of the Chinese novel, a subject that is yet to be fully defined and explored. Charles Witke gives similar warnings:

> Any group can absorb from a new group only as much as it can
> understand. Any new ideas can be incorporated only if the
> absorbing society is moving in the new group's direction in the
> first place. Otherwise, the absorbed group's concepts and its
> very language are simplified or adapted into the shape of the
> absorber's.[22]

The goal of cultural exchange is to open up wider vistas by mutually adjusting and mutually absorbing. Cultural exchange is not for the purpose of conquering one cultural mode with another established mode but to arrive at a full understanding of both modes through mutual respect. I cannot agree with Weisstein's closed attitude, and I refuse to believe that East–West comparisons would necessarily reduce to commonplaces and platitudes. Returning to the chart, the overlapping part of the two circles is still the focus for East–West comparatists. In other words I believe that fundamental patterns and structuring activities that rise above cultural bounds can be ascertained. I do not deny the possibility that a deep structure similar to that propagated by the linguists might surface. I only want to point out the perils lurking behind the assumptions in the application of models.

When Ezra Pound said in 1910 in the preface of his *Spirit of Romance*, "All ages are contemporaneous. . . . What we need is a literary scholarship, which will weigh Theocritus and Yeats with one balance,"[23] and when Picasso exulted over the cave paintings that seemed to leap out from time and space to assert themselves in vital rhythms, both were affirming the aesthetic core in art and literature that transcends cultural and temporal differences and linguistic limitations, a core of experience recognizable by all people from all ages. Such an experience is real; and that is why the American New Critics, spurred on the one hand by Kant, Croce, Coleridge, and the aesthetes of the late nineteenth century and, on the other, by the imagists' implied aesthetics of the concrete unmarred by abstract ideas, could proclaim an autotelic or autonomous aesthetic world within a poem. What the New Critics offered was the aesthetic structure in works of art. Although in their anxious effort to make claims for this aesthetic structure they have erred by shutting out all the historical elements that have gone into the making of this structure, we cannot deny the fact that they have successfully reminded historical critics of the equal importance of aesthetic considerations. As a result, almost all the later historical critics have absorbed in their criticism some degree of this formalistic approach.

It may not be out of place here to mention the battle between the French school and the American school of comparatists. Briefly, the French school (Van Tieghem, Carré, Guyard) emphasized historical evidence for every literary phenomenon and aimed at exhaustive information gathering to assure what they called *sécurité*. The investigations were often limited to "interrelationships," or influence studies, in which the accumulation of evidence brushed aside any aesthetic considerations. René Wellek (himself a staunch New Critic) attacked the French school for having totally ignored the literariness of a poem, the self-sufficient aesthetic core that rises above historical time. Together with Remak and Etiemble, he tried to promote comparative studies of genetically unrelated literatures. The perils inherent in both schools are by now too obvious to need repetition. What I would like to say here is that comparison and contrast of models from their indigenous sources can easily bridge the gap between the two schools, for any discussion of a model must necessarily include both the historical morphology of the model and its aesthetic structuring activities. For example, if we compare the uses of perspective and temporal structure in cubist and in classical Chinese landscape paintings (for the present purpose, let us focus only on the most salient features), it is not difficult to detect that both employ multiple or revolving perspectives as their compositional axes and both aim at the recomposition of synchronous moments of visual experience to constitute the sense of totality. And yet, there is between them such a degree of difference! The cubist painting is the recombination of fragments, while the Chinese landscape, simultaneously exposing the different sides of mountain scenery, is the recomposition of rocks, trees, and mountains, all recognizably intact and true to type, experienced at different times at different pitches (mountains seen looking up, down, across, around, etc.) during the painter's mountain stay and excursion (sometimes lasting over five years); the Chinese landscape is an environment re-created in its natural undistorted form and measure for the viewer to move in and about.

But here we must ask: Why fragmentation in the cubist paintings? Is fragmentation the reflection of mechanistic reality? Why no fragmentation in classical Chinese paintings? Each rock, tree, or mountain is realistically alive. Is it the reflection of the Chinese aesthetic emphasis on the self-so-ness (tzu-jan, nature as it is), the rhythmic vitality of natural objects as they are? The answers to these questions must come from the understanding of both the historical morphology and the aesthetic structure of each model. Thus and only thus can we avoid the pitfalls of "commonplace comparisons" of the early East–West comparatists.

For East–West comparatists of today, it has become even more imperative that they develop this awareness of models, particularly when neither of the two cultural horizons has expanded itself enough to absorb and include the circumference and structuring activities of the other. We have often come across these attempts: "The Romantic Poet Li Po," "Ch'ü Yüan Viewed from the Western Romantic Tradition," and so forth. Since there is not a "Romantic" moment comparable to that of nineteenth-century Europe in the classical Chinese period, we must first grasp the indigenous source of the Western model if we are to apply it at all to the Chinese works. We must know from inside the activities of the imagination so central to the Romantics. While this is no place to recapitulate all the aspects of this mental act, some of the essentials must be noted. In reacting against the empiricist philosophy, which holds that everything, including the mind, operates passively in accordance with some physical laws, the Romantics affirmed that the mind is active in perceiving and knowing the essence of the universe. Only poets are gifted with this imaginative faculty. Like the mystics in their epistemological search, they can perceive and know the metaphysical truth. But more than the mystics, they *perceive and express it simultaneously in language* and believe that perception should and can only be executed in poetic expression. Cognition, perception, and expression form one inseparable act. Hence, "Beauty is truth, truth beauty." The poets must be able to leap from the phenomenal world into the noumenal in their act of creation; the process often involves what Herbert Read once called metaphysical agony, precipitated by the overimportance given to the organizing power of the poet's individual mind. The "complete circle" of the medieval Christian cosmology now totally broken, the Romantic poets turned nature into a myth to provide for a framework within which a unified sensibility might be achieved. This, in turn, made it difficult for them to allow natural objects to emerge adequately as they are, a topic I discuss in great detail in my essay "The Morphology of Aesthetic Consciousness and Perimeter of Meaning in the Example of Pre-Romantic Concept of Poetry"[24] and chapter 4 of this book.

When a comparatist attempts to discuss Li Po or Ch'ü Yüan in terms of Romanticism, every attempt should be made to avoid judgments such as these: Ch'ü Yüan is a typical romantic poet, "a tragic figure, an outcast, incapable of fulfilling his ambitions in the secular world. Therefore, he finds solace in dreams, illusions and solitary travel."[25] This is to compare partial and surface resemblances as if they emerge from the same Romantic system! Had the scholar in question known the Romantic model at its root, she could have asked more pertinent questions. On what level, one may perhaps ask, and in what manner does the flight and quest in Ch'ü Yüan's *Li-sao* resemble the epistemological search of the Romantic poet, in spite of the fact that there is no metaphysical leap of the Romantic kind in Ch'ü Yüan? How do these quests and searches condition the syllogistical progression of both poetries? It is with awareness of this kind that the comparatist can find sounder and more workable points of departure from a model or models.

Indeed, the application of stylistic markers of a genre, movement, or period of one culture to the works of another is a very delicate matter. To begin with, there are many "narratives" about the morphology and meaning of a genre, a movement, or a period. Each narrative identifies a different set of markers, some of which may be mutually exclusive. Which narrative are we to follow when we turn to the works of a genetically unrelated culture?

Take the concept of baroque. Many competing definitions exist. In the words of Arnold Hauser, "the baroque embraces so many ramifications of artistic endeavor, appears in so many forms in the individual countries and spheres of culture, that it seems doubtful at first sight whether it is possible to reduce them all to a common denominator."[26] In fact, in the sphere of the visual arts alone, critics have come up with stylistic designations as diverse as "realist," "classicistic," and "decorative" baroques.[27] There is, according to Hauser, a vast difference between the baroque of courtly and Catholic circles and that of the middle-class and Protestant communities, ranging widely from the sensualistic, monumental-decorative to the stricter, formally more rigorous "classicistic" styles. The differences have much to do with the Counter-Reformation movement in Rome as well as the political and economic absolutism in France and Holland, involving very subtle and complex representations of power tensions and relationships.[28]

There is also this to be noted: In spite of Woelfflin's successful establishment of the term "baroque" as a period style designation, at least two things in his theoretical formulation need to be reconsidered, as aptly pointed out by Hauser. First, attempting to apply concepts of impressionism to the art of the seventeenth century, he singled out the "painterly," the "recessive," the "open form," and the "unclearness" at the expense of the classicist style, thus leading to the overemphasis on the unrestrained, the arbitrary, the unexpected, the wild, the accidental, the bold and startling, the discordant, and the contorted. Second, he considered the rise of the baroque—the development from strictness to freedom and so forth—to be a typical, consistently recurring process in the history of art, thus abstracting it out of concrete history.[29]

This formalistic emphasis led to very loose applications in other spheres of culture. Thus, we see the attempt to put Shakespeare, Jonson, Milton, Browne, Bacon, Crashaw, Donne, Dryden, and many others under one big umbrella and the conflation of metaphysical poetry, the gothic, Gongorism, and so on.[30] But baroque as a period style or genre was clearly culture-specific. Most, if not all, of the stylistic features are closely related to the socio-historical condition of the times. Aside from the heightened religious sense growing out of the tension between Reformation and Counter-Reformation and the glorification of power as part of political absolutism, there was a prevalent sense both of wonderment and bewilderment at a new sense of space brought about by Copernicus and Galileo. The replacement of geocentric Christian cosmology by heliocentric awareness was a form of displacement full of ambiguities. On the one hand, a new cosmos of infinite continuity of relationships of parts, at once heterogeneous and homogeneous, embraced humanity, affording it infinite new, expansive vistas. One the other hand, humans were also at a loss in the midst of this new relationship. As John Donne put it,

> And New Philosophy calls all in doubt,
> The Element of fire is quite put out;
> The Sun is lost, and th'earth, and no mans wit
> Can well direct him where to looke for it.
> And freely men confesse that this world's spent
> When in the Planets, and the Firmament
> They seeke so many new: then see that this
> Is crumbled out againe to his Atomies.
> 'Tis all in pieces, all coherence gone;
> All just supply, and all Relation:
> Prince, Subject, Father, Son, are things forgot.[31]

Much of the use of the conceit in the poetry of this period can be explained in the context of this ambiguous sense of replacement/ displacement. This is why this sensibility has been viewed both as a fault and as a merit; it was cited by Dr. Johnson as a means to allow "heterogenous" elements to be "yoked together by violence" but praised by T. S. Eliot as a marvelous sensibility by which poets were able "to fuse disparate elements together." This new cosmic sense caused individuals to shudder. Hauser's explanation of this shudder is quite to the point:

> At the end of this development the fear of the judge of the universe is superseded by the *"frisson métaphysique,"* by Pascal's anguish in face of the *"silence éternal des espaces infinis,"* by the wonder at the long unbroken breadth which pervades the cosmos. The whole of the art of the baroque is full of this shudder, full of the echo of the infinite spaces and the inter-relatedness of all beings.[32]

Indeed, this shudder is what the baroque is all about. The viewer is suddenly overwhelmed by sensualistic, bold, startling, fantastic, oversized, and almost improvisational details, which, aided by the intensification of optical and sensorial illusions, finally abandon themselves to the energy flow of a major theme or movement.

It is now clear that any discussion of baroque stylistic markers in works of other cultures must be conducted with full awareness of the historical complexity of this term. Thus, when James Liu entitled one of his studies *The Poetry of Li Shang-yin: Ninth-Century Baroque Chinese Poet*, we expect a discussion of this historical complexity together with a preliminary questioning of the feasibility of applying such a term to the work in question, but instead we find no discussion of the term in the main part of the book, which consists of translations of Li Shang-yin's poems and detailed analyses; Liu only made some passing comments in his essay "Li Shang-yin and the Modern Western Reader," using some general conclusions about baroque:

> Apart from ambiguity, Li Shang-yin's poetry shows a number of traits — conflict rather than serenity, tension between sensuality and spirituality, pursuit of the extraordinary or even bizarre, striving after heightened effect, tendency toward ornateness and elaboration — that would probably have been called "baroque" had he been a Western poet.[33]

But, precisely because Li Shang-yin was not a Western poet, we need to ask whether these stylistic markers mean what they meant in the culture-specific baroque of the West. I am not closing the door on the use of these stylistic markers; I just want to remind the user that he or she should ground these operative dynamics in their respective historicities before using them. Liu was aware of the problem and tried to offer a quasi-historical parallel:

> In cultural history, too, the ninth century in China is comparable to the seventeenth in Europe. Chinese literary historians customarily divide T'ang poetry into four periods, dubbed "early," "high," "middle," and "late" T'ang. This division, based mainly on the rise and fall of dynastic power, is somewhat artificial and not entirely satisfactory. It would be better to describe the development of T'ang poetry in terms of three successive phases: a formative phase . . . marked by experimentation and relative naivety, a phase of full maturity . . . characterized by great creative vitality and technical perfection, and a phase of sophistication . . . typified by tendencies toward the exuberant or the grotesque. It is not fanciful to see a parallel between these three phases of T'ang poetry and the quatrocento, cinquecento, and baroque periods of Italian art. Or we may draw a parallel between these periods of T'ang poetry and three successive periods of English poetry: The T'ang poets of the formative phase are comparable to English poets of the early sixteenth century like Wyatt and Surrey, those of the mature phase to the great Elizabethans, and those of the sophisticated phase to the

seventeenth-century poets traditionally called "metaphysical" and more recently labeled "baroque," such as Donne, Marvell, and Crashaw.[34]

One may want to ask how they are comparable? First, it is not difficult to find another stretch of cultural history that produces the same three phases of development, labeled by Liu as "formative," "mature," and "sophisticated," but it does not follow that the poetry produced in these three phases always comes out with the same "recurring" stylistic markers. Second, one wonders whether there is any truth in comparing these phases to those in Italian art and those in English poetry. How many readers will really feel that Li Shang-yin is like, say, John Donne? Third, most important of all, without the "shudder" before the newly discovered infinite space of the West, can we talk about a Chinese baroque at all?[35] Again, I am not saying that these stylistic markers cannot be used, but I would insist that those who do conduct their discussions with full awareness of their historical roots.

Since the use of models becomes a pedagogical problem only in studies between genetically unrelated cultures and before they come into direct confrontation, can we then say that, in the studies of recent Chinese literature—works after the May 4th Movement that have adopted Western forms and concepts as working models—we would not encounter this difficulty? Yes and no. First of all, one culture and its aesthetic horizon do not easily disappear merely because of the adoption of alien models. Very often, the poets may accept alien forms, attitudes, and thoughts only on the surface, whereas subconsciously the traditional aesthetic sense may continue to affect and condition the selection and operation of the alien models. One most interesting example is this: the Chinese romantic writers of the May 4th period adopted only the emotion-oriented romanticism (often in the extreme form of sentimentalism) and paid little or no attention to the more profound and, in fact, more central epistemological dimension (except perhaps Lu Hsün and Wen I-to, whose epistemological bent, if we can so call it, comes from a source different from the Western model). What cultural factors have made it so? Can we perhaps say the traditional Chinese emphasis on concrete reality-as-it-is, on phenomenal objects as final and complete by themselves, has made them resist this Western dimension? And what indigenous elements in the Chinese cultural milieu have made it possible for them to accept emotionalism with such unbridled enthusiasm?[36] When Leo

Ou-fan Lee in his *The Romantic Generation of Modern Chinese Writers* classifies these elements according to two prototypes, Wertherian, representing passivity and sentimentality, and Promethean, representing dynamism and heroism, he has indeed achieved a certain degree of success in delineating the temperament of these writers, but if he had proceeded with an awareness of the traditional aesthetic horizon to gauge the degree of conditioning involved in the adoption of these Western models, he could have given us an even more illuminating perspective into the cultural metamorphosis of this period.

When I say that the use of models is less problematic in studies of new Chinese literature, Joseph S. M. Lau's *Ts'ao Yü: A Study in Literary Influences* can be taken as an example. Ts'ao Yü deliberately modeled his plays after Ibsen, Chekhov, and O'Neill, and, as a result, we encounter very familiar structuring activities, both in characterization and plot. And yet, from the viewpoint of comparative literature, if such studies make no effort to compare and contrast cross-cultural models with traditional working models, they are less instructive and revealing; they do not lead to a wider convergence of cultural vistas.

The awareness of models can be useful to theorists and critics in yet another way. When a new literary movement is born — such as modernism, breaking away from Aristotelian discourse and conventional concepts of time and space — it either anticipates or grows toward a new expressive formulation. This new model is in its amorphous state, and its essential structuring activities are hardly recognized by readers still under the sway of established rules. If at this juncture we introduce literary and art models from different cultures — African, Oceanic, Amerindian, and Oriental — providing substantial differences from the traditional Western horizon and new resemblances to the emerging model, this will make readers see more clearly the strengths and weaknesses of their accustomed habits of mind. Perhaps they will also see the horizon offered by the new expressive needs and how they can positively complement what is lacking in their established model.[37]

2 Syntax and Horizon of Representation in Classical Chinese and Modern American Poetry

Legend has it that before composer John Cage began to lecture, he would shuffle his stack of notecards and proceed according to the resultant order. It was not exactly his faith in chance-as-order but the special way in which his lecture notes were prepared that made this procedure possible. Each note had to be a self-sufficient unit, free from sequential dependence on other notes. Only with this freedom could he begin with any notecard and always come out with a "coherent" lecture.

Now consider the palindrome poem in Figure 2, written in classical Chinese[1] by Chow Tse-tsung; it is a five-character regulated poem arranged in a circle. We can begin with any character, proceed clockwise or counterclockwise, and always come out with a new poem. There are at least forty versions in this text, and, according to the author, even if we also skip a character as we proceed, each five-character group will still form a perfect line. Clearly, this text cannot be translated into English and still work the same way. In English, as in all Indo-European languages, a sentence is almost always structured in a stipulated direction according to rigid syntactical rules. (For example, a subject leads to a verb to an object; articles govern certain nouns; past actions are to be cast in the past tense; parts of speech are clearly demarcated and determined, all in an act of predication to articulate and specify relationships.) Chow's poem can behave as it does because the classical Chinese language, as it is used in poetry, is free from syntactical rigidities—having no articles, personal pronouns, verb declensions, or connective elements such as prepositions and conjunctions and being indeterminate in parts of speech.

These facts quite often leave the words in a loosely committed

29

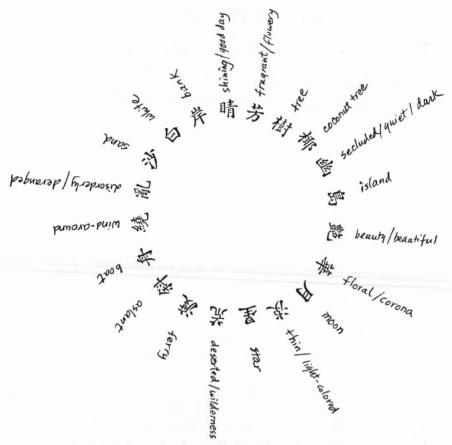

Figure 2.   Palindrome poem by Chow Tse-tsung

relationship with the reader, who remains in a sort of middle ground between engaging with and disengaging from them. Although not all Chinese lines can be syntactically as free as the present text, many Chinese poems capitalize upon this flexibility. This syntactic freedom promotes a kind of prepredicative condition wherein words, like objects in the real-life world, are free from predetermined closures of relationship and meaning and offer themselves to us in an open space. Within this open space we can move freely and approach words from various vantage points to achieve different shades of the same aesthetic moment. We are given to witness the acting out of objects and events in cinematic fashion and stand, as it were, at the threshold of various possible meanings.

In the real-life world, before we enter a "place," we cannot talk about "relationships" between or among objects. Objects have multiple spatial extensions, which remain indeterminate. Take, for example, a moon and a hut. If you look at them on level ground from a distance, the moon may appear *beside* the hut; but if you look at them from a high mountain, the moon may appear *below* it. Similarly, if you happen to be looking up at them from a deep valley, the moon may well be *above* the hut. Before we enter the scene and take up our viewing positions, the spatial relationships of "beside," "below," and "above" do not exist. Indeed, the spatial relationships will change as we move. The syntactic condition of classical Chinese poetic lines can often retain this indeterminate quality of not specifying viewing positions and spatial relationships, whereas English and most other Indo-European languages cannot. The lines

雞　　聲　　茅　　店　　月
cock/n. crow/n. thatch(ed)/n. inn/n. moon/n.

人　　跡　　板　　橋　　霜
man/n. trace/n. plank/n. bridge/n. frost/n.

give us objects in a real-life world in their barest, purest forms, as it were, uncontaminated by the author's subjectivity. We know from certain details—the cock's crow, the inn, the moon—that this is early morning and that a trip is involved. These details are given to constitute an atmosphere that strongly suggests the actuality of the situation, but we can never be certain where we should put the cock, the moon, the inn, and the bridge. Are we to visualize these, following the habits of English, in the following manner: (At) cockcrow, the moon (is seen above) the thatched inn; footprints (are seen upon) the frost (covering) the wooden bridge? We need not point out here that there are other possible ways of specifying the relationships between the moon and the inn. The moon, for instance, could be barely above the horizon. Not to determine fixed viewing locations, or not to use syntax to articulate such relationships, is to give back to the reader-viewer the freedom of moving into and about the scene, simultaneously engaging with and disengaging from the objects therein.

We can explain the predicative activities and habits of mind in Indo-European languages by the Western concept of perspective. Perspective refers to the fact that houses in the foreground appear bigger and houses receding into the background appear increasingly smaller until everything ends in an imaginary vanishing point. This is so because these objects are seen from a fixed location by one individual looking toward a fixed direction. But in almost all Chinese landscape paintings, we see scenes not only from the front but also from the rear; not one moment from one specific perspective but many moments from many viewpoints. In the words of Kuo Hsi of the eleventh century:

> A mountain looks this way close by, another way a few miles away, and yet another way from a distance of a dozen miles. Its shapes change at every step, the more the farther one goes. It looks this way from the front, another way from the side, and yet another way from the back. Its aspects change from every angle, as many times as the points of view. Thus, one must realize that a mountain contains in itself the shape of several dozen or a hundred mountains. It looks this way in spring and summer, another way in autumn and winter, the scene changing with the seasons. It looks this way in the morning, another way at sunset, yet another in rain or shine, the manner and appearance changing with morning and night. Thus, one must realize that one mountain contains in itself the manner of several dozen or a hundred mountains.[2]

Unlike Claude Lorrain, who directs the viewer by way of a clearly defined perspective, the Chinese artist proceeds from the belief that art should be in a sort of correspondence with the vital rhythms of nature. Just as we do not know a person by one encounter, we do not know a mountain by one viewing. The artist should, first of all, live with the "total" mountains and "total" rivers to know and feel first-hand their living reality by roaming in them for years, viewing and experiencing them in their different moments of appearance, in their various climatic and temporal conditions, and from all vantage points. After having lived with these experiential moments, the artist re-creates them all in a picture, avoiding one static compositional axis while offering simultaneously many axes to constitute a total environment in which the viewer is invited to roam and to consort with the *living* moments captured in corresponding vital rhythms. Therefore, the viewer is not restricted to seeing the scene from one static location *selected* arbitrarily by the painter. The viewer revolves, as it were, with the multiple perspectives available for viewing. In order to preserve this flexibility, the Chinese painter sometimes makes use of an emptiness that is at the same time a space of thingness, such as mists and clouds, to diffuse the distances, or manipulates the curving lines of mountains or other natural objects to camouflage the change of perspectives, subtly returning freedom of mobility to the viewer.

Aside from the diffusion of perspectives, the Chinese painter also avoids the use of a light source and chiaroscuro. Indeed, in the hands of Ni Tsan (1301–1374), the landscape becomes totally transparent.

Similarly, the syntactic flexibility found in many classical Chinese lines — indefinite positioning, indeterminate relationships, ambiguous and multiple functions of certain parts of speech, and so forth — allows the reader to retrieve a similar space of freedom for viewing, feeling, and reading, a space in which the reader stays in a middle ground, engaging with and disengaging from the objects appearing on the perceptual horizon. Take the common phrase *sung-feng* (松風, pine / wind). Are we to read it as "winds in the pines," "winds through the pines," or "pines in the winds"? Each of these English phrases imposes a clearly determinate or demarcated relationship between "pine(s)" and "wind(s)," but, by doing so, it has changed the original condition of our being placed in this spot, in which we see the pines and feel the winds simultaneously rather than being told or directed to see them only in a certain way. Take again another common phrase, *yün-shan* (雲山, cloud / mountain). Three or four possible ways of stating the relationships quickly come to mind: "mountains in the clouds," "clouds in the mountains," "clouded mountains," or "cloudlike mountains." But it is precisely because of the syntactically uncommitted relationship here between "cloud" and "mountain" that, as a mode of (re)presentation, such a phrase can subsume or evoke all four formations simultaneously. When the coextensive objects or images present themselves to our consciousness, clearly and transparently, we find ourselves, at the instant of this encounter, moving between them, tempted to articulate relationships between the two visual elements. But at the same time we refrain from doing so, knowing that predication or articulation of this kind will greatly reduce the fuller perceptual possibilities the instant has given us.

These kinds of asyntactical phrases abound in classical Chinese poetry. Here are some examples, all of which have led different translators to provide divergent formations in English:

1. *an-hua* (岸花) bank (as in riverbank) / flower
2. *ch'iang-yen* (檣燕) mast / swallow
3. *lou-hsueh* (樓雪) tower / snow
4. *kung-yün* (宮雲) palace / cloud
5. *lou-yün* (樓雲) tower / cloud
6. *hu-jih* (湖日) lake / sun

7. *feng-lin* (風林) wind / forest

8. *hsi-wu* (溪午) stream / noon [3]

Most of these examples work very much like the examples of "pine / wind" and "cloud / mountain" discussed above. In example 4, should we read it as "clouds surrounding the palace" or "clouds holding the palace"? In example 8, taken from the line "stream / noon / not / hear / bell" (given word for word here), are we to translate it as *"beside* the stream, *at* noon, (I? he? we?) do not hear the (monastery) bell"? What is lost here after we have determined the location (such as in *"beside* the stream") and the time (such as in *"at* noon")?

Or witness these two lines:

落　　花　　人　　獨　　立
fall(ing) / flower(s) / man / alone / stand

微　　雨　　燕　　雙　　飛
fine / drizzle / swallow(s) / pair / fly

Suppose we read or translate these as

Among the falling flowers, there stands a man.
Through the fine drizzle, swallows, in pairs, fly.

Reading these lines this way seems to have engendered some significant loss. In the Chinese, objects emerge and directly act themselves out before our eyes; they are clear, transparent, and true to their spatial extensions. In the translated lines, very much in the manner of Longfellow's "Under the spreading chestnut tree, the village smithy stands," the dramatic quality of immediate presence is gone, and the independence of the objects is disturbed, because between the reader-viewer and the scene we now have an interpreter pointing out relationships and explaining things. The reader's perception is now very much guided in certain directions stipulated by the subjective interests of the poet.

Try another two lines by Tu Shen-yen (600–700):

雲　　霞　　出　　海　　曙
cloud(s) / mist(s) / go out / sea / dawn

梅　　柳　　渡　　江　　春
plum(s) / willow(s) / (a)cross / river / spring

Are we to provide "missing links" according to the habits of English, such as those italicized below?

Clouds and mists *move* out *to* sea *at* dawn.
Plums and willows *across* the river *bloom in* spring.

There is something quite distorted in this version when compared to the original order of the immediate presencing of things. The word "dawn," for example, can be a noun indicating time, as in "at dawn," or a verb indicating the act of dawning. Similarly, the word "spring" has multiple meanings. The juxtaposition of "plums," "willows," and "spring" easily evokes "bloom," but clearly the word is imposed from outside the Chinese original. Compare the above translated version with the following experimental attempt:

Clouds, mists
out to sea:
Dawn.
Plums, willows
across the river:
Spring.

The difference in perception and reception is clear.

Now let us look at a short poem by the eighth-century Chinese poet Meng Hao-jan, laid out vertically, as it was done in the original, with word-for-word translations for the characters plus some tentative indications of their grammatical functions (using English classifications).

移 1. move (v)

舟 boat (n)

泊 moor (v)

煙 smoke (n, adj)

渚 shore (n)

日 2. sun (n)

暮 dusk (v)

客 traveler (n)

愁 grief (n)

新 new (adj, v [in Chinese])

野 3. wild, wilderness (n, adj)

曠		far-reaching, vast (adj)
天		sky (n)
低		low (v, adj)
樹		tree (n)
江	4.	river (n)
清		clear (adj)
月		moon (n)
近		near (v, adj)
人		man (n)

We can now tackle the question of the absence of personal pronouns. Who moves the boat to moor by the smoke-shore? Shall we assume, as have most translators, that the speaker "I" is always behind a poetic statement or image? What is the difference between putting the "I" into the poem and not putting it there? Just as Chinese painters avoid restricting their paintings to one perspective, the Chinese poet refrains from restricting the poetic state to only one participant. This freedom to begin a sentence without the use of any personal pronoun, a practice that is quite common in Chinese poetry, has the effect of returning to the reader-viewer the freedom to move into the ambience provided by the poet and take part in it directly. Indeed, the absence of the personal pronoun often offers the reader-viewer a doubleness in perception. Take the famous little poem by Li Po (701–762), "Jade Steps Grievance":

玉　　　階　　　生　　　白　　　露
jade / step(s) / grow / white / dew(s)

夜　　　久　　　侵　　　羅　　　襪
night / late / soak/(attack) / gauze / stocking(s)

卻　　　下　　　水　　　晶　　　簾
let / down / crystal / — / blind(s)

玲　　　瓏　　　望　　　秋　　　月
glass-clear / watch / autumn / moon

The verb that calls for a pronoun as its subject is "let down." If the reader supplies "she" as the subject, then the reader is standing outside looking in *objectively*, so to speak, at an object (the court lady). But "I" can also be supplied for "let down," in which case the reader is also *subjectively* looking out, being identified with the protagonist. In other words, the absence of a personal pronoun allows the reader to approach reality at once objectively and subjectively, simultaneously moving back and forth between the two positions.[4]

The previously considered poem by Meng Hao-jan contains a number of actions as well. Actions, the Westerner knows, take place in time, and yet the classical Chinese language is tense*less*. Why tenseless? Shall we cast these actions into the past, as do some of the examples that follow? The fact is that if the Chinese poet has avoided restricting actions to one specific agent, he has also refrained from committing them to finite time—or perhaps the mental horizon of Chinese poets does not lead them to posit an event within a segment of finite time. For what, indeed, is past, present, and future in real time? As soon as I pronounce the word "now," it is already in the past. The concepts of past, present, and future belong to the world of ideas; it is a human invention imposed upon Phenomenon,[5] or the undifferentiated mode of being, which we break into many linear orders as if they were authentic representations of the reality of time. The words of the Taoist Chuang-tzu are instructive here: "There is a beginning. There is a not yet beginning to be a beginning. There is a not yet beginning to be a not yet beginning to be a beginning."[6] Just as the concepts of "beginning," "middle," and "end" were proposed at the risk of cutting time into sections, those of "past," "present," and "future" are also artificial demarcations that break the undifferentiated mode of being into units and segments for subjective control.

It is obvious that we cannot approach this and most Chinese poems with the arbitrary time categories of the West. The Western ways of territorializing being conceal being rather than exposing it; they turn us away from the appeal of the concreteness of objects and events rather than bringing us into immediate contact with them.

The capacity of the Chinese poem to be free from the arbitrary temporal constructs of the West—to maintain a certain degree of close harmony with the concrete events in reality—can be illustrated by the way cinema handles temporality, for film is a medium that most felicitously approximates the immediacy of experience. Without mulling over the complex use of time and space in the art of film, let us address fundamental issues. For our purpose, a passage from Stephenson and Debrix's introductory book, *The Cinema as Art*, will make this clear. Cinema has "a natural freedom in temporal construction. . . . The lack of time prepositions and conjunctions, tenses and other indications . . . can leave the film free to reach the spectator with an immediacy which literature is unable to match."⁷ Time prepositions and conjunctions such as *"before* he came" and *"since* I have been here" do not exist in a film, nor in the actual events of life. There is no tense in either case. "When we watch a film," say Stephenson and Debrix, "it is just something that is happenning—now."⁸

Let us return for a moment to lines 3 and 4 in Meng Hao-jan's poem. We have already witnessed the doubling or tripling activity in words whose parts of speech remain indeterminate. In this case, the indeterminate relationship between the objects before and after "low" (or "lowers") and "near" (or "nears") opens very intriguing decision-making strategies. Take line 3. Is it the vastness of the wilderness that has lengthened the sky, lowering it to the trees, or is it the breadth of the stretch of the trees that seems to pull the sky to the wilderness? Should the translation be *"as* the plain *is* vast, the sky *lowers* the trees"? It seems that in reading it this way we will lose the immediate cinematic visuality in the original, a visuality that is promoted by a sort of spotlighting activity or mobile point of view offered the spectator. We will lose the acting out of the objects, the *now*ness and the concreteness of the moment, for, taking "low" as an adjective, the line can well be seen as three visual units—"vast wilderness, sky, low trees" —or, slightly modified but keeping to the visual order of the moment:

> Open wilderness.
> Wide sky.
> A stretch of low trees.

In this case, our perceptual activity almost mimics that of the movie camera, starting with a pan of the vast wilderness, followed by a tilting shot of the wide sky, then lowering and zooming closer to a stretch of low trees.

Now that we have a better sense of the play enhanced by the sparse syntax, the absence of personal pronouns as subjects, the tenseless quality of the Chinese verb elements, and so forth, we can be more adequately critical of most of the English translations of classical Chinese poetry, as the following examples will illustrate.⁹ (Italicized words indicate the translator's insertions to supply what he believed to be the missing links; italicized words in parentheses indicate the translator's interpretation or paraphrase of the original images.) In the examples below, the widely divergent renderings of the third line are especially notable.

I steer *my* boat *to* anchor
      by the mist-clad river
And *(mourn) the* dying day *(that brings me*
      nearer to my fate.)
Across the woodland wild *I see*
      the sky *(lean on) the* trees,
While close to hand the *(mirror)* moon
      (floats on) the shining streams.
                    Giles, 1898

Our boat *by the* mist-covered islet *we* tied.
    The sorrow *of absence the* sunset *brings* back.
    (Low breasting the foliage the sky loomed black.)
The river *is* bright *with* the moon at our side.
                   Fletcher, 1919

While my little boat moves on its mooring mist.
And (daylight wanes, old memories begin. . . .)
(How wide the world was, how close the trees to heaven!)
(And how) clear in the water the nearness of the moon!
                   Bynner, 1920

At dusk *I* moore*d my* boat *on* the banks of the river
With the oncoming night *(my friend) is* depressed
(Heaven itself seems to cover over the gloomy trees of the
    wide fields.)
(Only) the moon, shining on the river, is near man.
                   Christy, 1929

I move *my* boat and anchor in the mists *off* an islet;
With the setting sun the traveller's heart grows melancholy
    once more.
(On every side is a desolate expanse of water.)
(Somewhere) the sky comes down to the trees
And the clear water *(reflects)* a neighboring moon.
                   Jenyns, 1944

I need hardly point out that these translations are secondary elabora-
tions of some primary form of experience, the unfolding of some
schemata into separate parts. All the translators, starting with Giles,
must have been led by the sparse syntax in the original to believe
that the Chinese characters were telegraphic — shorthand signs for a
longhand message — and they thus took it as their task to translate

the shorthand into longhand, poetry into prose, and to add commentary all along to aid understanding, not knowing that the characters are "pointers" toward a finer shade of suggestive beauty that the discursive, analytical, longhand "unfolding" destroys completely.

It has been often said that Chinese syntax closely resembles that of English, namely, that they both follow the natural succession of an action, as in "John kicks a ball" (subject–verb–object). This is true to a certain degree, as, for example, in these two lines from a Li Po poem:

青　　山　　横　　北　　郭
Green / mountain(s) / lie across / north / wall

白　　水　　繞　　東　　城
White / water / wind around / east / city

These lines should translate easily into English. And yet, in the hands of Giles and Bynner, these lines become

Where blue hills cross the northern sky,
Beyond the moat which girds the town,
'Twas here. . . .

Giles, 1898

With a blue line of mountains north of the wall,
And east of the city a white curve of water,
Here you must. . . .

Bynner, 1920

Whereas in the original we see things working upon us, in the versions of Giles and Bynner we are *led* to these things by way of intellectual, directive devices ("where," "with," etc.). Clearly, what has happened here is that a different sort of hermeneutical habit of perceiving and reading has intruded upon a rather clear-cut condition or state of being. If distortion of aesthetic horizon can happen even in this "simple" case, namely, a subject–verb–object construction that should lend easily to translation in English, we can see why lines of asyntactical or paratactical construction, which abound in Chinese poetry, invite even greater deviations from the original order of impression. Ultimately, it is perhaps not English or other Indo-European languages per se that are guilty of such distortions but matters of perceptual orientation and priority that enter into such gross misreadings. Or, rather, it is a different sense of authentication we are dealing with.

The question of authenticating experience is a complex one. Clearly, different philosophical orientations and cultural and psychological conditions would lead to divergent modes of authentication. But even on the most rudimentary level, there is this to be noted: Our contact with the world is an *event* in which things concretely emerge from total phenomena, an active *happening* that defies containment, that is, at the moment of its unfolding, by concepts and meanings. Upon our contact with phenomena, what arises in our sentient network is not only intellectual or ideational activities but also visual, auditory, tactual, taste, olfactory, or even transsensual experiences. Quite often, we take in this compound moment in full *before* allowing it to terminate in ideas. One may argue that the reproduction of the sense of vision is the task of the painter, that of the sense of hearing is the task of the musician, and so forth. The forming of ideas is, as the logic goes, the task of the poet, as if to say the express objective of literature is nothing but articulating relationships among things and human beings. The making of meanings and ideas can, no doubt, be the end of a literary work, but it definitely is not its total aim. A literary work would do well to disclose the actuality of the moment of contact, the total sensing horizon. While it is a fact that poetry, as a linguistic artifact, cannot approximate many of the qualities of those reproduced by other media, such as colors, lines, and tones, this should not preclude a user of words from attempting to circumscribe the other sentient activities. Language, under suitable manipulation, can evoke the semblance of the visuality of painting and the tonality of music; in particular, it can approximate the morphology of the sensing process, but one must not allow the ideational activities to overwhelm or even impede the immediate emergence and presencing of things from total phenomena. Take this line from Tu Fu:

綠　　垂　　風　　折　　筍
Green / dangle / wind / break / bamboo shoots

Many readers are inclined to see syntactic inversion in this line and thus read it as "The wind-broken (tender) bamboo shoots are dangling green." This reading, or this way of writing (predication), ignores the grammar of experience at work. Imagine the actuality of the situation: the poet, traveling, encounters suddenly a green dangling. At this moment, he cannot tell what it is. It is only later that he finds that it is a young bamboo broken by the wind. "Green / dangle /

wind-broken / bamboo shoots" is the grammar of language following the grammar of experience. "The wind-broken bamboo shoots are dangling green," which adheres to the *conventions* of language but belies the experiential process, is the conclusion after the fact, not the actuality of the moment.

In a sense, it is the consideration of this kind of authenticating attempt in Chinese poetics that has led Chinese poets to bypass many of the syntactic restraints from which the Chinese language is not totally free, even though it is true that a large degree of syntactic flexibility in the Chinese language, as that demonstrated in the palindrome poem, has greatly enhanced the possibility of authentication. Thus, the prevalence of asyntactical or paratactical lines in Chinese poetry can be understood precisely as an attempt to readjust language (which is, by definition, restrictive) to fit in better with the moment of contact (by definition, open to multiple sensing channels and perspectives). Some examples are in order:

星　　臨　　萬　　戶　　動
Star(s) / come / ten thousand / house(s) / move.

Compare this line with "*While* the stars *are twinkling above* the ten thousand households," or "*When* the stars come, ten thousand houses move," or "The stars *cause* ten thousand houses (to) move." These readings have changed the visual events into statements about the events, which the Chinese presents to our consciousness as two cinematic shots. As a result, the English readings have restricted the interplay between them.

Central to this perceptual orientation is the attempt to promote the visuality of objects—to preserve the spatial tensions and counterpoints between them and to mimic the order of appearance of events by spotlighting phases of perception. Thus, to translate the lines

星　　垂　　平　　野　　闊
Star(s) / dangle / flat / plain / broad(ens)

月　　湧　　大　　江　　流
Moon / surge(s) / big / river / flow(s)

into either of the following[10]

> The stars lean down from open space
> And the moon comes running up the river.
> Bynner

Stars drawn low by the vastness of the plain
The moon rushing forward in the river's flow.
                                                    Birch

is to ignore the spatial coexistence and the dramatic presence of these
events. Although one finds great beauty in the translated lines, it is a
beauty of impressions that are different from those of the original.
We can now understand why one wants to resist the introduction of
analytical elements among visual units in the following lines:

月　　落　　烏　　啼　　霜　　滿　　天
1. Moon / set(s) / crow(s) / caw / frost / full / sky

野　　渡　　無　　人　　舟　　自　　横
2. (in) wilderness / ferry / no / man / boat / by itself / sideways

殘　　月　　曉　　風　　楊　　柳　　岸
3. waning / moon / morning / wind(s) / willow(s) / — / bank

Poems or even lines that emphasize the miming of the activities of
the perceiving act and focus on visual events in their various grada-
tions of color and light suffer the most in English translation. Let us
look at one such violation:

空　　山　　不　　見　　人
Empty / mountain / not / see / man
                    Wang Wei, 701–761

becomes, in Bynner's hand,[11]

There seems to be no one on the empty mountain.

The analytical or explanatory "There seems to be" is, of course, the
translator's interference in the direct contact between the "empty
mountain" and the viewer-reader. To put "no one" ahead of "empty
mountain" violates the life of the moment: We should notice the
emptiness, the openness, *before* we are aware of the other state of
being.

Let us look at a few more examples from Wang Wei, who is prized
for his ability to turn language into gestures miming the perceiving
act:

白　　雲　　迴　　望　　合
White / clouds / looking back / close up

青　　靄　　入　　看　　無
Green / mists / entering / to see / nothing.

There are changing perspectives in each line: "White clouds" (shot one), from a distance; "looking back" (shot two), viewer coming out of the mountain from the opposite direction, turning his head back; "close up" (shot three), viewer returning to same position as for shot one. The visual events are accentuated the way a mime, in order to suggest an event that is not visible, highlights gestures and movements to suggest the energy flow that originally supports that event. Arne Zaslove, in a demonstration-lecture in the Project for Music Experiment at the University of California, San Diego, in January 1973, gave an example that articulates most clearly the energy flow of the moment: "Supposing you are carrying a heavy suitcase with both hands." Zaslove proceeded to place both of his hands on the imaginary handle and lift the imaginary heavy suitcase. "You will find," he said, "that your whole body has to bend sideways toward your right to balance off the weight. If at this point you should bend toward the left, the miming act is false and becomes unrecognizable."

As signs, words function best when they capture the life mechanism of the moment of experience in ways similar to those described by Zaslove. Let us examine two more examples — the first from Wang Wei — that suggest the articulation of visual curves and movements:

大　　漠　　孤　　煙　　直
Vast / desert / lone / smoke / straight

"Vast desert," a panoramic view; "lone smoke" from possibly one single household, a single object in the midst of an immense expanse of emptiness; "straight," a windless condition true to the actuality of a desert. The line has the appeal of a painting; with the word "straight," it is almost sculptural.

Consider this line by Li Po from his poem "To See Meng Hao-jan off to Yangchou":

孤　　帆　　遠　　影　　碧　　空　　盡
A lone sail, a distant shade, lost into the horizon

Here we witness the progression of the boat moving slowly from the foreground and disappearing in the distance, suggesting both the duration of time Li Po has been standing by the Yangtze River watching his friend's boat move away and, indirectly, the deep bond of their friendship.

Now let us consider a few complete poems:

Dried vines, an old tree, evening crows;
A small bridge, flowing water, men's homes;

> An ancient road, west winds, a lean horse;
> Sun slants west:
> A heart-torn man at sky's end.
> > Ma Chih-yüan, ca. 1260–1341

In this poem, which operates pictorially rather than semantically, the successive shots do not constitute a linear development (such as how this leads to that). Rather, the objects coexist as in a painting, and yet the mobile point of view has made it possible to temporalize the spatial units.

And witness this poem:

> A thousand mountains — no bird's flight.
> A million paths — no man's trace.
> Single boat. Bamboo-leaved cape. An old man.
> Fishing alone. Ice-river. Snow.
> > Liu Tsung-yüan, 733–819

The camera first gives us a bird's-eye view with which we can at once take possession of the totality of the scene, as in all the classical Chinese landscape paintings, and then zooms in on one single object, an old man in the midst of the vast frozen river surrounded by snow. Unlike film, however, which often focuses on events to be strung together with a story line, the cinematic movement here reproduces the activities of the perceiving act of an intense moment, the total consciousness of which is not completed until all the visual moments have been presented — again, as in a classical Chinese painting. The spatial tensions here put us into the center of Phenomenon, allowing us to reach out to a larger circumference.

I once conducted a session on the structure of Chinese characters in an American grade school. After I had finished explaining how some of the Chinese characters are pictorially based, the signs matching the actual objects, a boy proceeded, naively, to pose a sagacious question: "All these are nouns — how are they to form ideas?" It seems legitimate to pose the same question about many of the Chinese lines above. I believe the question is answered, in part, in my earlier analysis of Liu Tsung-yüan's poem, in which the spatial tensions and relationships between the immeasurable cosmic scene and a speck of human existence (in the figure of an old man fishing) project, without comment, a picture of the condition of humanity in nature.

I answered the boy's question by bringing out another category of

Chinese characters. The three characters I chose were 時, 言, and 詩. The character 時 ("time") consists of the pictograph ⊙ "sun" and 业, a pictograph developed from an ancient picture of a foot touching the ground 业, which came to mean both "stop" (the modern form of which is 止) and "go" (the modern form of which is 之). What the ancient pictograph 业 means is, then, the termination of a previous movement and the beginning of another, a measured, dancelike activity. Thus, the earliest Chinese viewed the measured stop-and-go movement of the sun as the idea of time. The earliest pictographic stage of 言 was 舌, denoting a mouth blowing the tip of a flute. This character now means "speech," "message," or "word," which, to the early Chinese people, was to be in rhythmic measure. The third character means "poetry," which consists of two pictographs we are now familiar, namely, 舌 (rhythmic, measured message) and 业 (dancelike, measured, stop-and-go movement). In all three cases, two visual objects are juxtaposed to form an idea. As we may recall, this structural principle of the Chinese character inspired Sergei Eisenstein to conceive the technique of montage in film. In his "The Cinematographic Principle and the Ideogram," for example, Eisenstein says:

> The point is that the copulation . . . of two hieroglyphs of the simplest series is to be regarded not as their sum, but as their product, i.e., as a value of another dimension, another degree; each, separately, corresponds to an *object*, to a fact, but their combination corresponds to a *concept*. From separate hieroglyphs has been fused — the ideogram. By the combination of two "depictables" is achieved the representation of something that is graphically unpredictable. . . . Yes, it is exactly what we do in the cinema.[12]

The same structural principle continues to be at work in Chinese poetry. One line from a Li Po poem (discussed in great detail in my *Ezra Pound's "Cathay"*) is

浮　　雲　　遊　　子　　意
Floating cloud(s): wanderer's mood.

There, I asked whether the line meant that the clouds *are* or *are like* a wanderer's mood and decided that although no one would miss the resemblance of a wanderer's drifting to that of the clouds, "there is a flash of interest in the syntactically uncommitted resemblance" that would be lost by adding any words. Rather, I argued, Li Po has provided the simultaneous presence of two objects, the juxtaposition of two separate camera shots, resembling what Eisenstein called "not so much a simple sum of one shot plus another . . . as it does a creation. It resembles a creation—rather than the sum of its parts—from the circumstances that in every such juxtaposition the result is qualitatively distinguishable from each component element viewed separately."[13]

Here is another line that by the sheer fact of montage, by using independent but juxtaposed visual events, points to an idea without allowing the rhetoric of commentary to interfere:

國　　破　　山　　河　　在
Empire / broken / mountain / river / be (exist)

The reader feels, without being told, the contrast and tension in the scenery presented. Explanatory elaboration can only destroy the immediate contact between the viewer and the scene, as it does in this translation by Bynner[14] and in those by many others:

Though a country be sundered, hills and rivers endure.

Whether by using montage or a mobile point of view, the Chinese poets give paramount importance to the acting out of visual objects and events, letting those objects and events explain *themselves* by their coexisting, coextensive emergence from nature, letting the spatial tensions reflect conditions and situations rather than coercing these objects and events into some preconceived artificial order by sheer human interpretive elaboration. In a line like Li Po's,

鳳　　去　　臺　　空　　江　　自　　流
Phoenix gone, terrace empty, river flows on alone

do we need any more words to explain the vicissitudes of time versus the permanence of nature?

The success of the Chinese poets in authenticating the fluctuation of concrete events in Phenomenon, their ability to preserve the multiple relationships in a kind of penumbra of indeterminateness, depends to a great extent on the sparseness of syntactic demands. This freedom allows the poet to highlight independent visual events, leaving them in coextensive spatial relationships. And this language, this medium for poetry, would not have become what it is without the support of a unique aesthetic horizon—the Chinese concept of the loss of self in undifferentiated existence—ordained by centuries of art and poetry.

There is an inseparability of medium and poetics, of language and world view. How, then, can a language of rigid syntactical rules such as English successfully approximate a mode of presentation whose success depends on freedom from syntax? And how can an epistemological world view developed from Platonic and Aristotelian metaphysics, which emphasize the ego in search of the nonego and attempt to classify being in concepts, propositions, and ordered structures—how can such a world view turn around to endorse a medium that belies the function and process of epistemological elaboration?

The answer is that it cannot, that such a turn is impossible so long as the Platonic dichotomy of the phenomenal and the noumenal (appearance and reality) and the Aristotelian "universal logical structures" persist without adjustment. Nor can any attempt to turn the English language into one of broken, unsyntactical units as a medium for poetry succeed so long as no attempt is made to widen the possibilities of the Western aesthetic horizon to include the *other* world view, the Chinese mode of perception, at least coextensively with the Western world view. It is at this juncture that the discussion of convergence becomes most cogent and significant.

The adjustment of Western world views in modern times is the subject for a book in itself. Without going into the complicated history of this adjustment, it is sufficient to say one thing, namely, that all modern thought and art from the phenomenologists to as late as Jean Dubuffet's *Anticultural Positions* began with a rejection of abstract systems (particularly those of Plato and Aristotle) in order to return to concrete existence. Almost all the phenomenologists posed this problem, and Heidegger's request to return to the appeal of being gathered momentum in many later philosophers and artists.[15] Meanwhile, Bergson, who was, in essence, still an epistemological philosopher, pointed a way toward the "liquidation of the romantic self."[16]

For my purpose here, I will focus on a few statements by Anglo-American critics and poets at the turn of the century, statements that, as we will see later, have led to a subtle adjustment of the poetic language to the degree that it literally violates traditional syntactical structures. My central interest in this section is with some of the potentialities of this process of change in the English language.

Let us begin with Pater's famous statement in his book *The Renaissance*; there he says that it is "not the fruit of experience, but experience itself, [which] is the end, . . . to burn always with this gem-like flame."[17] While ancient thought sought "to arrest every object in an eternal outline," the modern spirit asserts that "nothing is or can be rightly known except relatively and under conditions. . . . [Modern man becomes] so receptive, all the influences of nature and of society ceaselessly playing upon him, so that every hour in his life is unique, changed altogether by a stray word, or glance, or touch. It is the truth of these relations that experience gives us, not the truth of eternal outlines ascertained once for all, but a world of gradations."[18]

"Experience itself" is the key; "a world of gradations," not "the eternal outlines ascertained once for all" of the Platonic ideas. Echoing Pater but developing ideas from Bergson, T. E. Hulme writes:

> The ancients were perfectly aware of the fluidity of the world and of its impermanence . . . but while they recognized it, they feared it and endeavoured to evade it, to construct things of permanence which would stand fast in this universal flux which frightened them. They had the disease, the passion, for immortality. They wished to construct things which should be proud boasts that they, men, were immortal. We see it in a thousand different forms. Materially in the pyramids, spiritually in the dogmas of religion and in the hypostatized ideas of Plato.[19]

Instead of consisting of "hypostatized ideas" and relying on the arrogant self, Hulme asks that poetry be "not a counter language, but a visual concrete one. It is a compromise of a language of intuition which would hand over sensations bodily. It always endeavours to arrest you, and to make you continually see a physical thing, to prevent you from gliding through an abstract process."[20] One of the methods to achieve this is through a process of selection: "Say the poet is moved by a certain landscape, he selects from that certain images which, put into juxtaposition in separate lines, serve to suggest and to evoke the state he feels. . . . Two visual images form what one may call a visual chord. They unite to suggest an image which is different to both."[21]

This is montage: juxtaposition of two visual events to create a third that is different from both. The method is, to Hulme, an alternative to the process of explanation in which syntax plays an important role. Syntax unfolds the intensive manifold, the vital reality, into extensive manifold, a mechanical complexity.[22]

In 1911, before he came into contact with Chinese poetry, Pound argued, "The artist seeks out the luminous detail and presents it. He does not comment."[23] After his contact with Chinese poetry, he wrote, "It is because certain Chinese poets have been content to set forth their matter without moralizing and without comment that one labors to make a translation."[24] Early in 1901, Pound advised William Carlos Williams in similar terms, and in 1916 he wrote emphatically to Iris Barry about "the necessity for creating or constructing something; of presenting an image, or enough images of concrete things arranged to stir the reader. . . . I think there must be more, predominantly more, objects than statements and conclusions, which latter are purely optional, not essential, often superfluous and therefore bad."[25] Pound was practicing a form of montage at the end of his early poem "Cino,"[26] without, I am sure, being fully aware of its permanence in his poetry as well as in the works of those after him. His contact with the Japanese haiku, Chinese poetry, and Chinese characters turned the technique into a central one in the *Cantos*. He began to use this technique consciously with his famous poem "In a Station of the Metro." Later, in the *Cantos*, the juxtaposition of images or objects was expanded into the idea that cultural moments acted as "luminous details," leading to the increased use of the Chinese ideogram as an amassing vortex.

Williams, in turn, wrote "no ideas but in things."[27] He went further to say that "a life that is here and now is timeless, . . . a new world that is always 'real,'" and that "no symbolism is acceptable."[28] The emphasis on the "here and now," the "real," and the "nonsymbolic" can be considered a true beginning to break away from the Platonic system, to become, in Kenneth Burke's words, a poet of contact.[29] Williams wanted to see "the thing itself without forethought or afterthought but with great intensity of perception."[30]

And Charles Olson and Robert Creeley, in step with Pound and Williams, postulated, "The objects which occur at any given moment of composition . . . are, can be, must be treated exactly as they do occur therein and not by any idea or preoccupations from outside the poem . . . must be handled as a series of objects in field . . . a series of tensions . . . space-tensions of a poem . . . the acting-on-you of the poem."[31]

Hulme was arguing for a poetic ideal before which the English language, with all its rigid syntax for elaboration and clarification, becomes helpless. Hulme called for the destruction of syntax to achieve the concrete. The earliest attempt, however, was made by Mallarmé. In order to arrive at a pure state of the poetry of essences, to freely transpose objects and words for his construction of a world so absolute that it has no strings attached to physical reality,[32] he dislocates syntax and, in his later sonnets, withdraws all the links that originally riveted the poem together.[33]

This absolutism of art, as well as his syntactical innovation, prepared the way for Pound and others to realize the poetic ideal that Hulme and Pound, each in his own way, postulated. The adjustment of conventional English made by Pound to approximate the curves of experience was a continuing process. Compare the two stanzas below, stanza (a) being the rearrangement of (b) — Pound's "The Coming of War: Actaeon" — back to traditional line format.

> (a) An image of Lethe, and the fields
>   Full of faint light, but golden gray cliffs
>   And beneath them, a sea, harsher than granite.

> (b) An image of Lethe,
>   and the fields
>   Full of faint light
>   but golden,
>   Gray cliffs,
>   and beneath them
>   A sea
>   Harsher than granite.

Breaking the traditional lines into small units graphically arranged serves to promote the visuality of the images, to isolate them as independent visual events, to force the reader-viewer to perceive the poem as consisting of spatial counterpoints, to enhance the physicality of objects (e.g., "sea" is literally and visually beneath the "gray cliffs," which protrude out from above), and to activate the poem through phases of perception (as does spotlighting or the use of a mobile point of view). These effects, modified and refined, dominate the entire *Cantos*.

In "The Coming of War: Actaeon," Pound used a space break to occasion a time break; he had not yet dealt actively with syntactical breaks. The latter aspect started with "In a Station of the Metro," and the discussion of the superpository technique in his 1914 essay "Vorticism" (by now too famous to need repetition here) launched him into more daring innovation.

"In a Station of the Metro" was modeled after the Japanese haiku, an example of which Pound examined in the same essay:

> The footsteps of the cat upon the snow:
> *are like* the plum blossoms

As Pound explained, "the words 'are like' would not occur in the original."[34] He precisely followed the example of that original in his "In a Station of the Metro":

> The apparition of these faces in the crowd;
> Petals on a wet, black bough.

To take away the words "are like" or "is like" is to disrupt syntax, giving prominence and independence to the two visual events, letting them coexist to define one another.[35] This poem's earlier version, which had appeared in *Poetry* in 1913, brings out Pound's obsession with the visual order and importance of the perceiving act. It runs:

> The apparition   of these faces   in the crowd;
> Petals   on a wet, black   bough.

Here we find both the space break and the syntactic break that Pound was later to employ in the *Cantos*.

In Pound's "South-Folk in Cold Country," which Pound mistranslated from the crippled Fenollosa notes,[36] we find:

> Surprised. Desert turmoil. Sea sun.

Here what we are interested in is the resemblance of this line, syntactically speaking, to some of the Chinese lines we have seen: syntactic break, superposition of one impression of bewilderment and disorder upon another, as well as synchronous images. More lines of this kind were to come in the *Cantos*, some lines of which I will simply quote without much comment:

> Rain; empty river, a voyage
> . . . .
> Autumn moon; hills rose above lakes
> . . . .
> Broad water; geese line out with the autumn.
> > from Canto 49

> Prayer: hands uplifted
> Solitude: a person, a Nurse.
> > from Canto 54

> Moon, cloud, tower, a patch of the battistero
> all of whiteness.
> > from Canto 79

Pound constructed Canto 49 out of a series of Chinese poems that were written by a Japanese in an album of paintings modeled after the Chinese art-motif of "Eight Views of Hsiao-hsiang." Here, Pound, using a crib[37] done by a Chinese in Italy, kept close to the Chinese syntax. One may perhaps say that with this poem Pound finally ordained his innovation not only for himself but for many others to come, including Gary Snyder.

At this point, it would be helpful to draw attention to one aspect of my conclusion in *Ezra Pound's "Cathay."* I argued that instead of simply pointing out the mistakes of the Fenollosa-Pound interpretation of the Chinese character, we should consider what aesthetic horizon they found in the structure of the Chinese character that excited them and how it helped them to reaffirm their own obsession with simultaneity and visual perspicuity.

> The fact is that even if the Pound-Fenollosa explanation of the ideogram were correct, as for instance in the case of EAST (東) and DAWN (旦), there is no way for the English language to reproduce them *literally* or *physically*. For if we try to reproduce the Chinese character 東 (sun behind tree or, as Pound has it, "sun rising, showing through tree's branches"), we cannot write the word "sun" literally on top of the word "tree," for one word will be crossed out by the other, whereas the Chinese character for sun (日) on top of the character for tree (木) easily forms a new Chinese character, EAST (東). In the case of the Chinese character for dawn (旦) (Pound's "sun above line of horizon"), we cannot reproduce it merely by writing:
>
> SUN
HORIZON
>
> This arrangement is still different from the Chinese which comes from the pictorial ☉. Any English reproduction of the elements in the two characters will involve the insertion of logical, directional links. Hence, the simultaneous presence of "sun" and "tree" in one picture is rendered into "sun *behind* tree" or "sun *rising, showing through* tree's branches." The insertion of logical, directional links between the objects immediately destroys the simultaneity of the elements in the Chinese characters and allows them to fall back upon the logic of succession. Why, then, was Pound so excited over the structure of the Chinese character?[38]

Clearly, as we look back on it, it was the *compositional* qualities of the Chinese character that helped to define the developing goals of Pound's project: simultaneity, montage, and visual perspicuity. That is why he considered Fenollosa's essay a piece of poetics rather than a treatise on the Chinese character as such. Pound seemed to be fully aware of the fact that to be true to the aesthetic ideal as proposed by the ideogram and by Chinese poetry, an ideal that he finds compatible with the compositional ideals of his poetry, he must relinquish logical and directional links. The examples given above attest to this attempt. Indeed, in his *Cantos* Pound progressively tried to take away these "links" to achieve what I call "leaps of logic" on an extensive scale, leading to a nonmatrixed presentation, a simultaneous "happening" or acting out of luminous cultural moments as patterned energies in montage or polyphonic orchestration. Recognizing later how the physical existence of the Chinese character can give forth an expressiveness of which English is incapable, he used actual Chinese characters as vortices, or even emblems, into which and out of which impressions and events constant rush.

Similar to Pound's graphic and syntactical innovation was the practice of his close friend William Carlos Williams, who was partially influenced by Pound and to an even greater degree inspired by Gertrude Stein's language experiments and by the Armory Show of 1913.[39] Stein's theory and practice had an incalculable influence on Williams and on poets and artists after him — Black Mountain poets, John Cage, Jerome Rothenberg, John Ashbery, to name just a few.

Stein's motto "Composition [as in Cézanne and as in Beethoven] as Explanation"[40] has taken several leads in the "revolution" of language in modern and postmodern times. Words, like colors and forms in painting, like notes in music, she argued, are not limited to being vehicles for meanings or ideas. They should perform exactly like colors, forms, and tones to form a composition. Just as colors (in painting) and sounds (in music) are given equal value, words should be allowed to fully express themselves. From Cézanne, Stein took the idea that

> in composition one thing was as important as another thing. Each part is as important as the whole. . . . To me one human being is as important as another human being, and you may say that the landscape has the same values, a blade of grass has the same value as a tree. . . . Just as everybody has the vote, including the women, I think children should, because as soon as a child is conscious of itself, then it has to me an existence and has a stake in what happens. . . . I became gradually more conscious of . . . a need for evenness. At this time I threw away punctuation. My real objection to it was that it threw away this balance that I was trying to get, this evenness of everybody having a vote. . . . Then in about the middle of [*Making of Americans*] words began to be for the first time more important

than the sentence structure or the paragraphs. Something happened. . . . I felt a need . . . of breaking it down and forcing it into little pieces. I felt that I had lost contact with the words in building up these Beethovian passages. . . . I began to play with words then. I was a little obsessed by words of equal value. . . . I had to recapture the value of the individual words. . . . I took individual words and thought about them until I got their weight and volume complete and put them next to another word, and at the same time I found out very soon that there is no such thing as putting them together without sense.[41]

We can now understand why Sherwood Anderson once said, "For me the work of Gertrude Stein consists in a rebuilding, an entire new recasting of life, in the city of words."[42] A revolution in language is also a revolution in consciousness. First and foremost for Stein, words must be emancipated from closed meanings, in particular, the way words are subordinated to the tyrannical system of grammar in a kind of master–slave relationship. Her *Tender Buttons* (1914) can be seen as a direct challenge to the conventional, hegemonic uses of language. Following the habits of English grammar, we often balk at her choices of words, because many of them appear at the most unexpected positions: for example, where the dictates of English grammar lead us to expect a noun, we find a verb or a verb-like word, and so on. Or, in almost all the pieces in *Tender Buttons*, we do not know how to break the sentence into groups of meaningful phrases: There seem to be many possible ways of regrouping them. These facts point to multiple readings. Consider this example:

ORANGE
Why is a feel oyster an egg stir. Why is it orange centre.
A show at tick and loosen loosen it so to speak sat.
It was an extra leaker with a sea spoon, it was an extra licker
    with a see spoon.[43]

First, in an effort to grasp "meaning" we might try grouping or re-phrasing this sequence of words: Should we read it in short phrases like the following?

> Why is a feel
> oyster
> an egg
> stir.
> Why is it orange
> centre.

> A show at tick
> and loosen
> loosen it
> so to speak
> sat.
> It was an extra leaker
> with a sea spoon,
> it was an extra licker
> with a see spoon.

This exercise by no means claims to be the only plausible reading. In fact, this piece invites other possible readings. This is the point of Stein's experiment. One thing is clear, however: We are forced to redivide the lines, not once, but many times, and each time we do it we are giving to each word a new, added dimension. In the process, a series of queries surges in our minds:

ORANGE
Why is a feel [verb or adjective?] oyster an egg stir. [Why no "?" Is this a statement? Can it be a statement?] Why is it orange [noun or adjective?] centre. A show at tick [internal rhyme?] and loosen loosen [imperative mood? sound play?] it [antecedent?] so to speak [internal rhyme or echo?] sat. [What or who sat?] It was an extra leaker [playful sound echo?] with a sea spoon [playful sound echo?], it was an extra licker [playful sound echo?] with a see spoon [playful sound echo?].

Certainly, there must be other queries as well in our minds. The indeterminateness of the grammatical functions of the words (or, rather, the nullifying of these functions) helps to liberate the words from normative demands for focused meaning. The feeling conveyed by such passages, according to William Carlos Williams, "is of words themselves, a curious immediate quality quite apart from their meaning, much as in music different notes are dropped, so to speak, into repeated chords one at a time, one after another—for themselves alone."[44]

If we consider the graphic and syntactical innovations of William Carlos Williams, we find a combination of strategies from Pound's Chinese examples and from those found Stein's language experiments. First, compare the line structure of the following sentence with Williams's graphic arrangement:

> so much depends upon a red wheelbarrow
> glazed with rain water beside the white chickens.

so much depends
upon

a red wheel
barrow

glazed with rain
water

beside the white
chickens.

In Williams's graphic treatment, the line breaks and spacing enhance
the visuality of different phases of the perception of the object as
words gain independence and liberation from the linearity of the
normal line structures. As a result, these independent visual events or
moments provide changing perspectives of the object as the reader-
viewer is transposed into the midst of a scene to witness the object's
various spatial extensions. The same is true of Williams's "Nantucket":

Flowers through the window
lavender and yellow

Changed by white curtains —
Smell of cleanliness —

Sunshine of late afternoon —
On the glass tray

a glass pitcher, the tumbler
turned down, by which

a key is lying — And the
immaculate white bed

This technique of combining line breaks and spacing with syntactic
breaks forces the reader to focus attention *at all times* — this is the
lesson that Olson and Creeley learned — on the urgency of every
moment as it occurs in the process of perceiving. Williams happily
approved the essay "Projective Verse" by Olson and Creeley as an
extension and clarification of his technique. The following passage by
Olson can indeed be considered a footnote to Williams's ideas about
the perceiving process:

ONE PERCEPTION MUST IMMEDIATELY AND DIRECTLY
LEAD TO A FURTHER PERCEPTION. It means exactly what it
says, is a matter of, at *all* points . . . get on with it, keep moving,
keep in, speed, the nerves, their speed, the perception, theirs,
the acts, the split second acts, the whole business, keep it
moving as fast as you can, citizen. And if you also set up as a

poet, USE USE USE the process at all points, in any given poem always, always, one perception must must must MOVE, INSTANTER, ON ANOTHER![45]

Williams's use of single words or short phrases as lines is most intriguing in the poem "The Locust Tree in Flower."[46] A comparison between the early version (1933, on the left) and the later one (on the right) will bring out most clearly the protean functions of space and syntactic breaks in Williams's poetry:

Among	Among
the leaves	of
bright	green
	stiff
green	old
of wrist-thick	bright
tree	broken
	branch
an old	come
stiff broken	white
branch	sweet
ferncool	May
	again
swaying	
loosely strung—	
come May	
again	
white blossom	
clusters	
hide	
to spill	
their sweets	
almost	
unnoticed	
down	
and quickly	
fall	

Like many of Williams's other poems, the early version, by dint of the space break, accentuates the different phases of the act of perceiving. But, like those poems, the early version also has a continuity (of syntax). The revised version is something else. First of all, "Among"—among what? "Of"—of what? These prepositions have become *position* words of another sort, putting us in the midst of ("Among") something that then changes in both perspective and in spatial relationship ("of"). The perspective changes again as we notice color ("green," a color so strong that it takes full possession of the viewer) and then again as we see age ("old")—as we notice, in other words, the qualities (and their growth and change) that mime the life process of the locust tree. This is a language that approximates the morphology of feelings: "Bright," "broken," "branch," with its rough progression of vowels, reflect the inner struggle of growth until "come," with its open vowel.

Williams's revised version matches Zaslove's description of how gestures and movements have to reflect the life mechanism of the moment in order to authenticate it. In this poem, too, as in the flexibility of Chinese syntax, as in the ambiguous ways in which Stein's words work, the usual allotment of grammatical function to each word is erased. Indeed, if one views Williams's poem from the standpoint of normative English grammar, one is bound to say, No, it's not English at all, it doesn't fulfill the syntactic requirements of the language. And yet, supported by a tensional distribution of energy reflecting the activities of the perceiving moment, these words serve quite adequately as a medium for poetic expression.

Robert Creeley fully understands this miming of "energy-discharge," as he puts it. He says that

> if one thinks of the literal root of the word *verse*, "a line, furrow, turning—*vertere*, to turn . . . ," he will come to a sense of "free verse" as that instance of writing in poetry which "turns" upon an occasion intimate with, in fact, the issue of, its own nature rather than to an abstract decision of "form" taken from a prior instance.
>
> The point is, simply enough, why does the "line" thus "turn" and what does inform it in that movement?[47]

Creeley, unlike Williams, is a subjective poet who writes about intimate moments he once "stumbled into"—"warmth for a night perhaps, the misdirected intention came right . . . a sudden instance of love"[48]—and as such, he very seldom emphasizes the visual events as Williams does. But he has the same obsession with promoting the physical presence of an experience (even though a subjective one), an obsession that has driven him to use in his poems—I think to his advantage—the kind of space breaks and syntactic breaks endorsed by Pound and Williams.[49]

For our purpose, one example from Creeley is adequate:

> In the court-
> yard at midnight, at
>
> midnight. The moon is
> locked in itself, to
>
> a man a
> familiar thing
> —"La Noche"

This is a poem that would not work if cast in a "normal" line structure. The repetition of "at midnight" would become rhetorical and superfluous, but when it is graphically separated as Creeley has done, leaving "midnight" and "the moon" in the center of the poem, "locked in" the arms of the poet's awareness, as it were, we can feel (physically feel) the "turning" from the outside world into the inner familiar moment in which the poet finds himself.

Space and syntactic breaks abound in contemporary poetry after Pound and Williams. Indeed, most of the poets in Donald Allen and George F. Butterick's *The Postmoderns: The New American Poetry Revised* (1982) have incorporated these strategies in their poetry. Obviously, this is no place for a thorough examination of the various ways in which each of these poets receives and makes use of these strategies. For our conclusion, let us look at some examples from Gary Snyder, a statement from Michael McClure, and a palindrome attempt by Robert Duncan.

It is a well-known fact that Gary Snyder has inherited the traditions of Han Shan and Wang Wei and has incorporated Pound's and Williams's language. The convergence of these influences is most clearly expressed in his translation of Wang Wei, done while a student at the University of California, Berkeley.[50]

空　山　不　見　人
Empty / mountain / not / see / man

但　聞　人　語　響
but / hear / men('s) / voice(s) / sound

返　景　入　深　林
reflect / shadow / enter / deep / forest
(sun's reflection)

復　照　青　苔　上
again / shine / green / moss / upon

Empty, the mountain—
　　　　not a man,
Yet sounds, echoes
　　　　　　as of men talking
Shadows swing into the forest.
Swift light flashes
On dark moss, above.

It is, therefore, not surprising that many of his lines come very close to the working dynamics of the Chinese line. Here, without further comment, are some examples:

Burning the small dead
　　　　branches
　broke from beneath
　　Thick spreading white pine
　　　　　　a hundred summers
snowmelt　　　rock　　　　and air
　　hiss in a twisted bough
　　　　　sierra granite;
　　　　　　mt Ritter—
　　　　black rock twice as old
Deneb, Altair
Windy fire.
　　　　　　"Burning the Small Dead"

First day of the world
white rock ridges
　　　　　　new born
Jay chatters　　　the first time
Rolling a smoke by the campfire
New!　　　never before.
bitter coffee, cold
dawn wind, sun of the cliffs.
　　　from "Hunting No. 15"

In the blue night
frost haze, the sky glows
with the moon
pine tree tops
bend snow-blue, fade
into sky, frost, starlight.
　　from "Pine Tree Tops"

In his *Scratching the Beat Surface* (1982), Michael McClure quotes a poem of Su Tung-p'o (1036–1101) in its word-for-word layout from my *Chinese Poetry* (1976). Then, McClure comments: "Professor Yip then versifies this way—*it is not as good*—but clearer" before he quotes my English rendering.[51] As if to echo Stein's statement that "there is no such thing as putting [words] together without sense," McClure goes so far as to accept the word-for-word format as more than adequate a medium for poetry, believing as he does with Stein that each word radiates more connections than conventional syntactical structures can handle.

Lastly, a palindrome attempt by Robert Duncan from his *Bending the Bow*:

The Fire   Passages 13

jump	stone	hand	leaf	shadow	sun
day	plash	coin	light	downstream	fish
first	loosen	under	boat	harbor	circle
old	earth	bronze	dark	wall	waver
new	smell	purl	close	wet	green
now	rise	foot	warm	hold	cool

This poem reappears a few pages later, reading backwards and vertically:

cool	green	waver	circle	fish	sun
hold	wet	wall	harbor	downstream	shadow
warm	close	dark	boat	light	leaf
foot	purl	bronze	under	coin	hand
rise	smell	earth	loosen	plash	stone
now	new	old	first	day	jump[52]

This chapter intends to be both radical, in the sense of being a root introduction to the aesthetic ground of the Chinese poetic line, and exploratory, in the sense of looking toward an ideal convergence of two languages and two poetics. The adjustment of language (in particular, the use of paratactical structures—space breaks and syntactic breaks—in Pound, Williams, and the postmodernists) can perhaps be seen as a strategy to force us to question the ways in which language forms our perceptions and, in doing so, to open ways for us once again to achieve the correspondence between word and thing, between language and being.

3   Language and the Real-life World

Behind many of the language experiments by poets and the discussions on language by philosophers is one central obsession: Can language authenticate experience in the real-life world? My last essay was an attempt to examine, through the lens of classical Chinese language and poetics, the working dynamics in the language adjustments of Anglo-American modernists. I have yet to probe into the philosophical and historical grounding of this obsession. This I will do in the present essay.

Before I go any further, a recapitulation of the problem is necessary. I will use just one brief example. Consider, for a second, the following elements of a given moment in a concrete environment: *stream, house, silence, no one around.* Consider these elements *before* you decide the relation of the house to the stream (by the stream? above the stream? overlooking the stream? etc.), *before* you judge the silence of the general surroundings to contrast with the sound of the stream, *before* you become aware, even in your own sense of solitude, of your own presence. As we can see, the prepredicative moment belongs to the original, real-life world, beyond human touch, beyond conception, and beyond language; the predicative acts belong to the mediating subject. Meanwhile, the act of predication—the determination and articulation of certain relationships among the indeterminate, emerging objects, and, indeed, thinking itself—becomes, as Hegel has argued, a form of negation of that which is immediately before us.

The immediate question is, then, this: Is it possible to have a line of poetic expression in which the prepredicative givenness can remain uncontaminated? For example, can we simply give the above-described moment, in English, as such—*stream house silence no one*—without feeling guilty of having violated some essential law of the English language? And yet, if there is another language that can give it simply as such, as in Chinese, 澗戶寂無人, what are we to understand from this phenomenon? What kind of philosophical or aesthetic position does this fact point to or evolve from? Why would giving it out as such in English evoke a sense of abnormality, even if we bend backwards to accept it as possible? These are aesthetic questions, but they are also philosophical and historical ones. William Carlos Williams once said,

> unless there is
> a new mind there cannot be a new
> line.[1]

Placing it against the perspective outlined above, the statement could be rephrased into several interrelated questions central to modern philosophy and poetics:

1. Can an original moment of the presencing of the real world come to disclose itself authentically before us *through language* without being pressed into some kind of Procrustean bed involving syntax, rhetoric, linguistic codes, and so forth?

2. Is originality at all possible, if, by originality, we mean a phrase or a line that is totally free from the restraints of language, which, being historical by nature, usually operates by herding all lived and varied experiences into the proper folds, clear-cut, clean, orderly, and reduced?

3. The limits of language being such, can we really see the world "with an ignorant eye," as Wallace Stevens aspires to?

The Orphic belief that language can call the world into being and Mallarmé's conviction that language is a magic wand that can make an object disappear, leaving itself trembling in communion with totality in the pristine world of nothingness, are examples that attempt to extend language's potentials through a process of mystification. While these views might have been possible, and even realizable, as in primitive society's once marvelous original contact and communication with the animal and plant worlds, language as we now use it, poetical or otherwise, often belies these magical conceptions. Language is a prison-house,[2] constantly coding, decoding, and recoding, at once *closed* as a system (as the structuralists want to see it) and *open*, changing and growing with overlaying significations, forming a net of continually interweaving and yet restrictive perceptual modes, from which poets who are determined to attain originality must extricate themselves. The prison-house of language is joined with that of thought.

For a new line of poetic expression to assert its independent presence, a poet must, first and foremost, recover the original ground, where we find the given as given, by liberating himself from the accustomed house of thought so that language acts not to disfigure things in their immanent presences but to make them disclose the dimension of their immediate thereness.

But let us return, for a moment, to the initial differences between the English predication of a moment in nature and the Chinese treatment of it. A common-sense Western logic will demand that the line *stream house silence no one* be rewritten in an order such as the following: "Silent is the hut beside the torrent: There is no one home."[3] In this version the original undetermined spatio-temporal relationships and conditions are now reduced to clear-cut, single perceptual possibilities. Other possibilities, all postreflective acts, include the following (randomly collected from existing translations): "The valley house deserted, no one there—";[4] "Hidden in a gorge, unnoticed";[5] "Families no longer live in this deserted valley."[6] These and many other possible versions, which are occasioned by the original components, treat those components not as things in their own right but only as *versions* of real beings, now reduced, changed, restricted. The freedom of the original components, the freedom with which they reach out in indeterminate multiple relationships, has been invalidated by these acts under the pretext of ascertaining their definable outlines and their hermeneutic margins.

However, once we are aware that the fruits of these acts (concepts and linguistic formulations) do not correspond to the original appeal and condition of the existential objects, we can begin to reverse the priority of our ground of understanding. This process of reversal consists of admitting the inadequacy of common sense and conceptual reason and, indeed, the inadequacy of language itself to authenticate the original world; this process of reversal also consists of realizing that the totalizing, ongoing, and changing process of all the pre-predicative beings must be continued within their undifferentiated modes, concrete and void of names.

Wu-yen tu-hua *and the Taoist Transparency of Language*

Reflection on the fundamental facts of the external world will immediately make us see that there is totality, or the totalizing process of the Great Composition of things in Phenomenon, and that this totality is changing and ongoing, whether we want to talk about it or not. From a complete awareness of this totalizing process comes the call to respect and preserve things in their pristine forms as they emerge from and merge into an undifferentiated oneness. Thus, the Taoist world view begins by rejecting the premise that the structure of Phenomenon (Nature), changing and ongoing, is the same as we conceive it. All conscious efforts to generalize, formulate, classify, and order it will necessarily result in some form of restriction, reduction, or even distortion. We impose our conceptions, which, by definition, must be partial and incomplete, upon Phenomenon at the peril of losing touch with the concrete original appeal of the totality of things. All such means of rationalization, Lao-tzu tells us, are deceptions:

> Tao, told, is not the constant Tao.
> Name, named, is not the constant Name.
> Nameless, the beginning of the world.
> Naming, the mother of a million things.
> Lao, 1[7]

> He who knows does not speak.
> He who speaks does not know.
> Lao, 56

The "Tao (Way) told" and the "name named" belong to the realm of concepts and linguistic formulations, from which things and beings are totally free. As Heidegger would put it twenty-three centuries later, "All essents are not affected by concepts."[8] Things self-generate and self-become. Since, strictly speaking, any thought of a thing becomes itself a verbal act, the deverbalized world (*wu-yen*, 無言, or *wu-yü-chieh*, 無語界) is the first step toward grasping the totality of things. Ideal knowledge is no knowledge. In Chuang-tzu's words:

> The knowledge of the ancients was perfect. How perfect? At that time they did not know that there were things. This is the most perfect; nothing can be added. Next, they were aware of things, but they did not yet make distinctions between them.

Next, they made distinctions, they did not yet judge them.
When judgments were passed, Tao was destroyed.

Chuang, 74

Chuang-tzu is particularly protective of the wholeness of the original
cosmic scheme, which classifications and conceptions tend to dissect
into separate units. The restrictiveness of words and ideas is further
articulated in the book of Chuang-tzu:

> What the world values is books. Books contain nothing but
> words wherein are found values of sorts. What words value is
> the sense of things. The sense of things reaches into something
> but that something is not to be conveyed by words. . . . What
> can be seen by seeing is forms and colors; what can be heard by
> hearing is names and sounds. How sad! Men of the world think
> that forms, colors, names, and sounds are adequate means to
> grasp the full feel of things. But forms, colors, names, and
> sounds are not adequate to grasp the full feel of things. "He
> who knows does not speak; he who speaks does not know."

Chuang, 488–89

Words are inadequate either to encompass the entirety or penetrate
into the invisible smallest parts:

> Viewing large things from the standpoint of the small, one
> cannot exhaust them. Viewing small things from that of the
> large, one cannot see them clearly. Fineness is the smallest of
> the small and the gigantic is the largest of the large; each
> different in its convenient way—this is natural. The idea of
> fineness and coarseness is restricted to things with form. Things
> so fine that they have no visible form cannot be demarcated by
> numbers. Things so large that we cannot encompass them
> cannot be exhausted by numbers. What words can speak of is
> the coarseness of things. What our sense can reach is the fine-
> ness of things. That which cannot be spoken of or sensed is that
> which coarseness and fineness cannot restrict.

Chuang, 572

Inherent in this recognition of the inadequacy of language is the
acceptance of humanity as limited and the rejection of the idea of
seeing humanity as preeminently the controller or orderer of things,
the consequence of which I shall explore presently. In the meantime,
let us turn to two contemporary philosophers, William James and
A. N. Whitehead, who delineated a world view that echoes, in some

measure, the Taoist holistic view but that also addresses the alienation of modern human beings. James says:

> The world's contents are given to each of us in an order so
> foreign to our subjective interests that we can hardly . . .
> picture to ourselves what it is like. We have to break that order
> altogether — and by picking out from it the items which concern
> us, and connecting them with others far away, which we say
> "belong" with them, we are able to make out definite threads of
> sequence and tendency. . . . Is not the sum of your actual expe-
> rience taken at this moment and impartially added together an
> utter chaos? . . . We have no organ of faculty to appreciate the
> simply given order. The real world as it is given objectively at
> this moment is the sum total of all its beings and events now.
> But can we think of such a sum? Can we realize for an instant
> what a cross-section of all existence at a definite point of time
> would be? While I talk and the flies buzz, a seagull catches a
> fish at the mouth of the Amazon, a tree falls in the Adirondack
> wilderness, a man sneezes in Germany, a horse dies in Tartary,
> and twins are born in France. What does that mean? Does the
> contemporaneity of these events with one another, and with a
> million others as disjointed, form a rational bond between
> them, and unite them into . . . anything that means for us a
> world? Yet, just such a collateral contemporaneity, and nothing
> else, is the real order of the world. It is an order with which we
> have nothing to do but to get away from it as fast as possible.
> As I said, we break it. We break it into arts and we break it into
> sciences. . . . We make ten thousand separate serial orders of
> it. . . . We discover among its various parts relations that were
> never given to sense at all . . . and out of an infinite number of
> these we call certain ones essential and law-giving and ignore
> the rest . . . [and say] the impressions of sense *must* give way,
> *must* be reduced to the desiderated form.[9]

James fully recognizes that we have no organ to apprehend what he calls the "collateral contemporaneity" of all the beings and events that exist and happen at any given moment. And yet the Western individual insists that they be represented in a way that fits the Western perception of a manageable sequence and order. In the words of Whitehead:

> The radically untidy, ill-adjusted character of the fields of actual
> experience is concealed by the influence of language, molded
> by science, which foists on us exact concepts as though they
> represented the immediate deliverance of experience. The result

is that we imagine that we have immediate experience of a
world of perfectly defined objects implicated in perfectly
defined events. . . . My contention is that this world, neat, trim,
tidy, exact, is a world of ideas, and that its internal relations are
relations between abstract concepts.[10]

For humans to be able to preserve or partake in the true order be-
fore dissecting and recomposing it, Chuang-tzu gives priority to the
preconscious, preconceptual, prelinguistic, nonverbal world where
its pristine form can come freely to us in its own way. Chuang-tzu
exalts the state before knowledge of ancient people, and Lao-tzu calls
for the return to childlike correspondence with the world ("Keeping
to the constant instinctive virtue, one returns to childlikeness"—Lao,
28). Both "ancient people" (before any polarization took place in their
consciousness) and children (in their naive condition) respond
directly to, and correspond in natural measure with, the appeal of the
concrete world without traversing through or into abstract concepts.
This tuned correspondence with the world of objects is described in
the book of Chuang-tzu as the Free Flow of Nature:

> The people have their constant instinctive nature: to weave for
> clothing, to till the fields for food. This is their shared virtue,
> one, total, undivided, and is called the Free Flow of Nature.
> Therefore, in a time of perfect virtue, people move slowly, their
> gaze one-minded. In such a time, mountains have no paths,
> lakes no boats or bridges. A million things emerge simultane-
> ously, one region joining another in a continuum. Birds flock,
> animals herd; grass and trees flourish. You can tie a cord to
> birds and animals to lead them along or climb up and peer over
> the nests of crows and magpies. In this age of perfect virtue,
> men live co-extensively with birds and animals, group side by
> side with a million things. Who would try to mark off superior
> men from inferior men? With the same "no knowledge" (*wu-
> chih*), their virtue stays put. With the same "no desire" (*wu-yü*),
> they remain simple and unhewn. Simple and unhewn—there
> we have the true nature of man.[11]

Chuang, 334–36

It is clear that for Lao-tzu and Chuang-tzu, Simple and Unhewn (*su
p'u*) is that realm of our original total consciousness that is open and
unblocked to the free flow of things and is lost to most people
through their acquisition of knowledge, one of the many forms of
systematization imposed upon our original nature. Our original

nature, had it been understood as such from the very beginning, would have continued in close measure with what it was; this would include adjusting our perceptual and expressive strategies.

Before we discuss this important prepredicative mode (and how it conditions perception and language), we must understand some of the key issues involved in the promotion of the Free Flow of Nature and the Simple and Unhewn.

To (re)present the original condition in which things and humans can freely emerge, first and foremost, humans must understand their position in and relation to the Great Composition of things. Since the human race is but one among millions of other beings in the totalizing fabric of Phenomenon ("Sky and earth came into being with us together; the myriad things and us are one" — Chuang, 79), we have no reason to give special privilege to humans and to their mental constructs as the sole authority on a subject that is larger than them and that they have no ability to fully encompass. The rebirth of our original condition depends, therefore, on the removal of formulated categories from our consciousness and on our affirmation of the million things in the concrete world outside concepts and language as "self-so-complete" objects, each functioning, generating, conditioning, and transforming itself according to its own nature. As "the air of nature blows on the million things in a different way so that each can be itself" (Chuang, 50), and as lengthening the duck's legs or shortening the crane's legs means pain and is a result of working against nature (Chuang, 317), we must leave all forms of beings as they are by nature. Each form of being has its own nature and place, just as a tree, by nature, grows upward, a river flows downward, a stone is hard, and water is soft. The legendary P'eng rises ninety-thousand miles (Chuang, 2). A little quail never gets more than ten yards (Chuang, 9). A certain tree lives many centuries, a mushroom only a short time (Chuang, 11). Each performs according to its own nature. How can we take *this* as *subject* (principal) and *that* as *object* (subordinate)? Merely one form of being among millions of others, what right do we have to classify other forms of beings? How can we impose "our viewpoint" upon others as the right viewpoint, the only right viewpoint? When we do that, are we not like the frog inside the well who claims that the partial sky he sees is the full sky? What right do we have to turn the original nature of another fellow being into something it is not? White clouds are white; green mountains are green. Green mountains cannot blame white clouds for being white. White clouds cannot blame green mountains for being green. The so-called possible and impossible are possible and impossible because they are said to be so.

> The "this" is also "that." The "that" is also "this." According to "that," there is a system of right and wrong. According to "this," there is also a system of right and wrong. Is there really a distinction between "this" and "that"? . . . Not to discriminate "that" and "this" as opposite is the very essence of Tao (Way). There you get the Axis of Tao. There you attain the Central Ring to respond to the endless.
>
> Chuang, 66

Thus, obliterate the distinctions and view things from both "this" and "that"—view things as things view themselves, which is the true balance of nature (Chuang, 70). In the words of Kuo Hsiang, the most important annotator of Chuang-tzu, "All things are what they are without knowing why and how they are . . . although things are different, yet they are the same in that they exist spontaneously as they are." "Since nonbeing is nonbeing, it cannot produce being. When being is not yet produced, it cannot produce other things. Who, then, produces things? They spontaneously produce themselves. . . . Everything produces itself and is not created by others. This is the Way of Nature" (Chuang, 50).

When Chuang-tzu claims that "Tao is everywhere," he does not mean any sort of human-invented concept, such as Logos or Creator, that determines the outlines of the beings in the phenomenal world but the self-realization of each form of being as it is, uninterfered with by abstract concepts or systems. This is the context in which Chuang-tzu says, "Sky and earth came into being with us together; the myriad things and us are one."

With this awareness of humanity's place in the free flow of things, we should turn our attention toward the unspeaking Other world rather than toward the speaking Self, the Other world being, of course, those absolutely lively, self-generating, self-transforming (*tu-hua*, 獨化) beings surrounding us. This particular mental horizon—oriented toward things rather than toward humans—entails a totally different set of attitudes, aesthetic assumptions, and strategies. The main aim is to receive, perceive, and disclose nature the way nature comes or discloses itself to us, undistorted. This has been the highest aesthetic ideal (*tzu-jan*, be-nature-thus-natural) in traditional Chinese art and literature. A brief review of the two directions of our perceptual priorities may be useful here.

In one, as the ego attempts to explain the nonego, the perceiver constantly imposes ideas or concepts on, or matches them with, images or objects in concrete Phenomenon, but in the other, as the ego loses itself in the undifferentiated mode of existence, into the totalizing flux of events and changes constantly happening before us, to "think" is to respond to the appeal of the presencing of things in their original state of freedom. Whereas the former tends toward the use of analytical, discursive, and even syllogistic progression coupled with a linear and temporal perspective, resulting in a sort of determinate, get-there orientation, the latter tends toward a dramatic nonconnective, simultaneous presencing of the multidimensional, multirelational objects instead of coercing them into some preconceived orders or structures. While the Taoist texts are full of parabolic expressions, the internal logic of the Taoist aesthetic leads to the deemphasis of metaphoric thinking and metaphysics, both of which have played a central role in much of Western poetry. A metaphor, on the most basic level, means that we use an object to designate an idea, a vehicle (thing named) for tenor (things meant). Metaphysics means to reach beyond *physis*, to borrow an interpretation from Heidegger, *physis* being the emergence of things, their emergence being seen to include both their "being" in the restricted sense of inert duration and "becoming."[12] But things in Phenomenon clearly need neither metaphor nor metaphysics to be what they are. A good example of this articulation is found in a large percentage of Chinese landscape poems such as those of Wang Wei, on which I have written in great detail in my *Hiding the Universe* and two other essays, "Aesthetic Consciousness of Landscape in Chinese and Anglo-American Poetry" and "The Morphology of Aesthetic Consciousness and Perimeter of Meaning in the Example of Pre-Romantic Concept of Nature."[13] Briefly, these poems are nonmetaphoric and nonsymbolic: The objects presented are nothing more than the objects themselves. The poet does not step in, but, rather, he allows the scenery to speak and act itself out. It is as if the poet has become the objects themselves.

But the complexity of the Taoist aesthetic is not fully circumscribed if we do not confront the subtle interplay of the built-in contradictions throughout the Taoist texts and if we do not try to see in what way the decreative process leads to or becomes the creative. This decreative–creative dialectic appears on the surface in the form of negation or renunciation: The Way of Nature is ineffable; language is inadequate; we should take no action (*wu-wei*, 無爲), have no mind (*wu-hsin*, 無心), no knowledge, no self (*wu-wo*, 無我); we should not speak about Tao; Tao (Way of Nature) is void and there is nothing in it. Paradoxically, in this seeming renunciation is the affirmation of the concrete total world, a world free from and unrestricted by concepts. The renunciation, then, is not negation but a new way of repossessing this original concrete world by dispossessing the partial and reduced forms the process of abstract thinking has thus far heaped upon us. Thus, without taking such actions as those defined by a closed system of abstract thinking, everything is done in accordance with our instinctive nature. Without exercising our conscious mind, we can respond fully to things that come into the orbit of our ken. With conceptual boundaries removed, our bosom is thus open, unblocked, a center of no circumference into which and across which a million things will regain their free flow and activity. It is clear that the Taoist perceiving-receiving activity must also be viewed from the standpoint of this decreative–creative dialectic.

> Do not listen with ears, but with the mind. Do not listen with the mind, but with the vital force (*ch'i*, or energy flow) within us. The function of the ear ends with hearing; that of the mind, with symbols and ideas. But the vital force is an emptiness ready to receive all things. Tao abides in the emptiness; the emptiness is the fast of mind.
>
> Chuang, 142

> Acting in the manner of man, it is easy to be artificial. Acting in the manner of nature, it is difficult to be artificial. I have heard of flying with wings, but not of flying without them. I have heard of knowing with knowledge, but not of knowing without it. Look at that which is empty. In the empty room, there is bright light, there is happiness. If you cannot stop there, your mind is galloping abroad though your body is sitting. If you can keep your ears and eyes to communicate within, and shut out consciousness and knowledge, then even the gods and ghosts will come to dwell with you, not to mention men.
>
> Chuang, 150

> Crush limbs and body, drive out hearing and vision, cast off form, do away with knowledge, and become identical with the Great Road — this is called Sitting-in-forgetfulness.
>
> Chuang, 284

Whereas many other modes of apprehending Phenomenon come to it with a handful of ready-made gauges, measuring and matching, the Taoist mind is blank, so to speak, thereby allowing the original nature of beings to have its full imprint, uninterfered with, undistorted. Such a state has also been compared to still water when it is the clearest (Chuang, 193)—a medium in which beings can mirror themselves. This condition of the mind resembles the trance-like consciousness of the mystics; in particular, it is close to the three stages of self-annihilation, forgetfulness, and the moment of lightning-like illumination or inspiration. Henri Brémond, discoursing on the war between Anima (deeper self, intuitionism) and Animus (surface self, intellectualism), describes the triple process this way: Since pure intelligence cannot reach the ultimate reality, it is by way of the annihilation of the surface self, the retreat of the rational power, that contact with the soul is possible. From the retreat comes a state of forgetfulness, a state in which all obstructions by the surface self are removed when inspiration finally occurs like a spark coming from the deepest source of our soul.[14] In his "On Making Everything Equal," Chuang-tzu describes a sage's state of mind while in communion with the music of nature:

> Nan Kuo Tzu Ch'i sat leaning on a table. He looked to heaven and breathed gently, seeming to be in a trance, and unconscious of his body. Yen Ch'eng Tzu Yu, who was in attendance on him, said: "What is this? Can the body become thus like dry wood and the mind like dead ashes? The man leaning on the table is not he who was here before." "Yen," said Tzu Ch'i, "your question is very good. Just now, I lost myself, do you understand? You may have heard of the music of man but not the music of earth; you may have heard of the music of earth, but not the Music of Nature."
>
> Chuang, 43–45

Indeed, the parallel with the three stages described earlier is intriguing. St. Teresa says, for instance, that in her mystical communion she neither sees nor hears. For Plotinus, "Unifying contemplation occurs when the soul closed its door on everything."[15] Blake, St. John of the Cross, Eckhart, and Pascal all have written about the retreat of the self as a precondition for merging with the ultimate. In a wider sense, we must consider the Taoist condition of *wu-hsin* (no mind) mystical—this is partly why Ch'an Buddhism later wholeheartedly took over this aspect as its central motto. It is at least mystical in William James's sense: "It is as if there were in the human consciousness a *sense of reality, a feeling of objective presence*, a perception of what we may call *'something there,'* more deep and more general than any of the special and particular 'senses' by which the current psychology supposes existent realities to be originally revealed."[16] And yet, the Taoist trance-like consciousness is at root different from Western religious mysticism: It does not work up to a leap into the noumenal or the metaphysical world; to the Taoist, as we may now understand, the phenomenal *is* the noumenal.

This quasi-mystical state is often described as *shen* (literally, spirit), a condition of mind after it has entered into the inner mechanism and activity of a thing or things. In Chuang-tzu's "The Fundamentals for the Cultivation of Life," a prince was astounded at a cook's skill in cutting bullocks, not only because every blow was done in perfect rhythm but because he seemed to have seen all the joints and cavities inside the body, for he knew exactly where to turn his blade before he encountered an obstruction. The cook explained, "What I love is Tao, which is more than mere skill. When I first began to cut up bullocks, I saw before me whole bullocks. After three years' practice, I saw no more whole bullocks. At present, I meet it with *shen*, not with my eyes" (Chuang, 119). Perhaps it is because of this mystical tincture amidst a poetics of the real and the concrete that all later literary and art theorists, Taoist and Confucian alike, from Lu Chi and Liu Hsieh to Chang Yen-yüan, Ssu-k'ung T'u, Su Tung-p'o, Yen Yü, and post-Sung critics, have made it the pivot of their theoretical formulation, for this decreative–creative dialectic helps to identify the ineffable and the real as one without resorting to human-invented dogmas as ways to explain beings and phenomena:

> In the beginning, suspend vision, bring back hearing, become lost in contemplation to reach out for contact—there spirit gallops into the eight limits of the cosmos, there the mind glides into millions of miles of space. Reaching the full feel of things, at first, a glimmer gathers into luminosity when all objects are brightened and clarified, each lighting up the other onward.
>
> The mind is cleared to crystallize contemplation.
>
> Trying the Void to demand for Being; knocking upon Profound Silence for sound.[17]
>
> Lu Chi (261–303)
>
> The perceptual activity travels far in spirit (*shen*). Completely stilled, contemplation centered, it reaches out to a thousand years. . . . The principle of perceptual activity is miraculous

when the spirit consorts with the external world. . . . To
develop one's perceptual activity, the most important thing is
emptiness and quiescence when one's five viscera will be
cleansed and the spirit purified.[18]

Liu Hsieh (ca. 465–520)

Drawings by rulers are dead. Keep to one's spirit (*shen*), con-
centrate on Oneness, there one finds true paintings. . . . He who
moves his thought and brush but is conscious of his painting as
painting misses it. He who moves his thought and brush
without being conscious of his painting as painting gets it, no
sticking in his hand, no stagnation in his mind; it becomes so
without knowing how.

Gather one's spirit, think freely — there is miraculous under-
standing of Nature. With both the external world and one's self
forgotten, with form cut off, knowledge done away with, even
if one's body becomes dry wood, one's mind, dead ashes, there
will be no hindrance to the miraculous principle of Nature. This
is the Tao of painting.[19]

Chang Yen-yüan (fl. 847)

Live plainly: wait in silence —
It is here the Scheme is seen.[20]
Ssu-k'ung T'u (837–908)

If you want poetry to be miraculous,
Nothing works better than being empty and tranquil.
In tranquillity, one perceives everything in motion.
In the state of emptiness, one takes in all the aspects.[21]
Su Tung-p'o (1036–1101)

The last attainment of poetry is entering into *shen*.

The highest kind of poetry is that which does not tread on the
path of reason, nor fall into the snare of words. . . . The
excellence is in . . . transparency and luminosity, unblurred and
unblocked, like sound in air, color in form, moon in water,
image in mirror.[22]

Yen Yü (fl. 1180–1235)

There is a *self-reflecting world* and there is a *selfless* world. . . .
The selfless world is achieved in quiescence and the self-
reflecting world is arrested from movement.[23]

Wang Kuo-wei (1877–1927)

The centrality and continuity of the Taoist decreative–creative dialectic is clear here and needs little comment. However, we must pause briefly and return to the initial contradictions. One can say that, within the Taoist activity of consciousness, a complete awareness of things as they originally are can be regained by this decreative–creative process but that the miraculous receptivity to the concrete world achieved by emptying out the trappings of our intellect is a state prior to expression. The ideal Taoist poet, when pushed to the logical end, should be silent and seek no expression, for the affirmation of the nonverbal world cancels out such a possibility. Chuang-tzu himself is fully articulate on this contradiction:

> Since all things are one, is there room for speech? Since I have spoken of "one," can there be no speech? One and "speech" make two; two and one make three. Proceeding from this on, even a skillful mathematician cannot exhaust it, let alone an ordinary man! Since, from nonbeing to being, we can get three, how much further we will go, moving from being to being. Thus, move not, let be. Tao knows no boundaries. Speech has no constancy.
>
> Chuang, 79

Tao cannot be told, and yet Lao-tzu and Chuang-tzu cannot help but use the word Tao to circumscribe it. While using it, they remind us that it should immediately be forgotten so that we can be one with nature again. The word "Tao" is used as though it were merely a pointer, a spark toward the original real world. But how can language, as a form of human invention, function in this way? What kind of negotiation can we have at all between the prepoem moment of total awareness and the act of expression?

There is an assumption in the Taoist decreative–creative dialectic that when we achieve our original condition and become one with Tao, everything else will follow its natural course. The hand and the mind will felicitously correspond, as in the case of the cook cutting the bullocks, or like the wheelwright chiseling the wheel: Every blow is exactly right (Chuang, 491). When we achieve our original condition, we will have in us a faculty akin to nature itself. To use Chuang-tzu's words: "To stop without knowing how it stops" (Chuang, 70). We all walk, and we walk without being fully conscious of our walking. This is one example of our natural condition. To arrive at this readiness, Chuang-tzu tells us: "Fishes (born in water, growing up in water) forget themselves in water. Men, (born in Tao, growing up in Tao) will forget themselves being in Tao" (Chuang, 242). Thus, the boatman can row a boat as if it were not there and regards the rapids as though they were dry land (Chuang, 642). And Lü Liang can dive into and emerge from water as if breathing air because, growing up by the water, he has conditioned himself to water's nature (Chuang, 656–58).

It is apt to recall here the idea of *tzu-jan* (i.e., be-nature-thus-natural). The Chinese poet exalts the moment when we can witness nature working itself out in a poem, one that structures and discloses nature the way nature structures and discloses itself. The tension between nature (effortless emergence of things) and art (human effort) is subtly avoided. In a stricter sense, art, by definition, can never be nature. What the Taoists imply from the very beginning is really restored naturalness or second nature, an activity or expressiveness akin to that of nature.

> Bend down — and there it is:
> No need to wrest it from others.
> With the Way in complete consort —
> The mere touch of a hand is spring:
> The way we come upon blooming flowers,
> The way we see the year renew itself.
> What comes this way will stay.
> What we get by force will drain away.
> A secluded man in an empty mountain,
> As rain drops, picks some blade of duckweeds
> Freely to feel the flash of dawn:
> Leisurely, with natural balance.[24]

Thus, the Taoist concept was echoed and expanded by the ninth-century poet-aesthetician Ssu-k'ung T'u and by many poets and critics throughout the centuries. Sometimes, "readiness," "spontaneity," and "free flow of energy" are synonyms used to describe the condition of becoming nature. In calligraphy or painting, which have to be executed in unhesitatingly quick brushstrokes because of the fluidity of the ink and the absorbency of the rice paper, the energy flowing out from the body to the executing brush must not be blocked. Similarly, in T'ai Chi exercise and movement, it is the free, natural energy flow of the body that we want to emulate in order to achieve a reconditioning of its function. To the Taoists as well as to many calligraphers, painters, and T'ai Chi masters, the unimpeded correspondence and coordination between the hand and the mind — natural action coming directly from natural condition — is an unshaken faith with nothing mysterious about it.

As we now see, the Taoists believe in the inseparability of consciousness and expression as it is reflected in those arts that emphasize *ch'i*, or energy flow. But in what way can we make the same claim for the creation of a poem when the poets, too, prize the energy flow as an important hallmark of their naturalness? Can we at all see language as an instinctive part of growth like our ability to walk? While Lao-tzu and Chuang-tzu have never explicitly said so, Taoist poet-critics certainly imply this possible comparison. For example, when Su Tung-p'o talks about his own style he paraphrases Chuang-tzu by saying:

> Writing should be like moving clouds and flowing water which have no fixed form but move [literally, walk] on where they have to move on and stop where they have to stop.[25]

> My writing is like water gushing out from an ample, deep spring. . . . It can move on a thousand miles a day without effort and turns with mountains and rocks and shapes itself according to the objects it encounters. This is something the artist is not conscious of. What he is conscious of is this: that it moves on when it has to move on and it stops when it has to stop.[26]

The suggestion is that expression (the felicity of language) can be as natural as water, an object of nature. In spite of this interesting analogy, there is no way in which we can avoid seeing language as a product of culture. As such, it will always contain predicative elements that are highly obstructive to the attainment of the cosmic measure of things. Our question now is: How are we to liberate ourselves from these elements so as to approximate (if we cannot re-create) the original, real world?

When I gave the example of a Chinese line 澗戶寂無人, saying that it comes closer to the real world than any "possible" English line, I did not mean that, from the very beginning, Chinese as a language was free from predicative elements. As a matter of fact, the Chinese language also has its restrictive elements. But the Taoist consciousness, dispossessing to possess, decreating to create, in an effort to promote the original, real world as the anchorage of our perception, has helped to reduce these elements to a minimum without bringing about a sense of unnaturalness. Chuang-tzu is fully aware of the problem of his own view of language:

Speech is not merely the blowing of winds. It is intending to say
something. But what it is intending to say is not absolutely
established. Is there really such a thing as speech? Is there really
no such thing as speech? Someone considers speech as different
from the chirping of young birds. But is there any distinction
between them, or is there no distinction? How is Tao obscured
that there should be distinction between true or false? How is
speech obscured that there should be a distinction between
right and wrong? Where is Tao not present? Where is speech
not appropriate? Tao is obscured by partiality. Speech is
obscured by vain show. Therefore, there are contentions
between the Confucianists and the Mohists. Each one of these
two schools affirms what the other denies and denies what the
other affirms. If we are to affirm what they both deny and deny
what they both affirm, there is nothing better than to use
transparency.

Chuang, 63

Language, no doubt, cannot be as natural as the blowing of winds or
the singing of birds. An interesting thought here, however, is that
poetics in both Eastern and Western cultures often likes to compare
poetry to winds and bird songs. This perhaps points toward an ideal,
the transcendence of the fetters of language so as to disclose more
freely. This idea is often advocated by lyricists. In a certain sense, the
Taoist vision can perhaps be called "lyrical vision." And yet, even
though language cannot become as natural as the blowing of winds
and the singing of birds, with a transparent understanding of the
relationship between language and the real order of the world, the
potentials of language can be adjusted to come closer to the natural
measure.

"To view things as things view themselves," considered according
to this transparent relationship, implies, then, the following: not to
put "I" in the primary position for aesthetic contemplation. This is
not difficult to understand: Phenomena do not need "I" to have their
existences; they all have their own inner lines, activities, and rhythms
to affirm their authenticity as things. Authenticity or truth does not
come from "I"; things possess their existences and their forms of
beauty and truth before we name them. (We need not know the
name of a certain flower before proclaiming it true and beautiful.)
Thus, subject and object, principal and subordinate, are categories of
superficial demarcation. A thing can be both object and subject at the
same time. "I" can be both subject and object. Positions can be freely

changed—subject and object, consciousness and phenomena interpenetrate, intercomplement, interdefine, and interilluminate, appearing simultaneously, with humans corresponding to things, things corresponding to humans, things corresponding to things extending throughout the million phenomena. "I" can view from this point outward, or "I" can view from that point inward, or from *this* place, *this* time and from *that* place, *that* time. *This* time, *this* place, *that* time, *that* place—none needs to be connected with another by causal relationship. Distance is not absolute. We can walk *toward* and *from* things. In this spatial horizon in which we can move about freely, the so-called distance is paradoxical; it *is and is not* there. As in many Chinese landscape paintings, perspective evaporates before the viewing eye. In Fan K'uan's "Travelers in the Valley," for example, while the figures, the forests, and rocks and hills in the lower right corner of the foreground of the long, hanging scroll appear very small (indicating that we are viewing them from afar), the mountain in the far distance behind them looms huge and imposing as if right before our eyes. In between, there is the mediation of a stretch of cloud, which is simultaneously solid (as a thing) and empty or void (as a visual unit in the painting), helping to diffuse our sense of distance. This painting shows the attempt to avoid a single, linear perspective so that viewers are allowed to view elements from different angles and moveable spatial relationships.

"To view things as things view themselves" also means this: Before the poet speaks and writes in language, it seems as if he has become each of the independent objects and identified with them, disclosing them according to their inner scheme and activities. To be identified with the million things can also be considered embracing the million things; thus, there is a unique sense of harmony and intimacy in our allowing the million things to change and play themselves out in their original gestures, forms, and appearances. In this kind of transparency between Phenomenon and human beings, there is naturally no clear-cut distinction, no hiding of their presences in abstract thinking characterized by positioning, naming, or conferring of definable and determinable meanings, no arbitrary imposition of right and wrong, no argumentation in "vain show." In this kind of transparency, language as a means of reflecting and tracing the activities of things will easily avoid predicative elements—definition, restrictive time and space, determined relationships—and will also avoid projecting by force self-invented meaning structures and systems upon the simple and unhewn phenomena; language will not infuse ego-reflecting elements into objects. Language is used to punctuate the vital rhythm and atmosphere of things as they emerge and act themselves out in the real world. What we call vital rhythm or atmosphere is often what we can only feel and not see, and so, it is even more important that it be free from the fetters of words. Thus, the Taoist artist stresses also the emptiness of language. What is written is fixed and solid; what is unwritten is fluid and empty. This empty and fluid wordlessness is an indispensable cooperator with the fixed and solid word. The full activity of language should be like the copresence of the solid and the void in Chinese paintings, allowing the reader to receive not only the words (the written) but also the wordlessness (the unwritten). The negative space, such as the emptiness in a painting and the condition of silence with meanings trembling at the edges of words in a poem, is made into something vastly more significant and positive and, indeed, has become a horizon toward which our aesthetic attention is constantly directed. By continually decreasing discursive and explanatory elements and procedures in the poetic line, by promoting the coextensive presencing of objects, the poets who possess what the Chinese call the "bosom" of Taoist consciousness help to bring forth a special type of nonmediating mediation, leading to an art of noninterference akin to the workings of nature, and a language that points toward the finer interweaving of unspeaking, concrete, changing nature, like the word "Tao," which we are to forget once it is pronounced, like the fish trap that can be forgotten once the fish is caught (Chuang, 944). The words become a spotlight that brightens objects emerging from the real world, showing them in full brilliance.

The Crisis of Language in the West: Contemplation and Change

When certain poetic lines that eliminate predication appeared in modern Anglo-American poetry with Pound, Williams, cummings, and the Projectivists following in the steps of Mallarmé,[27] people could not help but call them "deviations." In the words of Roland Barthes:

> Modern poetry destroyed relationships in language and
> reduced discourse to words as static things. This implies a
> reversal in our knowledge of Nature. The interrupted flow of
> the new poetic language initiates a discontinuous Nature,
> which is revealed only piecemeal. At the very moment when
> the withdrawal of functions obscures the relations existing in

the world, the object in discourse assumes an exalted place: modern poetry is a poetry of the object. In it, Nature becomes a fragmented space, made of objects solitary and terrible. . . . The word is left with a vertical object, it is like a monolith, or a pillar which plunges into a totality of meanings, reflexes and recollections: it is a sign which stands. The poetic word is here an act without immediate past, without environment, and which holds forth only the dense shadow of reflexes from all sources which are associated with it.[28]

With the same attempt to avoid predicative elements, why does modern poetry evoke the sense of deviation? The objects are nothing but unfamiliar, strange, and isolated. We can disagree with Barthes's formulation of nature, which is still one that is controlled and dominated by language, an order made up of what William James called "serials," which necessarily break up the "collateral contemporaneity" of all beings, but most readers still find it difficult to accept poetic lines found in modern poetry as being natural. Why?

Paradoxically and anachronistically, it was the anxiety over the inadequacy of language, over the question whether language can authenticate what is immediately before us, that ushered in the whole movement to reinvent language in the West. Indeed, the language crisis has also been an epistemological crisis, about which modern philosophers, aestheticians, and poets have obsessively agonized. Witness a blunt statement by Albert Camus in his "Sur un philosophie de l'expression": "It's a matter of deciding whether our language is a lie or truth."[29]

From Mallarmé through Stein, from Pound to the postmodernists, from Kierkegaard to Heidegger to Derrida, this question echoes like a call from profundity, at once apocalyptic and divine.

Mallarmé, almost distraught by the inadequacy of language, fitfully attempted to turn the denial into a privileged passage into totality. Languages to him are

imperfect because multiple; the supreme language is missing . . . the diversity of languages on earth means that no one can utter words which would bear the miraculous stamp of Truth Itself Incarnate. This is clearly nature's law . . . to the effect that we have no sufficient reason for equating ourselves with God. But then esthetically, I am disappointed when I consider how impossible it is for languages to express things by means of certain keys which would reproduce their brilliance and aura.[30]

Distressed by the impossiblity of language, Mallarmé sought to liber-
ate words from their bondage to the original world of objects that
conceptual reason has set and to allow them to move into and exist
like isolated things trembling in the zero of nothingness, in silence
and blank space where both objects and language (in the form re-
ceived from culture) would be negated, when Beauty, like a bouquet
totally new, rises magically and musically out of the words.[31] Through
this negative process, he wanted to give back to language its mystic
dimension: the Orphic world-creating power.

This attempt to essentialize objects by changing words into props
to define the ambience or into players to play themselves out in an
empty field or stage is to purge everything palpable of a lived experi-
ence. The world so produced has no identification with the real,
original world (notice that the flower Mallarmé created is not to be
found in the plant world!) but has, instead, become a shadow of the
Platonic scheme in reverse. Like the "shut windows" in his poems, if
the world is to be known, it can only be intuited through its absence.
There is, in this scheme of things, no reentrance into the free flow of
objects of the original world; instead, the objects have been taken out
of the concrete natural environment in which we find them and then
transported by the poet into a new (still conceptual) world of lan-
guage, in and for themselves, with no reference to the original world
for identification. "Everything exists in the world to finally culminate
in a book (the world created by the poet's language)."[32] There is no
attempt to retrieve the prepredicative appeal of the objects whereby
we can regain the original world.

> I am travelling . . . but in unknown lands, and if I had fled from
> the fierce heat of reality and have taken pleasure in cold imag-
> ery, it is because for a month now I have been on the purest
> glaciers of esthetics; because after I had found nothingness, I
> found beauty.[33]

Here we recall his famous sonnet:

> La vierge, le vivace et le bel aujourd'hui
> Va-t-il nous déchirer avec un coup d'aile ivre
> Ce lac dur oublié que hante sous le givre
> Le transparent glacier des vols qui n'ont pas fui!
>
> Un cygne d'autrefois se souvient que c'est lui
> Magnifique mais qui sans espoir se délivre
> Pour n'avoir pas chanté la région où vivre
> Quand du stérile hiver a resplendi l'ennui.

Tout son col secouera cette blanche agonie
Par l'espace infligée à l'oiseau qui le nie,
Mais non l'horreur du sol où le plumage est pris.

Fantôme qu'à ce lieu son pur éclat assigne,
Il s'immobilise au songe froid de mépris
Que vêt parmi l'exil inutile le Cygne.[34]

Mallarmé wants to create a nameless world out of language. Words
are like a magic wand by which the relationships between the objects
and the original environments in which we find them are made to
disappear. Objects are thus alienated from their original grounds and
made independent, with no past, no familiar connections to the real
world, so as to let them work out freely a new world of their own (an
aesthetic domain made from words). Although we can perhaps say
here that the swan is a metaphor for the poet himself, it is never-
theless not a swan that we can find in the real world; it can only exist
in the aesthetic world of words through which an almost mystical
blinding brightness is emitted. This swan, like the flower rising out of
the music of Mallarmé, is not an object of the feathered world.

Mallarmé disregarded the appeal of the original world and
usurped the position of the Creator. Mallarmé once quoted these
words from Genesis, "The word is the world," and by this proclaimed
God's work to be his own, placing expression above everything else
in the making of a poem. This fact makes his (as well as his fol-
lowers') dislocation of syntax (which once might have been intended
to reach out to the prepredicative immanence of word-objects) come
to us as a violent act and as a form of deviation.

We can see, too, that Mallarmé's distrust of language is, at the
same time, its promotion to a specially privileged status. This privi-
leged status is at root different from our consideration of language's
relation to the original ground, the givenness and presencing of
things as they are. But why did Mallarmé (and the subsequent
postsymbolists and modernists) do this? What historical changes had
brought about this reaction against the existing conceptions of lan-
guage? Here, we must first explore the complex socio-historical and
epistemological crisis in which Mallarmé found himself.

When Plato excommunicated the poet from his Republic, his
verdict was that what the poet imitates is only an illusion because his
object of imitation, the external world, is constantly changing, and, as
such, the appearances of things can only be shadows of some
permanent Reality (i.e., Logos, wherein resides the so-called Truth).

Our first reaction to this line of reasoning is that Plato, too, affirms that art is a human construction and hence cannot become nature (god-made). If we follow this line of thinking, we can also reach the conclusion that human intellect is limited and that language is insufficient in representation, but this is not Plato's logic.

In his hierarchy of values, Plato divides knowledge into three modes. The lowest mode is pure perception. It cannot lead to truth, because its objects are constantly changing appearances, which are not a fit locus for Truth. Here, Plato's view is clearly contrary to that of the Taoists, which affirms constant changes as the very Truth itself; Plato attempts to locate Truth somewhere else.

The highest mode in Plato's scheme is the contemplation of the Idea, transcendent and transensuous, by pure intelligence. What is called Truth resides in this abstract world beyond the concrete world of appearances. And only through philosophical thinking, not sense perception, can we expect to reach this Logos. This preference has directly affected the entire spectrum of perceptual (and consequently expressive) modes in the West.

Between Plato's lowest and highest modes is the thinking activity proposed by Pythagoras—mathematical and geometrical thinking—as the only path from pure perception to pure idea. In fact, mathematics and geometry were born from the ancient practices of observing the activities of the heavenly bodies. What they did was to proceed from hypotheses—these *were* hypotheses—to speculate on the structure of the universe and to measure the movement of its stars. This was the beginning of Western science. Thus, we know that what Plato calls philosophical thinking already contains the seeds of scientific logic. To know the universe involves going through some analytical and syllogistical processes. Such processes have dominated Western use of language ever since.

We must also notice that the so-called Truth (be it abstract Logos or the Law of Movement of the Universe) comes to us only as "notions" of Truth or "hypotheses" of Truth, and as such they are human structures in place of the "real" order of the concrete world of appearances itself. In other words, in Plato's hierarchy of knowledge, order is placed within man's thought or intellect, not in the external world. Plato created Logos, an abstract system, to play against what is given before us in its supposedly unorganized form. To do this is to alienate humanity from its original ground: Humankind is not seen as one of the millions of components that make up the total fabric of being but is promoted to be the paradigm of all orders.

Aristotle subsequently strengthened the centrality of human mental constructs in the cosmic scheme of things. His geocentric view of a finite universe, for example, exerted a long, unchallenged influence in the West. Following Empedocles's view on the various properties of the four elements, he concluded that earth, being the heaviest, therefore occupies the center, while water, air, and fire, being increasingly lighter, form the next three spheres surrounding earth, with a constellation of fixed stars on the outermost sphere, beyond which there is no other world. We now know that this view of the structure of the universe was built upon a mere hypothesis and has been proven wrong, and yet this human-made order dominated almost twenty centuries of Western scientific thinking, including the powerful Christian adoption of it in the Middle Ages, when finite humans and earth were pitched against God, the infinite and beyond. What do we learn from this historical fact? Aristotle conditioned almost all Western thinkers to seek order within humankind and to regard its mental constructs as absolutes. Thus, the "universal and logical structures" that a poet is supposed to be able to provide from existential experiences—an argument Aristotle used to counter Plato's preference of philosophy over poetry and his excommunication of the poet from his Republic—are to be taken as absolutes, when in reality they are nothing but human notions (conceptual worlds after abstraction).

The elevation of the ego's domination of the original world became so strong that even after the Copernican revolution, when both Aristotle's model of a finite universe and the medieval cosmology were supposed to be blasted (as John Donne puts it in his "An Anatomy of the World," "'Tis all in pieces, all coherence gone"), Bacon could go so far as to proclaim that "the artificial does not differ from the natural in form and essence,"[35] and Descartes could insist that "there are no differences between the machines built by artisans and the diverse bodies that nature alone compose."[36] In fact, even after the seventeenth century, many people continued to explain the universe in terms of machines.

The ego's domination of the original world also had other sociohistorical consequences. The principle of domination of nature was transposed to the human realm: Humans dominated other humans on the principle of exchange value (the use value of an object). This further removed the immanence of things as things as well as the immanence of people as people. With industrialization, which capitalized on the domination and exchange principles, the function of language, which had been suffering from the Platonic-Aristotelian process of abstraction, was further reduced to serving the ideology of a society that values above all the instrumental importance of things and human beings, such as seeing a tree not as a tree but as lumber and seeing a man not according to his natural being but according to his production potentials. The function of language, under this society, is not to approximate, authenticate, or derive animation from the cosmic scheme or the workings of nature but to carry practical knowledge. When Western philosophers and artists talk about the crisis of language, they are not engaging in a frivolous aestheticism; the crisis is directly bound to the crisis of ideology. Here, we must reexamine the ambiguous role of science in the history of consciousness.

Properly speaking, the crisis of modern consciousness began in the seventeenth century with the challenge of the hermeneutical framework underlying the once unified world view and consciousness that dominated medieval and Renaissance Europe, namely the Christian geocentric cosmology together with its hierachical structures. This challenge ushered in the extremely complex and ambiguous role of science. It was ambiguous because this history can be written as the dawn of humanism since the challenge brought with it the challenge of the power structure invested in the church and the prince. In one significant sense, this was the beginning of a process of liberating individuals from arbitrarily "constituted" but at root suppressive "beliefs"—the beginning of the demythologization of the so-called truths. And yet, the writing of this history is not without its biases. With the prioritization of the rational, emphasizing the kind of verifiability natural sciences had offered, a host of other so-called illogical, irrational, but in reality alternative forms of consciousness were exiled. Indeed, any other form of thinking deviating from this new emphasis had to be justified. Thus, we find artists and poets of subsequent centuries had to claim that literature can be as precise as science, as in Pound's "The Serious Artist," or to circle out a separate domain for poetry as in all symbolist and postsymbolist theories.

The crisis of consciousness emerged in yet another disturbing form. While the West must be thankful to Copernicus and Galileo for breaking the medieval mythico-political cosmological framework (since their challenges gave rise to the birth of the Enlightenment, which presented the possibility of leading Western society out of its ego-centered consciousness), the enlightened individual was, paradoxically, left in a new wilderness. Before the break, the world was cohe-

sive; all three levels—the macrocosmic, the earth, and the microcos-
mic—were rolled into one, with a network of interpretive markers,
arbitrarily constituted and antinatural though they were, that were
unified and understood throughout Europe. After the break, the truly
universal cohesive framework is yet to be found. We see a lot of
nostalgia for the so-called unified sensibility in Pound, Eliot, and
Hulme, for example. In a sense, all attempts since the seventeenth
century, from the Romantics through the symbolists and modernists
to the phenomenologists and existentialists, can be considered ways
of finding alternative explanatory systems, either working from
within or borrowing from non-Western traditions, to replace this lost
world. As it turned out, however, post-Enlightenment humanity had
to further accelerate the centrality of reason, leading to logical,
positivistic objectivity, or to affirm the subjectivity of the self as the
site, organically creative, by which the poet not only could know the
essences of the universe but could give it a new *raison d'être* and, at a
later stage of development, could make totally new worlds within an
ego-reflecting language.

The rise of science, which has fragmented the world, has also frag-
mented humankind. The demand of postindustrial specialization has
led to complex isolated entities of knowledge that the conventional
reductionist language can no longer comprehend. Eliot's words
characterize this situation well:

> We can only say that it appears likely that poets in our civili-
> zation, as it exists at present, must be *difficult*. Our civilization
> comprehends great variety and complexity, and this variety and
> complexity, playing upon a refined sensibility, must produce
> various and complex results. The poet must become more and
> more comprehensive, more allusive, more indirect, in order to
> force, to dislocate if necessary, language into his meaning.[37]

Similarly, the expressionist painters had to distort forms and shapes
of objects to fully comprehend this complexity. Language as an
expressive medium (for that matter, the language of all the arts) in
the postindustrialized period has many deficiencies. This is the other
reason that philosophers and poets desperately sought change and
reinvention in "the language of the tribe."

One of the consequences of specialization and compartmentaliza-
tion in the postindustrialized world is that the poet is left with no
role to play. The poet is no longer asked to speak for nature, or to
account for God's scheme of things, or to be a source of commu-
nication between society and God and between human beings.

Explication of the structure of the universe can be better done by the scientist. Suddenly, overnight, just like the poet in a low pub in one of Baudelaire's prose poems, the poet's halo has fallen into the gutter and is nowhere to be found. The poet has no altar in society. The rise of science and its demand for verifiability of statements about metaphysical or moral truths have put the question of self and values into great jeopardy. A. N. Whitehead epitomizes the discord in one sentence from Tennyson: "The stars blindly run." If the stars run blindly according to the law of celestial movement, do the molecules in our body also run blindly? If they do, we cannot be responsible for our moral actions. If they do, how are we to understand the exact meaning of self? Science has opened up a Pandora's Box. It has driven some to search for the meaning of human life (such as in existentialism, within the larger phenomenological philosophy) or to explore the structures and behavioristic patterns of the psyche (such as in psychoanalysis); it has also led some to recontemplate the relationship between humans and phenomena (such as in phenomenology) or to explain historical phenomena through scientific logical dialecticism (such as in Marxism). All these can be considered attempts to reposition the self in some coherent, meaningful contexts.

It was against the impotence of language to comprehend the fragmented complexities induced by reductionist scientific realism and against the ultimate denial of the poet's place in the cosmic scheme of things by the resultant reification of humankind that the affirmation of subjectivity became imminent. The romantic emphasis on imagination as an active organizing principle of the poet's mind over logic and reason, the mythologizing of nature as a replacement for Logos and God and as a companion model through which the full potential of the poet's mind can be glorified, the symbolist elevation of language as possessing Orphic power, offering a symbolic nature for nature itself (language *as* world, style *as* absolute, beauty *as* religion) —all these efforts must be seen as challenges to the reductionist threat of positivistic philosophy and as a protest against the reification of human beings by withdrawing into a solipsistic world of aesthetics, now proclaimed to be autonomous, complete, and brimming with the spirituality abandoned by postindustrial society.

The so-called reinvention of language was aimed at restoring the perceptual dimensions exiled by reductionist reason and by the reification of human beings. But this restoration could not be achieved by a tour-de-force elevation and mystication of language or by a self-willed rejection of the original world. The restoration had to begin

with a root understanding of what T. E. Hulme once called the ulti-
mate illness of the Western mind: the invasion and domination of the
original world by the ego in numerous arrogant forms:

> The ancients were perfectly aware of the fluidity of the world
> and its impermanence . . . but while they recognized it, they
> feared it and endeavored to evade it to construct things of per-
> manence which would stand fast in this universal flux which
> frightened them. They had the disease, the passion, for immor-
> tality. They wished to construct things which would be proud
> boasts that they, man, were immortal. We see it in a thousand
> different forms, materially in the pyramids, spiritually in the
> dogmas of religion and in the hypostatized ideas of Plato.[38]

Even though modern poets, beginning with Mallarmé, attempted to
discard the Platonic and Aristotelian discourses, they had not been
cured of the disease of positing their ego or self-consciousness as the
source of final order at the expense of disfiguring and exiling the
original world. This refusal to reenter the immanence of things made
impossible any attempt to liberate language from its prison-house.

Here, the Taoist horizon of transparency between consciousness
("I") and the world becomes particularly instructive. A brief recapitu-
lation of this horizon is in order. Between "the world as it is (self-so)"
and "the world as it is believed to be," the Taoists turn their attention
toward the former and reject the premise that the structure of the
world is the same as we conceive it. They understand, first, that
naming, meaning, language, and concept are restrictive acts, none of
which can fully authenticate the very original state of things, and all
of which will, one way or another, distort it; second, that the real
world, quite without supervision and explanation by human beings,
is totally alive, self-generating, self-conditioning, self-transforming,
and self-complete; and third, that humankind, being only one among
a million beings, has no prerogative to classify the cosmic scheme.
Hence, we should not put "I" in the primary position to dominate
and determine the forms and meanings of things; instead, we should
allow consciousness and the million things to freely exchange posi-
tions so as to coexist, to answer one another, to mutually illuminate
and be totally transparent.

In this transparency, because "I" view things as things view them-
selves, what emerges in the language is the easy avoidance of analyt-
ical, discursive, and syllogistic elements, giving us a nonconnective,
dramatic presencing of things; because the ego merges with and

diffuses itself in the undifferentiated composition of things, identifying with them and leaving them in the forefront of perception, it can eschew "ego-reflecting" elements and can retain multilinear, multispatial relationships with the ongoing continuity of the composition of things.

When the modern poets in the West attempted to eschew the analytical, the discursive, the syllogistic, the linear, and the determinate, they indeed achieved something quite close to the expressive strategies found in classical Chinese poetry, namely, direct, concrete acting out of objects, spatialization of time, and temporalization of space. These expressive strategies led to visuality of events in coextensive relationships with pictorial and sculptural appeal, indeterminate and nonrestrictive relationships leading to multiple suggestiveness and multifaceted space activity, simultaneity of objects leading to juxtaposition and superimposition.[39] But the full realization of this aim requires simultaneously the loss of self in the free flow of things and the attunement of the ego (self, consciousness) with the original transparent relationships in the total composition of things so as to leave the given as given, to view things as things view themselves in their *natural* environment. It follows, then, that until Western poets can adjust their perceptual priority and repossess the original real world, their stylistic innovations will not be natural and will be viewed by many readers as "deviations."

The movement to reorient consciousness so as to repossess the original world has been a continuous obsession for modern philosophers and poets in the West. As early as 1844, Kierkegaard questioned the abstract systems of the West (the world of ideas) and opted for concrete existence. In his *Concluding Unscientific Postscript*, he says:

> The difficulty that inheres in existence, with which the existing individual is confronted, is one that never really comes to expression in the language of abstract thought, much less receives an explanation. But abstract thought is *sub specie aeterni*, it ignores the concrete and the temporal, the existential process. . . . The questionable character of abstract thought becomes apparent especially in connection with all existential problems, where abstract thought gets rid of the difficulty by leaving it out, and then proceeds to boast of having explained everything.[40]

Abstract thought cannot comprehend and authenticate concrete existence. This, as we now look back on the first section of this chapter, is the main theme in William James's insistence upon "collateral contemporaneity" and Whitehead's "immediate deliverance of experience"; both want to prevent the total "real" world from being broken up into serial orders or reduced to "desirated" forms. In later years, Heidegger demanded a return to a pre-Socratic understanding of *physis* (the emergence of things) instead of indulging in *meta-physis*. In between came T. E. Hulme's Bergsonian resistance to scientific reduction of the indescribable world into counters, along with the imagists' emphasis (not yet fully articulated) on the real and the natural symbol as adequate symbol.[41]

The various philosophical orientations outlined above suggest a potential for reaffirming the innocence and immanence of things, if it could be made acceptable to postindustrialized humanity. A new "line" of poetic expression (such as those that eschew determinate syntactical relationships) needs a new "mind" to become authentic and natural. It is this need that has made the works of Heidegger meaningful, particularly because of his attempt to recover the original ground of being by pointing toward the given as given, undoing slowly the reductionist concepts, classifications, and logos-centered orders. It is on this level that we find the Taoists and Heidegger sharing, and even speaking, the same language. I will outline here two attempts toward this new orientation, one by Heidegger in philosophy, the other by William Carlos Williams in poetry.

As if to echo one of Chuang-tzu's writings, "On Making Everything Equal," in which most of the Taoists' germinal ideas are articulated, Heidegger says in his *Introduction to Metaphysics*,[42] "All essents [beings] are of equal value and we must avoid singling out any particular essent, including man."

> For what indeed is man? Consider the earth within the endless darkness of space in the universe. By way of comparison it is a tiny grain of sand; between it and the next grain of its own size there extends a mile or more of emptiness; on the surface of this grain there lives a crawling, bewildered swarm of supposedly intelligent animals, who for a moment have discovered knowledge. And what is the temporal extension of a human life amid all the million years? Scarcely a move of the second hand, a breath. Within the essents as a whole there is no legitimate ground for singling out the essent which we called mankind and to which we ourselves happen to belong.
>
> *Introduction to Metaphysics*, 3–4

Humankind being such, it should not be placed in the primary position of dominating and controlling the world. In fact, humans do not have this faculty, for the essents are not affected by concepts. "To be sure, the things in the world, the essents, are in no way affected by our asking of the question 'Why are there essents, rather than nothing?' Whether we ask it or not, the planets move in their orbits, the sap of life flows through plant and animal" (5). "Our questioning is after all only a psycho-spiritual process in us which, whatever course it may take, cannot in any way affect the essent itself" (29). Heidegger suggests that we return to the condition before language happened, for "as long as we dwell on the word form and its meaning we have not yet come to the 'thing'" (87)—return to what Maurice Merleau-Ponty, the chief disciple of Husserl and Heidegger, later called "the world [that] is always 'already there' before reflection begins—as an inalienable presence."[43] When we use the word "being" to discuss this inalienable world, the word escapes us as something intangible. "All the things we have named *are*, and yet when we wish to apprehend being, it is always as though we were reaching the void. The being after which we inquire is almost like nothing—being remains unfindable . . . in the end, the word 'being' is no more than an empty word. It means nothing real, tangible, material. Its meaning is an unreal vapor" (*Introduction to Metaphysics*, 35). In a sense, Heidegger feels, like the Taoists, that the word "being" is used only as a provisional pointer: Once we reach the inalienable world of things, the word should be crossed out. (This is comparable to Chuang-tzu's "Forget the words when you get the sense of things; forget the fish trap once the fish is caught.")

Heidegger is deeply aware of the problematics of language. His dialogue with a Japanese (given in chapter 1) is a demonstration of how Westerners have been caught in the prison-house of language. The first step to be taken is to break the concepts of the universe and their restrictive language modes and procedures so that things can return to the condition by which they achieve determinable being by being indeterminate (91). In his "Hölderlin and the Essence of Poetry," Heidegger points out that the poet possesses both the most dangerous and the most precious language. Most dangerous because it often alienates things from their original real condition; most precious because if we can undo the illusions it carries, it can help us disclose the real emergence of things.[44]

As can be expected, one of the first things Heidegger must do is to recover the pristine meaning that exists between name and thing by an etymological exercise, trying to resurrect some Platonic-Aristotelian concepts in pre-Socratic terms.

1. *Physis* (the root for the word "physics"): "What does the word *physis* denote? It denotes self-blossoming emergence (e.g. the blossoming of a rose) opening up, unfolding, that which manifests itself in such unfolding and preserves and endures in it; in short, the realm of things that emerge and linger on . . . emergence . . . in celestial phenomena (the rising in the sun), in the coming forth of man and animal from the womb. . . . This power of emerging and enduring includes 'becoming' as well as 'being.' . . . It is experienced primarily through what in a way imposes itself most immediately on our attention and this was the later, narrower sense of *physis: ta physei onta, ta physika*, nature.[45] . . . Philosophical inquiry into the realm of being as such is *meta ta physika*; this inquiry goes beyond the essent. . . . The fundamental question of this work is of a different kind from the leading question of metaphysics. Taking what was said in *Sein und Zeit* as a starting point, we inquired into the *'disclosure of being.'*" (14; 16–17; 18)

2. *Aletheia* (often translated as Truth): "Since the essent as such *is*, it places itself in and stands in *unconcealment, aletheia*. We translate, and at the same thoughtlessly misinterpret this word as 'Truth'. . . . For the Greek essence of truth is possible only in one with the Greek essence of being as *physis*. On the strength of the unique and essential relationship between *physis* and *aletheia* the Greeks would have said: The essent is true insofar as it is. The true as such is essent. This means: The power that manifests itself stands in unconcealment. . . . Truth is inherent in the essence of being. To be an essent—this comprises to come to light, to appear on the scene, to take one's [its] place, to produce something." (102)

3. *Eidos* or *idea* is not something abstract. "They call the appearance of a thing *eidos*." (60)

Heidegger's reinterpretation of these concepts is his way of destroying existing closures of meaning so as to recover a pristine understanding of the relationship between consciousness and the world. This gesture reminds us of Kuo Hsiang's commentary on Taoists texts that were mystified over time. Kuo Hsiang helped to clear away the possible mystical as well as metaphysical meanings unduly attributed to the words *Tao* (which misled many Western translators to

translate it as God or Logos), *T'ien,* literally sky, now clearly anno-
tated as nature (Chuang, 10), and "Divine Mortals" and "Holy Men,"
now annotated as names referring to those who understand and
allow things to assume their own nature and run their own course
(Chuang, 22–25). He unequivocally said in his preface: "Above, there
is no Creator; below, things create themselves." This clarification
prepared the way for the landscape poets of the Six Dynasties to see
mountains as mountains.

Heidegger's efforts can be seen as an attempt to clear away the
metaphysical burdens of the past. Like the Taoist return to the
original uncarved world, Heidegger encourages the re-recognition of
physis, the emergence and unconcealment of things before the
closures of abstract meanings (i.e., the prepredicative condition of
things). This led him to pronounce a new beginning for Western
aesthetics. A poet should not be obsessed with *aletheia* (in the
traditional sense), or concepts, or hypotheses about the real world
but should converse and communicate directly with the living appeal
of things as they are. In his *Poetry, Language, and Thought,*[46] Heidegger
has this to say about thought and creativity:

> To think "Being" means: to respond to the appeal of its pres-
> encing. The response stems from the appeal and releases
> toward that appeal.
>
> PLT, 183

> Poetry calls things, bids them come. . . . Bidding is inviting. It
> invites things in, so that they may bear upon men as things. . . .
> The things that were named, thus called, gather to themselves
> sky and earth mortals and divinities. This gathering, assem-
> bling, letting-stay is the thinging of things. The unitary fourfold
> of sky and earth, mortals and divinities, which is stayed in the
> thinging of things, we called — the world. In the naming, the
> things named are called into the thinging. Thinging, they
> unfold world, in which things abide and so are the abiding
> ones. By thinging, things carry out world. . . . Thinging, things
> are things. Thinging, they gesture — gestate — world.
>
> PLT, 199–200

According to Heidegger, between human beings and things, be-
tween thing and thing, there is a kind of mirroring that both "sets
each of the four free into its own but . . . binds these free ones into
the simplicity of their essential being toward one another" (*PLT,* 179).
"World and things do not subsist alongside one another. They pene-

trate each other. Thus, the two traverse a middle. In it, they are at one. Thus at one, they are intimate. . . . The intimacy of world and thing is not a fusion. Intimacy obtains only where the intimate — world and thing — divides itself cleanly and remains separated. In the midst of the two, in the between of world and thing, in their *inter*, division prevails: a *dif-ference*" (*PLT*, 202). Subject and object penetrate each other and are both one and separate. Subject and object are interchangeable.[47]

By affirming the prepredicative condition of things as our perceptual priority, and by rejecting the premise that humankind can or should dominate the original world, Heidegger (the later Heidegger in particular) and the Taoists are speaking the same language. It is clear of course that the mode of presentation adopted by Heidegger is different from that of the Taoists. The latter, and Chuang-tzu in particular, use language of poetic dimension, full of visual imagery or visual events to strike the reader's receptor directly, whereas Heidegger has to use a complex and sophisticated argument to desophisticate. His *What Is a Thing?*, for example, is a thick tome in which he tries patiently to undo the logical structures that previous philosophers had artificially constructed.

If we claim that William Carlos Williams's view of poetry and his language strategies are inspired by Heidegger, this is definitely incorrect. On the one hand, his artistic manipulation comes from Mallarmé's double view of language: While denouncing language as inadequate, Mallarmé ordains it with a privileged, world-creating status. In a certain sense, Williams remains a Mallarméan expressionist. He picks up from Gertrude Stein the idea of nullifying grammatical functions so as to retain the multiplicity of meanings in a sentence. This destruction of linearity in part helps him to extend the Mallarméan concept of the supreme language. On the other hand, he has also inherited Hulme's rejection of abstract thought for concreteness and Pound's antidiscursive imagistic thinking. Thus, Williams pronounces "No ideas but in things." But more important, it was William James's emphasis upon the real order of the world and Whitehead's insistence upon "immediate deliverance of experience" that led modern American poets, Williams and the postmodernists in particular, to embrace things as they really are in the original real world. Thus, when he says, "A life that is here and now is timeless. That is the universal I am seeking: to embody in a work of art, a new world that is always 'real.' . . . No symbolism is acceptable," and when he insists on seeing "the thing itself without forethought or afterthought but with great intensity of perception," we feel that Williams, in his own way, through his specific channels, basically arrived at a perceptual-expressive mode that highlights "what is, is real." I have already discussed in the previous chapter the aesthetic assumptions of the use of space breaks and syntactic breaks in Williams's poetry. However, a full examination of the dialectical relationships between his perceptual orientation and his language strategies must be reserved for another occasion. Here, I find Hillis Miller's analysis of Williams in terms of Heideggerian phenomenology is adequate to bring out Williams's convergence with the Taoist aesthetic disposition. Let me simply summarize from Miller's quotations from Williams.[48]

1. [At twenty, Williams recognized an] "inner security"... "a sudden resignation to existence . . . which made everything a unit and at the same time a part of myself" (SL, 147).[49] . . . He abandoned his private consciousness. . . . "Why even speak of 'I' . . . which/interests me almost not at all?" (P, 30)

2. Consciousness permeates the world, and the world has entered into the mind. It is "an identity—it can't be/otherwise an/interpenetration, both ways" (P, 12)

3. The Romantic . . . opposition between inner world of subject and outer world of things . . . disappears. . . . [His is] a space both subjective and objective, a region of copresence in which anywhere is everywhere, and all times are one time. . . . All things exist simultaneously in one realm, and though they may interact they are not related causally. The idea of causal sequence is replaced by the notion of a poetry which "lives with an intrinsic movement of its own to verify its authenticity" (SE, 257) [Compare the Taoist idea of self-generating, self-transforming nature.]

4. "I feel as much a part of things as trees and stones" (SL, 127). . . . He belongs to "a wordless/world/ without personality" (CEP, 280) [Compare the Taoist emphasis on "no-self" (*wu-wo*) and the nonverbal world (*wu-yen*).]

5. "Whenever I say 'I', I mean also you" (SA, 4) [Compare "*This* is also *that, that* is also *this*" of the Taoists.]

These dispositions are no doubt consonant with those of the Taoists and Heidegger, but I am not suggesting that their world views are exactly the same. Although Williams had translated some Chinese poems and had read about the Chinese artistic temperament by way of Pound, there is not enough evidence to believe that Williams read and understood Taoism. Similarly, although Heidegger, at a later stage of his thinking, read Lao-tzu and, in one interview, even said that had he known the works of the Taoist-derived Ch'an Buddhism he would not have written what he had written, there is no evidence that he made any systematic study of Taoism. But precisely because of this, we feel it even more meaningful that Heidegger and Williams arrived at a similar orientation. Culture, like language's double edges that Heidegger talks about, will, as it develops, no doubt widen the possibility of communication, but it will also create alienation and incommunicativeness. Like any linguistic formulations, culture is established by a process of centering and privileging, thus excluding that which is on the margin, and by circling out a domain for sharper definition, thus rejecting that which freely flows in the open. What does this convergence between an intellectual horizon formed in the third century B.C. in China and those represented by Heidegger and Williams twenty-three centuries afterwards mean? It means a possible ground upon which we can repossess the original, real-life world by sharing the same questions asked concerning our consciousness and the world. But we must also mark this: The reverse of Williams's statement "unless there is/a new mind there cannot be a new/line" must also be true. A new mind needs a new line to be transformed. Without breaking down the prison-walls imposed by certain Western language practices, the sensibility leading toward the repossession of the original world cannot be reborn.

4   Aesthetic Consciousness of Landscape in Chinese and Anglo-American Poetry

> Romantic nature poetry . . . was an anti-nature poetry, even in Wordsworth who sought a reciprocity or even a dialogue with nature, but found it only in flashes.[1]

This statement made by Harold Bloom in 1970 has probably vexed many readers who consider Wordsworth the high priest of nature. Indeed, for decades, when referring to nature poetry or landscape poetry, many critics like to look at Wordsworth as the counterpart of either T'ao Ch'ien (365–427) or Hsieh Ling-yün (385–433). That they have been so compared is, no doubt, due to the facts that, first, they employ landscape as their primary material for poetry; second, they focus what we may call aesthetic attention upon natural objects — mountains, rivers, trees, birds, and so on; third, they are supposed to seek a return to nature and harmony with it; and, last, their poetries bear certain structural resemblances, such as the use of excursion (in Wordsworth and in Hsieh) as a means to disclose objects in nature. (Hsieh's poems were first given a generic classification as "Excursion Poems" before he was acclaimed as the initiator of Chinese landscape poetry.) Indeed, we may even find part of M. H. Abrams's description of the "Greater Romantic Lyric"[2] applicable to Hsieh in the sense that his poetry begins with landscape and ends with awakening or recognition.

And yet, in spite of these resemblances, many of the comparative studies of this poetry remain illusive and superficial. Upon closer examination of the two models on the basis of their indigenous sources, including comparison and contrast of their historical morphology and their aesthetic structuring activities, we will encounter significant root differences, both in terms of the conception of genre and in terms of perceptual-expressive procedures. The Chinese poets' consciousness of landscape as an aesthetic object in and of itself is a perceptual-expressive as well as genre possibility hardly circum-scribed by that of the English nature poets. To understand the exact projection and curve of this poetry, we must look into the historical formation of this aesthetic consciousness in both traditions.

Let it be understood first that not all poems containing landscape are necessarily landscape poems. For example, the large paragraphs of landscape description in Homer, those in the *fu* (rhymeprose) of the Han Dynasty, or the landscape passages in the long narratives of the classical Latin period only serve as a background against which human events take place. Landscape plays only a secondary or subordinate position; it has not become the main object for aes-thetic contemplation.[3] We call a poem a landscape poem not only because landscape has become the primary aesthetic object but also because landscape can be seen as an aesthetic object in and of itself. For landscape to become so involves, therefore, our acceptance of it as it is, self-so-complete. In what sense and in what way is such an acceptance made possible in China? To what degree can we say English and American poets have or have not cultivated such an acceptance? How does this acceptance or incomplete acceptance affect the contour of the different poets' approaches (perception and expression) to nature and, more specifically, to landscape?

There is a famous *kung-an* (*kōan*) in the Ch'an (Zen) Buddhist *Transmission of the Lamp:*

> Thirty years ago before I was initiated into Ch'an, I saw moun-tains as mountains, rivers rivers. Later when I got an entrance into knowledge, I saw mountains not as mountains, rivers not as rivers. Now that I have achieved understanding of the sub-stance, mountains are still mountains, rivers still rivers.[4]

This can be taken as representing three stages of our perception of reality. The first stage, "seeing mountains as mountains, rivers rivers," is comparable to the innocent or naive mode of apprehending reality. This mode is naive in the sense that it is not cluttered by intellectuality; it is perception like that either of a child or of people in primitive societies before any epistemological activity enters into their consciousness. This kind of consciousness responds directly to the concrete data of nature. A child's consciousness is often without language or at least without conscious intellectual language. A child lives in a sort of coexistence with the thousand things in nature but does not seek consciously to disclose them in poetry. When the child does, the poem often focuses on the most salient features of the concrete presences of things. Like the poems by primitive peoples, a child's poetic utterances often seek to identify objects in their full, original, indigenous status. However, when a conscious attempt to express this response in language is made, we find ourselves moving into the second stage of perception, "seeing mountains not as mountains, rivers not as rivers," in which epistemological activity is at work. This activity leads us away from the fresh, direct appeal of landscape to seek in the world of ideas for relationships and meanings. The third stage, "seeing mountains still as mountains, rivers still rivers," must then be considered an achieved perception in which we affirm landscape in its original existence as independent and self-sufficient. This article of faith necessarily demands that we abandon language and intellectualization to return to objects as they are. In a practical sense, both the first stage, from which we might be irrecoverably exiled, and the third stage, which remains open to us as a possible choice, offer no possibility for poetic expression, since poetry is invariably bound up with language. In both these stages, experience, not expression, is called for. Still, the perceptual differences involved here, which we can, for the moment, term *noetic* and *noematic*, would give rise to different expressive procedures, in spite of the intrusion of language. Noesis, in Husserl's sense, is the way or ways to look at an object, noema. We can see, imagine, and dream about a tree, but the tree remains what it is. Noetic formulations are products of the mind, not those of nature. To put it more simply, if the poet should start with the second stage of investigation, the process of disclosing landscape will be conditioned by the poet's constant attempt to articulate and clarify relationships between himself or herself and the objects in nature. If, on the other hand, the poet should start with the third stage, in which such relationships are transparent and need no further explanation, this disclosing mode will admit little or no intellectualization.

Let us, for the sake of illustration, compare a poem by Wang Wei, an eighth-century landscape poet in China, and Wordsworth's "Lines Composed a Few Miles above Tintern Abbey." Wang Wei's poem, "Bird-Singing Stream," is very brief.

> Man at leisure. Cassia flowers fall.
> Quiet night. Spring mountain is empty.

> Moon rises. Startles — a mountain bird.
> It sings at times in the spring stream.[5]

Wordsworth's poem is relatively long, 162 lines. We will quote here the first twenty-two lines:

> Five years have past; five summers, with the length
> Of five long winters! and again I hear
> These waters, rolling from their mountain-springs
> With a soft inland murmur. — Once again
> Do I behold these steep and lofty cliffs,
> That on a wild secluded scene impress
> Thoughts of more deep seclusion; and connect
> The landscape with the quiet of the sky.
> The day is come when I again repose
> Here, under this dark sycamore, and view
> These plots of cottage-ground, these orchard tuffs,
> Which at this season, with their unripe fruits,
> Are clad in one green hue, and lose themselves
> 'Mid groves and copses. Once again I see
> These hedge-rows, hardly hedge-rows, little lines
> Of sportive wood run wild: these pastoral farms,
> Green to the very door; and wreaths of smoke
> Sent up, in silence, from among the trees!
> With some uncertain notice, as might seem
> Of vagrant dwellers in the houseless woods,
> Or of some Hermit's cave, where by his fire
> The Hermit sits alone.
>
> *PW*, 2:259

The 140 lines that follow recount *how* "these beauteous forms" had given him "sweet sensations" and quietude, *how* he felt the presence of elevated thoughts interfused with a sense sublime, *how* between mind and objects there had been lively traffic, *how* nature becomes "the anchor of [his] *purest* thoughts," "the guide, the guardian," and "soul of all [his] moral being." Wordsworth once said,

> the visible scene
> Would enter unawares into his mind
> With all its solemn imagery.
>
> *The Prelude*, 191

Presumably, Wordsworth's ideal poem should also be one that allows the visible scene to enter "unawares" into his mind, but the poet who has fulfilled this ideal is Wang Wei and not Wordsworth. The discursiveness of the latter belies the perceiving process he seems to be arguing for. Three-fourths of the poem is spent in relating *how* external nature *affects* his mind and *how* his mind consorts with and complements nature. If, however, we should take the first twenty-two lines as a separate entity, we would have a landscape more or less free from explanation. In it he can even claim to have disclosed, so to speak, unconditional faith in the landscape as it is, a landscape that comes to us in a sort of spontaneity and immediacy: these waters, these cliffs, this sycamore, these orchard-tufts.[6] There is even a certain degree of trance-like consciousness with which the poet, like Wang Wei, receives the appeal of things in a kind of "wise passiveness" ("Expostulation and Reply," *PW*, 6:57). The implications of this famous motto by Wordsworth (coupled with "We murder to dissect" — "The Tables Turned," *PW*, 6:57) were never realized in his poetry, nor did he literally achieve the ideal state in which, as Geoffrey Hartman puts it, "cognition and perception is one."[7] The fact is, of course, that for Wordsworth landscape alone is not adequate to constitute the aesthetic object of his poetry. This is clearly expressed in his poetry, especially in his preface to *The Excursion* and throughout *The Prelude*, in which he repeatedly emphasizes the mind as the mediator and maker of meaning. "Minds that have nothing to confer/Find little to perceive" (*PW*, 2:35).[8] The complexity of this perceptual procedure, involving syllogistic progression and exploratory thinking, must be dealt with later in this essay. Suffice it to say here that his perceptual-expressive procedures differ greatly from those of Wang Wei. Briefly, in Wang Wei, the scenery *speaks* and *acts*. There is little or no subjective emotion or intellectuality to disturb the inner growth and change of the objects in front of him. The objects spontaneously emerge before the reader-viewer's eyes, whereas, in Wordsworth, the concreteness of the objects gives way to abstraction through the poet's analytical intervention. In large measure, Wordsworth begins with the second stage of investigation, a *noetic* approach to the phenomenal world, and Wang Wei's can be considered a *noematic* disclosure.

To fully understand the parameters of these two modes of perception and presentation, we must trace the morphology of these attitudes from their respective indigenous traditions. Here, the question of the adequacy of landscape must be rephrased as follows: Can natural objects in their mere physical existence express themselves without the poet's injecting into them ideas or emotions? Can landscape in its naive, innocent, original form, without involving the world of concepts, occupy us directly? This question is not only central to the discussion of landscape poetry but is also central to the phenomenological discussion of Being by such philosophers as Heidegger and others. The latter aspect has been treated in chapter 3. Let us now take up the former aspect. If the poet's answer to the above question is positive, he will attempt to release the objects in Phenomenon from their seeming irrelevance and bring forth their original freshness and thingness—return them to their first innocence, so to speak—thus making them relevant as "self-so-complete" objects in their coextensive existence. The poet merges with and, in some sense, becomes the objects before the act of composition and focuses attention upon them in such a way as to allow them to leap out directly and spontaneously to us, unhindered. Clearly, such a perceptual horizon is dominant in much of Chinese landscape poetry, particularly in poets like Wang Wei, Meng Hao-jan, Wei Ying-wu, and Liu Tsung-yüan (all T'ang poets). The centrality of this attitude is also reflected in a number of proverbial philosophical and critical phrases: Chuang-tzu: "Tao (Nature's Way) is everywhere"; Sun Cho (320?–380?): "The mountains and rivers are the Tao"; post-Sung critics: "What we see is where the Tao resides"; and Shao Yung (1011–1077): "View things as things view themselves."[9]

Most Chinese critics would claim that the ancient Chinese were always delighted by the natural sublimity of mountains and rivers; they were referred to as "beautifully alive" or "divinely beautiful," harboring sacredness and demanding reverence; they were compared to kind and wise men.[10] Indeed, such a view finds many echoes in later poems, such as this by Tu Fu (712–770):

> How about the Mount of Mounts?
> From Ch'i to Lu, never-ending green.
> Great Transformation centers here divine beauty.
> Shade and light divides here dusk and dawn.
> Rolling chest: in it are born layers of clouds.
> Eyelids strained to open by incoming birds from afar.
> Ah! to stand atop the highest peak
> To see: how tiny the rest of the hills!
> > "Looking at Mount T'ai-shan"

But, in spite of this view, in most ancient Chinese poems, such as those in the *Shih Ching* and the *Ch'u Tz'u*, mountains and rivers were still used decoratively and illustratively as a background. Its emergence from this subordinate position to a prominent and independent object for aesthetic consideration had to wait until the radical cultural change of the third and fourth centuries. This is no place to recount and detail all the social forces that stimulated this change. Briefly, this period witnessed a reaction against the dead rigidity and superficiality of the Han codification of the Confucian system, the revival of Taoism, the popularization of Buddhism by way of Taoist interpretations, large groups of intellectuals seeking affinity with nature by residing in mountains where they could enjoy them in their untrammeled fullness, and, perhaps most important of all, their engagement in *ch'ing-t'an* (pure talk or philosophical bull-sessions) on Tao (Way or Nature's Way). Many scholars have written on some of these historical factors,[11] but little has been done in the way of understanding the aesthetic implications of this change in literature.

As we can see, the central force in shaping the consciousness of landscape in medieval China is the Taoist aesthetic horizon, in particular, Lao-tzu and Chuang-tzu as promoted and explicated by Wang Pi (226–249) and Kuo Hsiang (died ca. 312). Kuo Hsiang's explication was especially influential on the Orchid Pavilion poets (the first landscapists), on Hsieh Ling-yün, and even on the Buddhist monk Chih Tun, whose participation in *ch'ing-t'an* sessions had turned him almost completely Taoist in his outlook. Kuo Hsiang's annotations of Chuang-tzu's view of Phenomenon had indeed become the woof and warp of medieval Chinese thinking, providing new departure for creativity.

Here, a highlighting of some of the related points from my discussion on Taoism in chapter 3 is in order. The Taoist philosophy begins by rejecting the premise that the structure of Phenomenon is the same as we conceive it. All conscious efforts in ordering it will result in superficial structures imposed upon undifferentiated existence and hence distorting it. Human classifications and conceptions cannot represent the cosmic scheme, the total Composition of Nature; the concrete, undivided existence must be retained and must not be dissected into separate entities. Since all imposed orders are forms of distortions of Phenomenon, we must give it back its original forms, understanding that "Ducks' legs are short; lengthening them means pain. Cranes' legs are long; shortening them means suffering" (Chuang, 317). We must leave them as they are by nature. Each form of being has its own nature, its own place; how can we take *this* as *subject* (principal) and *that* as *object* (subordinate)? We as human beings are but one form of being among a million others. What right do we have to classify other forms of beings? How can we impose "our" viewpoint upon others as the right viewpoint, the only right viewpoint? White clouds are white; green mountains are green. White clouds cannot blame green mountains for being green. Green mountains cannot blame white clouds for being white. In Kuo Hsiang's annotations, "All things are what they are without knowing why and how they are. . . . Although things are different yet they are the same in that they exist spontaneously as they are" (Chuang, 55). "Since nonbeing is nonbeing, it cannot produce being. When being is not yet produced, it cannot produce other things. Who then produces things? They spontaneously produce themselves. By this is not meant that there is an 'I' to produce. The 'I' cannot produce things and things cannot produce the 'I'. The 'I' is self-existent. Because it is so by itself, we call it natural. Everything is as it is by nature, not made to be so. . . . Who can be the Lord that commands things? Everything produces itself and is not created by others. This is the Way of Nature" (Chuang, 10). When Chuang-tzu talks about the "Piping of Nature," it is not something mysterious and transcending Phenomenon but the very Free Flow of Composition of a million things, each functioning, generating, conditioning according to its own nature. Here, Kuo Hsiang's commentary to this concept was most representative of the view of the times and was most cherished by the poets:

> Pipes and flutes come in different lengths and notes in different pitches. Hence, a million differences and variations of long and short, high and low, tones. Although tones vary in a million ways the principle of their natural endowment is the same. Thus, among them, no distinction of good and bad things. . . . Notes change in a thousand, a million fashions, harmonizing their differences, each always assuming its natural role, each performing its natural part.
>
> Chuang, 45

To put all things on an equal footing and to allow their various natures to take their course is the path to preserve the completeness of the cosmic scheme. Hence, one of the initiators of Chinese landscape poetry, Wang Hsi-chih (321–379), and other Orchid Pavilion poets can say:

> Looking up: blue sky's end.
> Looking down: green water's brim.
> Deep solitude: rimless view.
> Before the eyes, Pattern displays itself.
> Immense, Transformation!

> A million differences, none out of tune.
> Pipings all variegated:
> What fits me, none strange.
> Wang Hsi-chih, "Orchid Pavilion"

This poem can be considered the poetic restatement of Kuo Hsiang's interpretation of Chuang-tzu. Landscape is worthy of our wandering in it and viewing it because "what we see is where the Tao resides" ("Before the eyes, Pattern displays itself"), because "a million differences, none out of tune." Mountains and rivers are the very pattern of nature (in China, landscape poetry is called the "poetry of mountains and rivers"); they are by themselves complete.

The singular contribution of Kuo Hsiang in the revival of Taoism was his reaffirmation of Chuang-tzu's "Tao is everywhere" and that it is "self-rooted." He redefined many key Taoist terms and helped to clear away the possible mystical as well as metaphysical meanings surrounding the words *Tao, T'ien,* "Divine Mortals," and "Holy Men."[12] He unequivocally said in his preface: "Above, there is no Creator; below, things create themselves." This clarification prepared the way for pronouncements like "seeing mountains as mountains" by Ch'an Buddhists (who are Taoist-oriented) and for most of their paradoxical form of communication via anti-communication, as in this round of priest–disciple exchange:

Q: What is the general idea of Buddha's law?

A: Spring comes, grass green by itself.

I. A. Richards once explained the structure of metaphor in terms of vehicle and tenor. The view that landscape qua landscape is Nature's Way points to the merging of vehicle and tenor: The tenor is contained in the vehicle, or the vehicle is the tenor, the container is the contained, the thing named is the thing meant. This explains why a large portion of Chinese poetry is nonmetaphorical and nonsymbolic.[13] Because of this merging, it does not require human intellect to interfere or mediate. It is no accident that a Taoist should stress the Fast of the Mind (Chuang, 14) or Sitting-in-Forgetfulness (Chuang, 384), for it is by emptying out all traces of intellectual interference that one can fully respond, as does a mirror or still water, to things in their concreteness, to their spontaneous, simultaneous, and harmonious presences. It is a bosom empty but open, into which a million things can return. In order to achieve cosmic measure or the natural measure of things, we have to give back to natural objects their own freedom of activity, their own indigenous expressive emergence, we have to merge into, move with, and tune in with the million things constantly changing before us.

> The Sage roams in the path of a million changes — a million things a million changes in accordance with the laws of a million changes. Changes are infinite, and so would be the Sage.
>
> Kuo Hsiang's commentary on Chuang-tzu's concept of change (Chuang, 246)

Abiding by concrete things in their constant growth and change, we arrive at a sense of infinity without the burden of having to constantly struggle to match a set of assumed permanent forms.

But this view, to allow the uninterfered emergence of things, could, from another perspective, be labeled as antispeech and antiart. A poet must mediate between Phenomenon, which has its self-so-complete existence, and language, which is a human-conceived entity, in order to produce a poem. Therefore, it is not surprising to find that, among the early landscapists, as in Wang Hsi-chih's poem quoted earlier, vehicle and tenor are still separate, in spite of the fact that the tenor points back to the vehicle for identification.

The truth of the matter is that in many of the landscape poems of this period, the *consideration* of *how* landscape by itself is Nature's Way is latent in the poets' aesthetic consciousness, as for example in Hsieh Ling-yün's "Scene from South Hill to North Hill Passing the Lake . . .":

> Dawn: off from the south cliff.
> Sundown: rest on the north peak.
> Boat left ashore, to pore into distant islands.
> Staff laid aside, to lean on a thick pine.
> Sidepaths lean and long.
> Round islets bright and clear.
> Looking down: tips of tall trees.
> Harkening above: water rushes from large valleys.
> A criss-cross rock splits the stream.
> A dense forest blocks all paths.
> Sky thaws: thundering rains[14]: how about them?
> Vegetation rises up in profusion.
> First bamboo-shoots wrapped in green sheaths.
> New reeds hold purple fluffs.
> Seagulls sport on spring shores.
> Pheasants play in mild winds.
> Cherish Transformation: mind will be unbounded.[15]

Embrace things: love will deepen.
One need not regret that men of the past are distant.
Sad it is to find no one of like mind.
To roam alone is not emotional relief:
Appreciation now abandoned — cosmic scheme: who knows?

The poet's sight and hearing are filled with the epiphanies and ac-
tivities of mountains, rivers, and other natural objects. In the words
of Wang Hsi-chih, "We look up: immense, the universe! We look
down: so full, things and things!" A million things, a million fashions
of delight. "But what do these activities mean" is still a question for
Hsieh. His question: "Sky thaws: thundering rains: how about
them?" His answer: these activities in their natural measure give rise
to profuse vegetation. Each natural being, bamboo shoot, reed, sea-
gull, and pheasant, following its own natural endowment and role,
emits its energy of growth. By perceiving these beings as endowed
with natural energy, our minds will be boundless with change and
transformation. It is clear that this poem is still not free from traces of
explanation, but the form this explanation takes is unique; it resem-
bles the *kung-an* (*kōan*) verbal exchange in Ch'an Buddhism of a later
time. Compare the priest–disciple exchange, quoted above, to Hsieh:

Sky thaws: thundering rains: how about them?
Vegetation rises up in profusion.
First bamboo-shoots wrapped in green sheaths.
New reeds hold purple fluffs.
Seagulls sport on spring shores.
Pheasants play in mild winds.

and further to Wang Wei (701–761):

You ask me the way to the Pattern.
Fisherman's song deep into the cove.
    "Answer to Vice-Prefect Chang"

The employment of a concrete scene in place of explanatory elabora-
tions is a mode of expression continuously practiced by Chinese
poets. With the identification of vehicle and tenor, the last few lines
of commentary in Hsieh's poem, by its implication, must become,
then, a sort of appendage. The core consciousness of the poem is the
disclosure of landscape as it is. The Taoist emphasis on the priority of
things necessarily deemphasizes the role of commentary in poetry.
Thus, as we move from the third and fourth centuries to the T'ang
Dynasty, we witness a continuous decrease in the use of statements.

The acceptance of landscape as self-so-complete logically excludes the necessity of discursiveness, as can be observed in an interesting computation done by Ami Yuji in his *Chūgoku chūseki bungaku kenkyū* (*A Study of Medieval Chinese Literature*, 1960), in which he lays out the ratio between lines of scenery and those of statement in pre-T'ang poetry. A quick review of some of these will help to affirm this aesthetic consequence:

		No. of Lines	
Poet*	Poem	Scene	Statement
Chan Fang-sheng	Sailing into the South Lake	4	6
Hsieh Ling-yün	Scene from South Hill . . .	16	6
Pao Chao	Ascend Lu-shan	16	4
Hsieh T'iao	Roaming the East Field	8	2
	Viewing the Three Lakes	6	2
Shen Yo	Roaming Chung-shan	all scenery	
Fan Yün	To Ling-ling Country . . .	all scenery	
Wang Yung	The River Song	all scenery	
K'ung Chih-kuei	Trip to Mount T'ai-ping	all scenery	
Wu-Yün	Miscellaneous poems	all scenery	

*in chronological order

With this affirmation of the priority of things in their natural measure arose a whole art of focused attention upon landscape's live emergence from Phenomenon. For these Chinese poets, the function of language is solely to punctuate the very vital rhythm of the emergence of things, to approximate their cuts and turns, their patterning and the way they leap out fresh and alive from their seeming irrelevance. Thus, we find that Pao Chao discloses "earth's veins" from deep torrents, "sky's network" from spearing trees.[16] Some of the most famous of Chinese landscape poems by Hsieh Ling-yün are characterized by his ability to unfold for us, like landscape painters, the different phases and gradations of limpidity or transparency ("White clouds embrace dark rocks / Green bamboos charm clear ripples"), seclusion ("Linked cliffs: roads seem blocked / Thick bamboo-groves: paths are lost"), brightness ("Dense groves hold lingering gleam / Distant peaks hide an arc of light"), and light in the sense of lightness and in the sense of brightness ("Cloud and sun brighten each other / Sky and water both freshened and clear"). Or witness the play of distance in Hsieh T'iao ("Sky's end: mark a homing boat / Among clouds, indistinct, smoke or trees") and movement in stillness ("Fish sport: new lotus flutters / Birds scatter: last flowers fall"), or listen to the silence in sound, as in Wang Chi ("A bird sings: the mountain becomes quieter"). All these reflect what the Chinese critics would call "spiritual interest," or interest evoked by the vital rhythm of the natural measure of things, a fundamental expressive emphasis in poets like Wang Wei, Meng Hao-jan, Wei Ying-wu, and Liu Tsung-yüan and in Southern Sung landscape painters. Indeed, this expressive interest is dominant even in descriptive poets like Wang Yung (468–485), whose interest in landscape remains somewhat on the surface:

> Forests break off. Mountains stretch on still.
> Islands end. The river opens wide again.
> From clouded peaks, celestial village emerges.
> Source of the stream: sycamores and cedars.

The visual order of the natural objects as they come to us (or as we come to them) is closely reproduced, transparent, quickened, and direct, allowing the reader-viewer to move into the scene, unblocked.

Wang Wei's poetry is noted for its different gradations of visual distinctiveness:

> The river flows beyond the sky and earth.
> The mountain's color, between seen and unseen.
> > "Floating on the River Han"

> White clouds — looking back — close up.
> Green mists — entering — become nothing.
> > "Mount Chungnan"

> Vast desert: a lone smoke, straight.
> Long river: the setting sun, round.
> > "An Envoy to the Barbarian Pass"

These Chinese poets want to structure nature in accordance with nature's way of structuring itself or to disclose nature in accordance with nature's way of disclosing itself. To do so requires the poet's removal of the conscious self — that is, the Taoist conceptions of the "Fast of the Mind" and "Sitting-in-Forgetfulness" — to focus attention upon objects not from the poet's point of view but from that of the objects, a *noematic* awareness in which little conscious and intellectual activity is allowed to expand. This state of mind, of no conscious mind, no doubt resembles a trance-like consciousness:

> Empty mountain: No man.
> But voices of men are heard.
>> Wang Wei,
>> "Deer Enclosure"

> Man at leisure. Cassia flowers fall.
> Quiet night. Spring mountain is empty.
> Moon rises. Startles—a mountain bird.
> It sings at times in the spring stream.
>> Wang Wei, "Bird-Singing Stream"

> High on the tree tips, the hibiscus
> Sets forth red calyces in the mountain.
> A stream hut, quiet. No one around.
> It blooms and falls, blooms and falls.
>> Wang Wei, "Hsin-i Village"

In this consciousness, Kuo Hsiang says, "a million things return to one's bosom"; this is so because, free from the burden of thought, from the unrest of metaphysics, the poet has another hearing, another vision, so to speak (which the poet, in turn, gives us). The poet hears voices that conscious thinking selves normally do not hear and sees activities we are normally not aware of. This is precisely what Lu Chi (261–303) meant when he said, "In the zero of silence, to search for sound." It is also what Ssu-k'ung T'u (837–908) meant when he said, "Wait in silence—It is here the Scheme is seen."

The state of stillness, emptiness, silence, or quiescence is ubiquitous in the landscape poems of Wang Wei and his contemporaries. The "voices" one hears are those one hears in absolute silence—voices from unspeaking, self-generating, self-conditioning (*wu-yen tu-hua*) nature outside the world of language. In this poetry, discursiveness is out of place; in this poetry, each object discloses its original spatio-temporal extensions and relationships in a manner that is luminous, fresh, and pictorial, as in Liu Tsung-yüan's "River-Snow":

> A thousand mountains—no bird's flight.
> A million paths—no man's trace.
> Single boat. Bamboo-leaved cape. An old man
> Fishing by himself: ice-river. Snow.

Likewise, the famous Japanese haiku poet Bashō (1644–1694) approximates movement in stillness and sound in silence in his famous poem:

> Ancient pond—
> A frog jumps in:
> Sound of water.

Or he allows the silent world to emerge monochromatically:

> Spring:
> Unnamed mountain's
> Morning mist.

Thus, the Taoist *noematic* emphasis on nature's measure and scheme, as well as its denunciation of the egoist enterprise (i.e., that of the ego ordering the nonego), helps to bring forth a special type of non-mediating mediation by decreasing discursive, analytical, and explanatory procedures. This poetic strategy leads toward an art of pure landscape poetry of noninterference, *tzu-jan* and self-so-complete.

What kind of answer do we find in Western poets to our initial questions: Can natural objects, in their mere physical existence, express themselves without the poet's injecting into them emotions or ideas? Can landscape in its naive, innocent, original form, without involving the world of concepts, occupy us directly? We remember that Wordsworth once said: "Minds that have nothing to confer/Find little to perceive." He was even more specific.

> Objects . . . derive their influence not from properties inherent
> in themselves, but from such as are bestowed upon them by the
> minds of those who are conversant with or affected by those
> objects. Thus, the Poetry, if there be any in the work, proceeds
> whence it ought to do, from the soul of Man, communicating its
> creative energies to the images of the eternal world.
>
> Letters, 705[17]

The two themes (or the two variations of one theme) from his preface to *The Excursion* (or "The Prospectus to *The Recluse*") and the conclusion of *The Prelude* are almost proverbial; I quote them here only as a reminder:

> How exquisitely the individual Mind
> . . . to the external World
> Is fitted:—and how exquisitely, too—
> Theme this but little heard of among men—
> The external World is fitted to the Mind.
>
> *PW*, 5:5

> . . . and we may teach them how;
> Instruct them how the mind of man becomes
> A thousand times more beautiful than the earth
> On which he dwells, above this frame of things.
>
> *The Prelude*, 537

Despite Wordsworth's emphasis, at one point, on looking steadily at his object the way an artist looks at a model or an actual landscape, he definitely posits the aesthetic object of his poem within the poet's mind rather than within the landscape itself—in other words, in the mode of *noesis* rather than that of *noema*. Nature or innocence cannot be attained without traversing through thought. In the words of Geoffrey Hartman, "There is some confrontation of person with shadow or self with self. . . . Wordsworth cannot find his theme because he already has it: himself. Yet he knows self-consciousness to be at once necessary and opposed to poetry."[18] Nature or landscape is a subject for his mind to explore, a field in which he can identify the growth of his mind; at the most, landscape, serving as an object for aesthetic contemplation, is significant to him only to the extent that it helps to reveal the powers of his imagination in his epistemological search for transcendence. It is natural that such a search should be reflected in his exploratory rhetorical structure. Donald Wesling describes his style most cogently: "The tentative exploratory thinking in the body of 'Tintern Abbey' moves through a process of intellection which deepens the reference of the opening description—the distinction of Wordsworth is that at best landscape is inseparable from such sequences of generalization."[19] At this point, one may want to ask: In what sense can we talk about Wordsworth's landscape and Chinese landscape poems in the same breath? Indeed, it is apparent that Wordsworth's poems reveal a mode of approaching landscape very different from that of the Chinese poets. And yet, to say that Wordsworth had no genuine aesthetic interest in landscape would probably be wrong. There are many moments in which we find him totally absorbed in landscape, allowing us to be "usurped" by it, as, for example, this fragment:

> Many a time
> At evening, when the earliest stars began
> To move along the edges of the hills,
> Rising or setting, would he stand alone
> Beneath the trees or by the glimmering lake,
> And there, with fingers interwoven, both hands

Pressed closely palm to palm, and to his mouth
Uplifted, he, as though an instrument,
Blew mimic hootings to the silent owls,
That they might answer him; and they would shout
Across the watery vale, and shout again,
Responsive to his call, with quivering peals,
And long halloos and screams, and echoes loud,
Redoubled and redoubled, concourse wild
Of jocund din; and, when a lengthened pause
Of silence came and baffled his best skill,
Then sometimes, in that silence while he hung
Listening, a gentle shock of mild surprise
Has carried far into his heart the voice
Of mountain torrents; or the visible scene
Would enter unawares into his mind,
With all its solemn imagery, its rocks,
Its woods, and that uncertain heaven, received
Into the bosom of the steady lake.

The Prelude, 189, 191

In spite of certain analytical traces, we feel the activities of nature—solemn and beautiful—which emerge limpidly before our eyes in a moment of the obliteration of sense[20], a moment in which the question of vehicle and tenor has no precedence but, instead, a strong communion between the perceiver and the perceived is at work. But, like the marvelous Snowden mountaintop passage in Book 14, where the poet presents, for a moment, a pure landscape where there is not a trace of "encroachment," nature cannot be left alone in its original, self-sufficient form; it is seen as "the emblem of a mind / That feeds upon infinity" (*The Prelude*, 515). The earlier version is even more assertive: "The perfect image of a mighty mind, / Of one that feeds upon infinity, / That is exalted by an underpresence" (514). He continues later: "This spiritual Love acts not nor can exist / Without Imagination, which, in truth, / Is but another name for absolute power / And clearest insight, amplitude of mind, / And Reason in her most exalted mood" (521). As pointed out by Fred Randel in his "The Mountaintops of English Romanticism,"[21] passivity in the reception of scenery is continually questioned by the Romantic poets. This norm of unrest reaches back to Petrarch's having to apologize for his indulgence in pure landscape on top of Mount Verntoux near Avignon in 1335 instead of remembering that the human soul is beyond comparison the subject of admiration.[22] Among the Romantics, according to Randel, Coleridge furthered this theme and prepared the way for subsequent poets, including Wordsworth, to agonize over "whether man's whole soul is most fully engaged in a solitary sublime experience or in a social and ethical interaction."[23]

It is clear that while Wordsworth had a strong feeling for sensible objects as they really existed, he could not come to an unconditional acceptance of them as such. Hence, even within the more landscape-oriented passages, the disclosure of natural objects is carefully guided by his active perception of them. Wordsworth gives them to us in terms of *how he* comes upon them, in a sort of linear progression, rather than letting the objects come forth both diachronically and synchronically. Let us dwell upon the Snowden scene for a second. After the introduction of time and weather, the poet "began to climb"

> with forehead bent
> Earthward, as if in opposition set
> Against an enemy, I panted up
> With eager pace.

When he arrived at the top:

> and lo! as I looked up
> The moon hung naked in a firmament
> Of azure without cloud, and at my feet
> Rested a silent sea of hoary mist.
> A hundred hills their dusky backs upheaved
> All over this still ocean; and beyond,
> Far, far beyond, the solid vapours stretched.
>
> *The Prelude*, 511, 513

The series of goal-directed pointers like "began to climb," "panted up," "looked up," "beyond," and so on resemble the traditional one-dimensional perspective in painting: chosen time, chosen point-of-view. The phrase "as if in opposition set / Against an enemy" further polarizes his relation with nature and cancels the possibility of merging into it or "to view things as things view themselves." Here, it is instructive to reintroduce Hsieh Ling-yün's poem "Scene from South Hill to North Hill Passing the Lake . . ." for comparison. The title seems to promise a procedure exactly like that of Wordsworth — the use of "excursion" to disclose objects in nature, but closer examination reveals a clear difference. The contemporary critic Lin Wen-yueh lays out a common structural pattern found in the landscape poems by Hsieh and his contemporaries. Her chart for the first ten lines can serve as a point of departure for our discussion[24] (I have added the notes on yin and yang):

Dawn: off from the south cliff.	Dawn South	Yang*
Sundown: rest on the north peak.	Dusk North	Yin
Boat left ashore, to pore		
into distant islands.	Water/River	Yin
Staff laid aside, to lean on a		
thick pine.	Mountain	Yang
Sidepaths lean and long.	Mountain	Yang
Round islets bright and clear.	Water/River	Yin
Looking down: tips of tall trees.	Mountain	Yang
Harkening above: water rushes		
from large valleys.	Water/River	Yin
A criss-cross rock splits the stream.	Water/River	Yin
A dense forest blocks all paths.	Mountain	Yang

*also sight and hearing

One explanation of this structural pattern is, no doubt, the use of parallelism, as duly observed by Lin. But the rise of parallelism, which later became a common rhetorical device, was based upon nature itself. The primordial pair of Yang and Yin, Ch'ien (Sky) and K'un (Earth), sunshine and darkness, and so forth was derived from the ancient Chinese people's observation of cosmic forces at work in nature; it is through their cooperation — one complementing the other the way one parent complements the other — that produces the things in the world. Having one oppose the other would lead to the breakup of the original union and the destruction of totality. More important, objects disclose themselves to us diachronically (as we approach or emulate them) and synchronically (as they approach or emulate us). This explains the fact that the poet looks both *at* and *from* objects in nature, hence the changing perspectives and nontemporal sequence in Chinese landscape poetry. Like the Chinese landscape painter who uses multiple or revolving perspectives to represent his or her total experience of the mountains (as they are viewed from different vantage points and in their various appearances and moods), the Chinese landscape poet attempts to lay out all moments of experiencing a mountain reality spatially, as in this example from Wang Wei:

The Chungnan ranges verge on the Capital,	(viewer on level ground looking from afar — moment 1)
Mountain upon mountain to sea's brim.	
White clouds — looking back — close up.	(viewer coming out from mountain — m2)

Green mists — entering — become nothing.	(viewer entering — m3)
Terrestrial division change at the middle peak.	(viewer atop peak looking down — m4)
Shade and light differ with every valley.	(viewer on both sides of mountain — m5)
To stay over in some stranger's house —	(viewer down on level ground — m6)
Across the water, call to ask a woodcutter.	

In Wordsworth, however, we find the dominance of linear and syllogistic progression, like the use of a single perspective in traditional Western painting, both of which are examples of the process of the ego in search of the nonego.

When Plato denounced concrete appearances for his abstract Ideal Forms, he had already rejected the pre-Socratic faith that people, plants, and animals shared one undifferentiated world and language. This was the first polarization between self and nature. When Aristotle tried to save the poet from being excommunicated from Plato's Republic and introduced "logical structures" or "universal structures" as achievable forms of permanence, humans had separated themselves from the rest and acclaimed themselves to be the active generators of order, turning the infinite into finitely manageable units (such as Aristotle's model of the universe), reducing the untrammeled natural vastness into rationalized, explainable enclosures. The Greek emphasis on balance, symmetry, and restraint deterred Roman and later poets from accepting nature in its original, wild condition. With the rise of Christianity, any conception of infinity had to be anchored in God; delight in pure landscape was almost considered sinful because, like other sensuous pleasures, it would lead human beings away from their efforts to achieve communion with God. As a result, there was an unprecedented triumph of symbols over sensations in the hermeneutical framework in which objects in nature were implicated. Indeed, natural objects were employed almost exclusively for allegory, as signs for abstract ideas, as objects of personification, and as means for didacticism.[25] Here, we must reconsider the basic metaphorical structure — vehicle and tenor, signifier and signified, the literal and the symbolic — underlying metaphor, symbol, allegory, myth, and emblem in the context of Western writing, particularly in pre-Romantic periods.

Metaphor or metaphoric thinking has been seriously questioned by contemporary writers and philosophers. Beda Allemann in his "Metaphor and Antimetaphor" enumerated a series of attacks on metaphor, undertaken by as diversified a host of writers as expressionists like Carl Sternheim, Theodor Tagger, and Gottfried Benn, the futurist Marinetti, Paul Celan, Robbe-Grillet, and the Russian Formalists.[26] We can add Pound of the imagist period, Williams, and many postmodern poets. What were some of the things that bothered these writers? What kind of epistemological or hermeneutical crisis were they responding to? I will not be able to examine all the above cases. For our purpose, three examples will suffice. In Allemann's essay, the following piece of prose by Kafka is quoted:

> The poplar in the fields swaying in the wind, which you have called the Tower of Babel — for you refused to believe that it is a poplar. . . . Look what you are doing! Out of sheer rashness you are not satisfied with the true names of things, they are not enough for you, and now, in a great hurry, you pour arbitrary names out over them.[27]

As if to answer Kafka, Pound has this to say:

> I believe that the proper and perfect symbol is the natural object, that if a man use "symbols", he must so use them that their symbolic function does not obtrude; so that a sense, and the poetic quality of the passage, is not lost to those who do not understand the symbol as such, to whom, for instance, a hawk is a hawk.[28]

But this plain truth — to give back objects their immanence, to call a poplar a poplar, a hawk a hawk — is not so easy to assert. Witness Alain Robbe-Grillet's defense:

> If I say, "The world is man," I shall always gain absolution; while if I say, "Things are things, and man is only man," I am immediately charged with a crime against humanity.

The crime, Robbe-Grillet explains, is that he has broken a solidarity implicated in a system of anthropomorphic analogies, that he has ignored metaphoric thinking, which is supposed to lead him back to "a notion of hidden unity," and that he has allowed the world of objects to remain "entirely external." But analogical or metaphoric thinking is always affective, hence

> the world of the things has been so thoroughly contaminated by my mind that it is henceforth susceptible of any emotion, of

any character trait. I will forget that it is I, I alone, who feels melancholy [when I speak of the melancholy of a landscape], or suffers solitude; these affective elements will soon be considered as the *profound reality* of the material universe, the sole reality . . . worthy of engaging my interest in it.

And this reality, the universe of significations, "leads infallibly to the [idea] of a nature common to all things . . . a *superior* or *higher* nature. The idea of an interiority always leads to the idea of a transcendence."[29]

Here, we are not talking about metaphor as a mere literary device, as a figure of speech commonly used in both Western and Chinese poetry, but as a problem of epistemology and hermeneutics. An apple to the Chinese, to the pre-Socratics (Homer, for example), and to people of many other cultures is a fruit, sweet, crisp, and shiny, but to the pre-Romantics it has the entire burden of original sin—metaphor, myth, allegory, and emblem all rolled into one. Similarly, the garden—Andrew Marvell's "The Garden," for example—is invested with layers and layers of symbolic significances, the Virgilian *locus amoenus*, the biblical *hortus conclusus*, the lost Eden (again, the burden of Adam's Fall), the achieved Christian paradise, and so forth. Like man, "a little world made cunningly of elements," the garden, too, can be a perfect world reflecting the macrocosm. Ben Jonson's garden estate poem "To Penshurst" begins with God and the four elements, followed by various hierarchies, in order of importance, of angels, (God-ordained) princes, men and women (the former in command of the latter), animals, plants, and so on, with this interesting detail: The fish happily jumps to the hook, for within the predestined network of things, the fish is allotted to be eaten by men. In Pope's "Windsor Forest," the grand cosmic pattern of harmonious confusion and agreement through differences governs "nature," the physical universe, human society, humankind, and the arts. This pattern is fundamental even to the political state:

> . . . Draw to one point, and to one centre bring
> Beast, Man, or Angel, Servant, Lord, or King.
> "Essay on Man," iii, 301–2

In the pre-Romantic periods, almost none of the objects in nature was seen as it is. As Owen Barnfield puts it, the literal was always implicated in the symbolic.[30] Through a series of analogies, the four elements—fire, air, water, earth—were seen to have made up man's body, including the making of the four humors, constituted the plant and animal as well as the mineral worlds, and thus to have linked everything in a network of symbolic markers within a cartography referred to as macrocosm-geocosm-microcosm. All creatures were God's imprints and signatures.[31]

In this connection, one most unimaginable aspect for the Oriental mind is that mountains should have been considered in seventeenth-century English literature as "shames," "ills," "warts," "wens," or "blisters" (a subject thoroughly studied by Marjorie Nicolson in her book *Mountain Gloom and Mountain Glory*). They were seen as such because the appearance of mountains after the Deluge destroyed the balance, symmetry, and order of God's work. In a curious way, Adam's Fall (microcosm's blemish) was linked to the Deluge (the disfiguring of Earth's perfect globe, giving rise to "ugly" mountains) and later to the breaking of the circle (the geocentric macrocosm blasted by Copernicus and Galileo). Both Nicolson and Basil Willey are of the opinion that the eighteenth century was plunged into a huge crisis of consciousness because of this curious blend of pessimism. In the words of Nicolson:

> Each of these "decays" aroused opposition. Against the orthodox conception of the decay of Nature in man was the humanistic defense of the essential goodness of man. In opposition to the decay of Nature in the earth, we find one group of theologians staunchly insisting that the earth was *not cursed*, that this still is the world that the Lord has made, and other men, like Hakewill, declaring that, even though God may or will destroy it, Nature in itself has no seeds of decay, but operates upon orderly laws. If momentarily the "new philosophy," which seemed to prophesy the decay of the cosmos, called all in doubt, the implications of the Galilean discoveries were to lead . . . to exultation rather than despair.[32]

"Opposition" is perhaps not the best word to describe the situation. The eighteenth century literally had to "justify" humankind, nature, and the infinite interstellar world in order to overcome the pessimism and sense of "displacement" brought about by the earlier period. In this connection, Shaftesbury played a pivotal role. Aside from his very important argument for the innate goodness of man, an argument that helped precipitate the reception of Confucianism in this period, he, through an imaginary dialogue between Theocles and Philocles conducted while going through an interstellar and terrestrial excursion, resurrected in hyperbolic terms a nature in its superabundant variety and irregularity hitherto disallowed or dampened in literature and art.[33] While this "liberation," aided by the new sense of sublime occasioned by the translation of Longinus and the elated descriptions of the Alps by travelers, made it possible for a poet like James Thomson to write, with Miltonic drive, extended descriptions of nature in which the poet surrenders to a scene and accepts its mysterious power as such, this nature was still permeated with all the attributes of God—with or without naming him. Thus, when Romantic poets like Wordsworth began to appropriate landscape as their primary aesthetic material, consciously or unconsciously, they too had to justify its role in the order of things, for, as Kant (following Plato) would say, pure perception of phenomena is not sufficient; real knowledge consists of the poet's faculty of imagination to see into the essence of the ontological world, to move beyond the phenomenal to the noumenal. This epistemological search, often weighted with agony and unrest for meaning beyond the phenomenal (in this case, landscape) is ubiquitous among the Romantic poets. Hegel sees this most clearly:

> The hour that man leaves the path of mere natural being marks the difference between him, a self-conscious agent, and the natural world. The spiritual is distinguished from the natural . . . in that it does not continue a mere stream of tendency, but sunders itself to self-realization. But this position of severed life has in its turn to be overcome and the spirit must, by its own act, achieve accord once more. . . . The principle of restoration is found in thought, and in thought only: The hand that inflicts the wound is also the hand that heals it.[34]

The craving for radical innocence together with all its unresolved conflicts and contradictions continued to obsess modern philosophers and poets. Kierkegaard's rejection of abstract system (the world of ideas) for concrete existence, Heidegger's demand to return to pre-Socratic conceptions of *physis* (emergence of things) instead of *metaphysis*, and, in between, the imagists' not yet articulated emphasis on the natural symbol as adequate symbol (Pound: "A hawk is a hawk"; Williams: "No ideas but in things," "a world that is always real")[35] — these positions arose from a central concern of *how*, in Kenneth Rexroth's words, the Western poet can bypass epistemological procedures.[36] The *how* has become part of the rhetorical justification of the poet's object-oriented poem. Take, for instance, these lines by Rexroth (italics mine):

> The holiness of the real
> Is always there, accessible
> In total immanence.
>   "Time Is the Mercy
>   of Eternity"

> The seasons revolve and the years change
> *With no assistance or supervision,*
> The moon, *without taking thought,*
> Moves in its cycle, full, crescent, and full.[37]
>   "Another Spring"

We recall here Wallace Stevens, whose entire poetic effort can be characterized as attempting to see the original "mere being" with "an ignorant eye." But his affirmation of the self-sufficient presences of terrestrial objects as they are also has to take the form of rhetorical justification (italics mine):

> The palm *at the end of the mind,*
> *Beyond the last thought,* rises
> In the bronze decor.

> A gold-feathered bird
> Sings in the palm, *without human meaning,*
> *Without human feeling,* a *foreign* song.

> *You know then that it is not the reason*
> *That makes us happy or unhappy.*
> The bird sings. Its feathers shine.

> The palm stands on the edge of space.
> The wind moves slowly in the branches.
> The bird's fire-fangled feathers dangle down.
>   "Of Mere Being"

Instead of conceiving reality as having an ontological status, Stevens perceives or tries to perceive it in its prethinking or preontological context of synchronous presences of beings. He finds it difficult to present this world because, unlike the real world, he has to make a choice in the ordering:

> it was not a choice
> Between excluding things. It was not a choice

> Between, but of. He chose to include the things

> That in each other are included, the whole,
> The complicate, the amassing harmony.[38]

The paradox here is as Hegel had stated it: "The principle of restoration is found in thought, and thought only: the hand that inflicts the wound is also the hand that heals it." It is in this sense that Stevens, like the Romantics, is still troubled by the question of epistemology. In "The Poems of Our Climate," after having presented concretely and transparently a world consisting of clear water, a brilliant bowl, and pink and white carnations, Stevens continues, "one desires / So much more than that. . . . Still one would want more, one would need more, / More than a world of white and snowy scents. / There would still remain the never-resting mind."[39]

The persistence of this desire for epistemology and the priority given to humankind as the sole order-generating agent deter many poets from accepting the concrete world as such. John Crowe Ransom is of particular interest here. In attacking imagism, he understands beautifully how marvelous and remarkable objects by themselves can be:

> [Idealists] object that an image in an original state of innocence is a delusion and cannot exist, that no image ever comes to us which does not imply the world of ideas, that there is "no precept without a concept." . . . But there is this to be understood too: the image which is not remarkable in any particular property is marvellous in its assemblage of many properties, a manifold of properties like a mine or a field, something to be explored for the properties; yet science can manage the image, which is infinite in properties, only by equating it to the one property with which the science is concerned; for science at work is always *a science*, and committed to a special interest. It is not by refutation but by abstraction that science destroys the image. It means to get its "value" out of the image and we may be sure that it has no use for the image in its original state of freedom. People who are engrossed with their pet "values" become habitual killers. Their game is the images, or the things, and they aquire the ability to shoot them as far off as they can be seen, and do. It is thus we lose the power of imagination, or whatever faculty it is by which we are able to contemplate things as they are in their rich and contingent materiality.[40]

In spite of this richness, we are later told, the best kind of poetry, or the "right" kind of poetry, is what he calls "metaphysical poetry" in which the poet's mind is assigned a miraculous role.

Our whole study would have reached an impasse if, after all this intense awareness of objects as they are by various poets and philosophers, no further steps had been taken. The view that objects are immanent by themselves and need no human supervision to be what they are anticipated the possibility of bypassing epistemological procedures all together. This positive step was first taken by Williams in such poems as "Nantucket," "Sycamore," and "The Red Wheelbarrow," in which, to use Hillis Miller's words, there is no symbolism, no reference to a world beyond the world, no interaction of subject and object.[41] As I have argued in chapter 3, this final break from the dominance of a Platonic world of ideas and concepts, a break that involves the questioning of the artificially "constituted" transcendence and affirmation of the immanence of things, prepared the way for poets like Gary Snyder, Charles Tomlinson, the later Rexroth, the later Robert Creeley, Robert Bly, Cid Corman, Lew Welch, James Wright, and many postmodern poets to meet, receive, and present landscape in its own terms with a humility and freedom from egoistic intrusion quite unmatched by previous landscapists.[42]

Here, I would like to consider briefly the works of Rexroth, Tomlinson, and Snyder, through which I hope to reveal the trajectory of this change. All three poets, each in his own way, have produced pure landscape poems of *noematic* emphasis. Part of their change to this aesthetic consciousness is, no doubt, due to their exposure to Chinese poetry and art, but, more relevantly, they were more disposed to pure landscape than poets of earlier generations because of the slow change of perceptual orientation outlined above and in chapter 3. They had been relatively freed, so to speak, from Platonic-Aristotelian perceptual constructs as well as from the "burdens" of Christianity so that they could see more clearly the implications of the Chinese model.

Kenneth Rexroth

Rexroth was probably the first American poet after Pound who embraced Chinese culture with almost complete passion and seriousness. He tried to read almost anything about Chinese culture and literature. In his *An Autobiographical Novel, Assays, Classics Revisited,* and many reviews on things Chinese, he generously acknowledged his debt to Chinese culture and art, to Chinese poetry in particular. He related how Pound's *Cathay* led him into Chinese literature, how as a young boy he read with elation Waley's Chinese translations, which had incalculable influence on him, and how an hour of talk with Witter Bynner, translator of T'ang poetry, changed his interest and led him to read and fervently translate Tu Fu, whose works have become an important marker of his art.[43] As he puts it:

I have saturated myself with his poetry for thirty years. I am sure he has made me a better man, as a moral agent and as a perceiving organism.[44]

I have had the work of Tu Fu by me since adolescence and over the years have come to know these poems better than most of my own.[45]

In fact, Tu Fu, according to Rexroth, is in some ways "a better poet than either Shakespeare or Homer,"[46] and his poetry comes from "a saner, older, more secular culture," as it "embodies more fully the Chinese sense of the unbreakable wholeness of reality. . . . It can be understood and appreciated only by the application of what Albert Schweitzer called 'reverence for life'. What is, is what is holy."[47] Rexroth was greatly excited to find a sounder universe from Joseph Needham's book on Chinese science:

The dominant influence in this volume seems to be the organic philosophy of Whitehead, shorn of its Platonic excrescences. It serves as an available bridge to the comprehension of a world in which Nature works by "doing nothing" instead of passing laws, in which the universe moves as a great web of inter-relatedness of which man and his imperatives are only part. This is basically a true picture of the Chinese universe. It is a universe full of strange and wonderful things. It is a universe Western man is going to have to understand if we are going to survive happily together.[48]

We recall that in his poem, "Another Spring" (quoted earlier), which was constructed with images and lines from various poems from the T'ang Dynasty,[49] he affirms the self-generating, self-immanent other world outside ourselves that needs no thought nor supervision. It is clear that his stance is Taoist-oriented. Thus, in an interview conducted by Cyrena N. Pondrom in March 1968, he repeatedly emphasizes that "poetry deals with much more concrete things. It possesses an intense specificity—the intense specificity of *direct* contact and *direct* communication; rather than dealing intellectually and discursively with permanent archetypes it does so directly via Whitehead's 'presentational immediacy.'"[50] To resort to argument as a form of mastering life and experience is to doom oneself. "Man kills himself by defining the indefinable, grasping the inapprehensible. We do not apprehend reality, since this implies an outstretching effort; rather it apprehends us. We are simply in *reality*. We are in being like fish in water, who do not know water exists."[51] The last statement is a free translation of Chuang-tzu's "Fish forget themselves in water; men forget themselves in Tao [Nature's Way]" (Chuang, 272).

By returning to their natural function, human beings can enter into direct mutual emulation with objects. All evidence shows that Rexroth accepted the Chinese aesthetic horizon, but the early Rexroth accepted it with a certain trepidation. In spite of large paragraphs of landscape in his early poems, there still remain presentational difficulties. First, as we have observed above, he has to introduce into his poems rhetorical justification. Second, he still clings to the method of equivalence (a subtle form of metaphoric structure) by merging landscape somewhat mysteriously into eroticism, which, according to Rexroth, is another form of direct experience.[52]

> Beyond the hills
> The moon is up, and the sky
> Turns to crystal before it.
> The canyon blurs in half light.
> An invisible palace
> Of glass, full of transparent
> People, settles around me.
> Over the dim waterfall
> The intense promise of light
> Grows above the canyon's cleft.
> A nude girl enters my hut,
> With white feet, and swaying hips,
> And fragrant sex.
>
> "Mirror"[53]

I must say, however, that Rexroth was very sincere in his attempt to emulate Chinese poetry. He once said that he wrote poetry according to a kind of Chinese rule:

> that is, it is a certain place, at a certain time. . . . "A gong sounds far off among the pines" — it is a monastery in the mountains. What this does is to put the reader in a poetic situation. It puts him in a place, just like it puts him on the stage, makes him one of the actors. He is in the poetic situation. . . . This is the fundamental technique of Chinese poetry.[54]

Indeed, we find many of his poems trying to emulate this "rule." His

"Yin and Yang," inspired by Tu Fu, is such a poem disclosing different activities in spring within the movement of the natural cycle. This desire to become "Chinese" was finally more fully realized in his *New Poems* (1974):

> The air has the late summer
> Evening smell of ripe foliage
> And dew cooled dust. The last long
> Rays of sunset have gone from
> The sky. In the greying light
> The last birds twitter in the leaves.
> Far away through the trees, someone
> Is pounding something. The new
> Moon is pale and thin as a
> Flake of ice. Venus glows warm
> Beside it. In the abode
> Of peace, a bell calls for
> Evening meditation.
> As the twilight deepens
> A voice speaks in the silence.
>
> "Star and Crescent"

The objects and events in nature (echoing Chinese motifs) have a fairly spontaneous emergence without the poet's disruptive commentary. Here is another example, from the same book, of self-sufficient landscape poetry, in which objects exist in a kind of "presentational immediacy" without going through, in Rexroth's words, "permanent archetypes intellectually and discursively":

> A cottage in the midst
> Of a miniature forest.
> The only events are the distant
> Cries of peacocks, the barking
> Of more distant dogs
> And high over head
> The flight of cawing crows.
>
> "A Cottage in the Midst"[55]

Charles Tomlinson

When Charles Tomlinson published his "Nine Variations in a Chinese Winter Setting" in *The Necklace* in 1955, an elated Donald Davie had this to say about the poem:

> [The poem] is no piece of fashionable chinoiserie. Nor has it anything to do with translations from the Chinese by Arthur

Waley or Ezra Pound. It is an exercise in rendering the perceptions of one sense by vocabulary drawn from the other:

> Pine-scent
> In snow-clearness
> Is not more exactly counterpointed
> Than the creak of trodden snow
> Against a flute.

Scent and sight and sound flow together. . . . What emerges from the stanza is not scent or sound or sight but a quality that is all of and none of them, that comes to life only when all of them, each in its own rich identity, comes into perception together.[56]

Davie concludes by saying this is the elaboration of the symbolist "paysage interieur" and the suggestion by Stevens's "Thirteen Ways of Looking at a Blackbird." Tomlinson's own confession gives us a different impression. I offer it here not to refute Davie's most searching analysis but to complement and deepen it. In a letter to me, dated January 1, 1975, Charles Tomlinson says:

You asked about my poetic attitude. I think primarily it was getting the human being into a right relation with nature, where the individual ego was not a predator and where nature could speak for itself inside a relationship — not simply as background or symbolism. When I was a boy I saw a Chinese painting (in a book an aunt brought from Shanghai) entitled "Pine Scent in Snow-Clearness," it hit me at the time that the line was going to be "my attitude." I was fascinated by a title that said so much and yet was so free of the mere subjective. I couldn't have explained it that way then. But I clung to that line for years, feeling it as a kind of pure talisman, something proof against all sentimentality — all the slush the radio poured out in those days. Finally, I used it in *The Necklace*. I think now my "attitude," granting to nature its own being, had political extensions — basically, it was anti-fanatic (hence, my "Assassin" and "Prometheus" poems), anti-Promethean, suspicious of the merely excited, and yet sensuously aware, deep in colour, form, texture. And yet how much of it I owe to that single phrase, and how right it should have begun with a Chinese painting now that I find myself writing to you. I always thought that phrase "Pine scent, etc." a wonderful instance of sensibility responding to nature, without mere self-involvement, responsive and responsible.

It is fair to say that behind this "attitude" is a comment on the whole system of analogies that Robbe-Grillet criticizes, on the whole Platonic-Aristotelian as well as medieval burden discussed earlier, and on the egoistical sublime of Wordsworth and other Romantics. It is also clear that this "attitude" is not a surface echo of the Chinese title but one of deep resonance with the Chinese landscapists. Here are two of his landscape poems:

> Look down. There is snow.
> Where the snow ends
> Sea and where the sea enters
> Gray among capes
> Like an unvaried sky, lapping
> From finger to finger
> Of a raised hand, travellers
> Skirt between snow and sea.
> Minute, furtive and exposed,
> Their solitude is unchosen and will end
> In comity, in talk
> So seasoned by these extremes
> It will recall stored fruits
> Bitten by a winter fire.
> The title, without disapprobation,
> Says "Merchants."
>
> "On a Landscape by Li Ch'eng"

> White, a shingled path
> Climbs among dusted olives
> To where at the hill-crest
> Stare houses, whiter
> Than either dust or shingle.
> The view held from this vantage
> Unsoftened by distance, because
> Scoured by a full light,
> Draws lucid across its depth
> The willing eye: a beach,
> A surf-line, broken
> Where reefs meet it, into the heaving
> Blanched rim of bay-arcs;
> Above, piercing the empty blue,
> A gull would convey whiteness
> Through the sole space which lacks it
> But, there, scanning the shore,

Hangs only the eagle, depth
Measured within its level gaze.
"Icos"[57]

In these poems, Tomlinson has achieved a good degree of freedom from the "mere subjective" and from "mere self-involvement" and brought back to the natural objects color, form, and texture with cinematic visuality. "Icos," in particular, is reminiscent of Wang Wei's "Crossing the River to Ch'ing-ho" in its cinematic handling of various images. Here is Wang Wei's poem:

Boating on wide river:
Confluent water reaches sky's end.
Sky-waves suddenly open up:
Towns: millions of houses.
Farther on: cities are visible.
Instantly, mulberries and hemp.
Backview of native country:
Teeming water merges with cloud-mist.

Both poems achieve unblurred visual immediacy while clear and un-blocked images, like different phases of perception capturing chang-ing gradations of color and light, unfold before the viewer. However, when put among Wang Wei's other poems, "Icos" will appear more consciously controlled in the way the camera is guided. Perception is consciously organized into shots. In this sense, Tomlinson, like Williams, from whom he learned this organization, maintains a certain degree of continuity with the tradition of linear movement in Western poetry, although there is this important difference: Both Williams and Tomlinson are careful in varying this movement with striking changes of perspective at key points as well as with sharp twists and turns to reflect the various shifts in perceptual activity. Tomlinson's discussion of Williams's rhythmical line structure is equally applicable to his own poetry. Following Pound's character-ization of Williams's lines as full of "jerks, sulks, balks, outbursts and jump-overs," he describes Williams's art as one "where the attention is frequently turned upon outward things, the sound structure of the poems which embody that attention is an expression of strains, breath pauses, bodily constrictions and releases." He compares this to the act of walking: "The good walker should be able to change pace, stop, start, turn, step up and down, twist or stoop, easily and quickly, without losing balance or rhythm. . . . The Williams poem finds analogies for most of these movements."[58] With this art of attention to the changing speeds and tensions in the act of perceiving outward things as they disclose themselves, the garrulous ego and "the never-resting mind" are very much effaced. In this sense, Tomlinson's poems come close to the Chinese sense of allowing nature to "speak for itself."

Gary Snyder

Snyder's long and deep identification with Chinese culture and poetry is too well known to need recounting here. His translation of Han Shan ("Cold Mountain Poems") turned Han Shan and himself and their lifestyles into a modern legend; and the two together became a sort of popular cultural hero to college youths of the 1960s and 1970s through his fictionalization in Jack Kerouac's *The Dharma Bums* (1959).

When I met him in 1972, I asked him why he was so interested in Chinese landscape poetry. He said, "I grew up in the forests of the Pacific Northwest. When I was about 10, my parents took me to Seattle to see an exhibition of Chinese landscape paintings. I loved them instantly because these were mountains and rivers I recognized; they were as real as those I saw." The mountains he saw every day were real and alive rather than allegorical, symbolic, or artificial. This virgin contact with nature and the confirmation of this nature by Chinese landscape paintings prepared him to become one of its staunchest apologists.

> Among the most ruthlessly exploited classes: Animals, trees, water, air, grasses.[59]

> So many mountains, on so clear a day, the mind is staggered. . . . From Canada to Oregon, and ranges both east and west—the blue mass of the Olympics far over hazy Puget Sound— [My companion, who is a poet, said:] "You mean there's a Senator for all this?"[60]
> Unfortunately, there isn't a senator for all that. And I would like to think of a new definition of humanism and a new definition of democracy that would include the non-human, that would have representation from those spheres. This is what I think we mean by an ecological conscience.[61]

Gary Snyder's position is clear. If poetry speaks at all, it should speak for and from the silent but lively world outside humankind. It should be at once the voice of humanity and the voice of nature. "We must find a way . . . to incorporate the other people . . . —the creeping people and the standing people, and the flying people and the swimming people—into the councils of government" (*TI*, 108). Poetry must be at once mysterious (as voices from an awe-inspiring sacramental world long lost to modern humans), aesthetic (as "a pure perception of beauty"), and moral-political (as an assertion of the rights of the nonhuman).[62] Thus, one of Snyder's essay titles reads "The Politics of Ethnopoetics" (*OW*, 15).

His commitment, too, is clear: It is not the "return to nature" of armchair philosophers, nor the sublimation and glorification of self through the use of nature. It is certainly not the view of the U.S. Forest Service—"treat it right and it will make a billion board feet a year"—which sees forests as crops and scenery as recreation (*EHH*, 12). Snyder means a *literal* return to nature (or re-habitation [*OW*, 57]), to relearn and reexperience humankind's original relationship with the cooperative, interdependent, interdefining, interrelated, total composition of things. He means humanity's ceremonial participation in holistic communionism (*RW*, 39) to recover its original "natural being" (*EHH*, 155), so that "men, women, and children . . . follow the timeless path of love and wisdom, in affectionate company with the sky, winds, clouds, trees, waters, animals and grasses" (*EHH*, 116). "Gratitude to Wild Beings, our brothers, teaching secrets, / freedoms, and ways; who share with us their milk; / self-complete, brave and aware / *in our minds so be it*" (*TI*, 24).

It is no accident that his early Amerindian studies, his love for Taoism and Chinese landscape poetry, and his Ch'an Buddhist training all converge into one center of awareness where humankind becomes truly "moral" by trusting its natural being and by "following the grain" (*EHH*, 115). There are clear similarities among his three areas of deep interest. The primitive mode of perceiving nature is concrete, viewing things (w)holistically as self-complete (*TI*, 24); it was a state of total harmony between human beings and nature before polarization. On this level, it resonates with the Taoist aesthetic discussed earlier and in chapter 3. Ch'an Buddhism, Taoist-oriented, attempts to teach us, through intuition and poetry, to live and function within Nature's way. All these contributed to Snyder's complete identification with nature and made him cherish "an attitude of openness, inwardness, gratitude; plus meditation, fasting, a little suffering and some rupturing of day-to-day ties with the social fabric" (*OW*, 37).

Snyder's call for the retreat of the dominating ego and readjustment of humankind's relation with the "living, exciting, mysterious" phenomenal world, which continuously fills "one with a trembling awe leaving one grateful and humble" (*EHH*, 123) easily led him to a kind of nonindividualistic poetry:

> Down valley a smoke haze
> Three days heat, after five days rain
> Pitch glows on the fir-cones
> Across rocks and meadows
> Swarms of new flies.
>
> I cannot remember things I once read
> A few friends, but they are in cities.
> Drinking cold snow-water from a tin cup
> Looking down for miles
> Through high still air.
> "Mid-August at Sourdough
> Mountain Lookout"[63]

A set of simple and unassuming images from nature, relatively free from rhetorical embellishments, open up an ambience into which the reader is invited to move about, to stop for a moment, during which the reader may expand the horizon by reflecting upon it. This is followed by a brief comment like a personal aside, but it is not a comment that would disturb the objects around him. The reader's attention is almost immediately reverted back to the original scene, which now stretches into the distance as nature acts itself out. The operative dynamics in this poem work very much like the Chinese poems both in the first part of this chapter and in chapter 2. Snyder once said: "A poet sort of faces two directions: one is to the world of people and language and society, and the tools by which he communicates his language; and the other is the non-human, non-verbal world, which is the world of nature as nature is itself, before language, before custom, before culture. There are no words in that realm."[64] This paraphrase of the Taoist-Ch'an Buddhist idea of unspeaking, self-generating, self-conditioning nature is the best commentary on the poem just quoted. Commentary like this sometimes slips into his landscape poems, such as this passage from his "Piute Creek." Somewhere in the midst of the gorgeous landscape, the poet says:

> All the junk that goes with being human
> Drops away, hard rock wavers
> Even the heavy present seems to fail
> This bubble of a heart.
> Words and books

> Like a small creek off a high ledge
> Gone in the dry air.
>
> A clear, attentive mind
> has no meaning but that
> Which sees is truly seen.[65]

Like Tomlinsons's title for his book of poems, *Seeing Is Believing*, "that which sees is truly seen" is very much like the Taoist "what we see is where the Tao resides." In many of his landscape poems, Snyder effortlessly dropped the commentary as, for example, in these two poems:

> in the blue night
> frost haze, the sky glows
> with the moon
> pine tree tops
> bend snow-blue, fade
> into sky, frost, starlight.
> the creak of boots.
> rabbit tracks deer tracks
> what do we know.
> > "Pine Tree Tops"
>
> Earth a flower
> a phlox on the steep
> slopes of light
> hanging over the vast
> solid spaces
> small rotten crystals;
> salts.
> Earth a flower
> by a gulf where a raven
> flaps by once
> a glimmer, a color
> forgotten as all
> falls away.
> a flower
> for nothing;
> an offer;
> no taker;
> snow-trickle, feldspar, dirt.
> > "For Nothing"[66]

Overwhelmed by the richness of the presences of objects in nature, the poet finds himself wavering at the edge of speech. Should he break the spell of this expressive silence and elaborate on this richness for the reader-viewer? Should he let the objects express their presences and speak for themselves? Thus, he stops short at an indecisive phrase: "what do we know." Should we read it as a question or as a statement? Nature has continually offered itself: "an offer; / no taker." Forget your mind, forget your words, there —

snow-trickle, feldspar, dirt.

there —

Fisherman's song deep into the cove.

5 "Secret Echoes and Complementary Correspondences" — A Chinese Theory of Reading

Reading a Chinese Poem

When we open a book and read its words, phrases, and sentences, other books—from antiquity, from the recent past, or even in foreign languages—will be opened simultaneously, and words, phrases, or sentences from these will at once appear in our consciousness along with those in front of our eyes, trembling, ready to speak to us. As a voice leaps out from the black type and white spaces to speak to us, other voices answer—as echoes from the distance, or as a quiet prompting, or as a loud protest—moving us beyond here and now into other spaces and other times. By so doubling, these other voices bring about changes, like a huge symphony playing inaudibly to our inner ear, converging into a confluent, dense music.

This reading experience is also the experience of the poet, who must, in the process of writing, become his own reader and listen inwardly to his own voices, now externalized, over and over again. Let us take, for example, the first poem, "Masculine Whole," of Ssu-k'ung T'u's (837–908) *Ars Poetica, The Twenty-four Orders of Poetry*:[1]

雄　　　　　　渾
(masculine; heroic)　(undifferentiated whole)

1. 大　　用　　外　　腓
   great; large / use / outside / change(s)
   　　　　　(changes outside)

2. 眞　　體　　內　　充
   true / body / inside / fills full
   　　　　(fills inside)

3. 返　　虛　　入　　渾
return (to) / void; emptiness / into / undifferentiated
　　　　　　　　　　　　　　　　　　　whole

4. 積　　健　　爲　　雄
amass;　　　/ strength / become / masculine; heroic;
accumulate　　　　　　　　　　　　strong

5. 具　　備　　萬　　物
possess / get ready / ten thousand / things in the world

6. 橫　　絕　　太　　空
lie across / exhaustively / Primary / Space

7. 荒　　荒　　油　　雲
wild (thrown about);　/　flowing　/　cloud(s)
vague; indistinct

8. 寥　　寥　　長　　風
wide on all sides;　　/　long　/　wind(s)
spreading far and wide

9. 超　　以　　象　　外
transcend; / by means of / forms; / outside;
exceed　　　　　　　　　　　　(beyond forms or the givens)

10. 得　　其　　環　　中
get; attain / its; that / ring / center

11. 持　　之　　非　　強
hold　/　it　/　not　/　by force

12. 來　　之　　無　　窮
come　/　it　/　no　/　end
　　　　　　　　　(limitless)

Take the first phrase "Great use." Immediately, Chuang-tzu (ca. 399–295 B.C.) the Taoist speaks from antiquity:

> There are hawthorns, pear trees, orange trees, pomelo trees, gourds, and others. The fruits are knocked down when they are ripe, and the trees are abused. The large branches are broken, and the smaller ones torn away. The life of these plants is suffering, because of their productive ability. They, therefore, cannot complete their natural term of existence, but come to a premature end in the middle of their time, and bring upon themselves destructive treatment from society. It is so with all things. For a long time I learned to be useless. There were several occasions on which I was nearly destroyed. Now I succeed in being useless, which is of the *greatest use* to me.[2]

What does the last phrase "being useless, which is of the greatest use" mean, and how is it related to "Great use changes outside" in the poem?

When Chuang-tzu used a word or a phrase, each of the words or phrases arose in his consciousness only after they were linked to certain experiences, some of which came to him through other words or phrases. Or we can say that each word already carried in itself the "meanings" of other "worlds," "things," or "texts." What is the relationship, we may ask, between "being useless . . . is of the greatest use" and the famous Taoist pairs *wu-wei/wei* (無為/為, nonaction/action) and *wu-chih/ta-chih* (無知/大知, no knowledge/great knowledge)? Ssu-k'ung T'u's phrase "Great use" is lifted from Chuang-tzu's chapter "The Human World," in which a central theme is "to receive the myriad things with a void bosom" through "the Fast of the Mind," where "bright light" comes through "an empty room," where one's mind "can gallop abroad while one's body remains sitting."[3] In Ssu-k'ung T'u's poem, we find an easy echo: "Return to the void into the Undifferentiated Whole." Thus, clearly, "being useless" and "emptiness or void" must be related. As a matter of fact, "being useless is of the greatest use" cannot and should not be understood in terms of the normal moral or value judgment; it escapes all ready-made conceptions. More importantly, it cannot be extended to mean "poetry is useless." This kind of black and white demarcation, according to the Taoists, is the beginning of dissolution and fragmentation.

And yet, in spite of this reasoning, we cannot stop the negativity of this phrase from making itself felt. Interestingly, as if long anticipated, Chuang-tzu hid in another chapter an answer to this challenging voice:

> Chuang-tzu was walking on a mountain, when he saw a large tree with huge branches and luxuriant foliage. A woodcutter was resting by its side, but he would not touch it. When he was asked about the reason, he said that it was good for nothing. Then Chuang-tzu said: "This tree, because of its uselessness, is able to complete its natural term of existence." Having left the mountain, Chuang-tzu lodged in the house of his friend. The friend was glad and ordered his waiting lad to kill a goose and boil it. The lad said: "One of our geese can cackle, and the other cannot; which of them shall I kill?" The host said: "Kill the one that cannot cackle." Next day, his disciple asked Chuang-tzu, saying: "Yesterday we saw the mountain tree that can complete its natural term of existence because of its uselessness. Now for

the same reason, our host's goose died. Which of these positions would you, master, prefer to be in? Chuang-tzu laughed and said: "I would prefer to be in a position which is between the useful and the useless. This seems to be the right position, but is really not so. Therefore, it would not put me beyond trouble. But he who makes excursion in *Tao* and *Te* is not exposed to any trouble. He is above the reach of both praise and detraction, now like a dragon, now like a snake. He changes with time and has no insistence. He is now high and now low, taking harmony as the measure. He enjoys himself at ease with the author of things. He treats things as things, and is not being treated as a thing by them. What can involve him in trouble?"[4]

Things are different (each possessing its own nature, occupying its own place) and yet undifferentiated (when we stop imposing upon them the distinction between subject and object, right and wrong). "Great use" (or "small use"), "usefulness," and "uselessness" are not to be determined by *one* predetermined yardstick.

Hui-tzu said to Chuang-tzu: "The king of Wei sent me some calabash seeds. I planted them and they bore a fruit as big as a five-bushel measure. I used it as a vessel for holding water, but it was not solid enough to hold it. I cut the calabash in two for ladles, but each of them was too shallow to hold anything. Because of this uselessness, I knocked them to pieces." "Sir," said Chuang-tzu, "it was rather you did not know how to use large things. . . . Why did you not make of it a large bottle-gourd, by means of which you could float in rivers and lakes?"[5]

Everything has its own natural endowment, its own natural inclination, its own suitability. If we leave each thing to perform its own natural inclination, then everything can be free in its own development and movement. The conceptions of "great use" and "small use" are born from an accentual system that denies each thing the possibility of remaining the way it is according to its natural measure. Chuang-tzu, to deframe the fetters inherent in an accentual system, therefore, begins by diffusing viewpoints; he asks that we do not discriminate *that* and *this* as opposites so as to open up a middle ground, a *huan-chung* (ring/center), whereby we can respond to the endless changes:

The possible is possible; the impossible is impossible. *Tao* evolves and sequences follow. Things have names and are what they are. What are they? They are what they are. What are they not? They are not what they are not. Everything is what it is, and does what it can do. There is nothing that is not something. There is nothing that cannot do something. Therefore, a beam and a pillar are identical. So are ugliness, beauty, greatness, wickedness, perverseness, and strangeness. Separation is the same as construction. Construction is the same as destruction. But all things, without regard to their construction and destruction, may again be united into one. . . . Therefore, the sages harmonize the systems of right and wrong, and rest in the evolution of nature. This is called following two courses at once.[6]

As we can now see, in Ssu-k'ung T'u's poem the phrases like "ring/center," "ten thousand / things in the world," and "come/it/no/end" (or, "What comes this way comes without end") are not independent at all, and they cannot be isolated to assume autonomous circles of meanings. From the beginning, they brought along with them echoes from other texts. Similarly, the word *hun* (渾, "Undifferentiated Whole") must be read together with the Taoist notions of "void/empty," of "Not to discriminate *that* and *this* as opposites," and of "following two courses at once." The appearance of this word, like the appearance of any other word, is already infiltrated or invaded by words and phrases from other texts. It is this interillumination and intercorrespondence between these words and phrases, including the stories and parables that gave rise to them, that has helped to weave the continually changing and developing "meanings" of the word *hun*.

Echoes come not only from Chuang-tzu but from other writers as well. When the word "void" occurs, we hear Chuang-tzu's voice and, simultaneously, the voices of Lu Chi (261–303) and Liu Hsieh (ca. 465–520):

Erected in the center-domain (center of the ring) . . . suspend vision, bring back hearing, become lost in contemplation to reach out for contact — there spirit gallops into millions of miles of space.

Trying the Void to demand Being; knocking upon Profound Silence for Sound.[7]

Lu Chi, "Wen Fu"

The perceptual activity travels far in spirit. Completely stilled, contemplation centered, it reaches out to a thousand years . . . The principle of perceptual activity is miraculous when the

spirit consorts with the eternal world . . . to develop one's
perceptual activity, the most important thing is emptiness and
quiescence.[8]

Liu Hsieh, *The Dragon-Carving of the Literary Mind*

With these echoes, then, the phrases in Ssu-k'ung T'u's poem, "All
phenomena now contained / it stretches proudly across space" (pos-
sess / get-ready / ten thousand / things in the world; lie across /
exhaustively / primary / space), now receive much larger symphonic
play from different levels of overlay. Indeed, even more voices and
echoes, from all directions, came to dominate the poet's conscious-
ness (and, in turn, ours) — voices from essays on poetry and painting
written before Ssu-k'ung T'u's time. And — at least for readers such as
us — this would be true not only of those written before but also those
written afterwards. The many works modeled after *The Twenty-four
Orders of Poetry*, such as Yang T'ing-tzu's *Explaining the Twenty-four
Orders of Poetry* (1815) and Tseng Chi-tse's (1839–1890) *To Develop
Twenty-four Orders of Poetry*, offer us emulative and commenting
voices. And if these anachronistic voices help to disclose certain hid-
den "meanings" in Ssu-k'ung T'u's text, then we feel that we cannot
be so sure such voices did not *at one point* possess the poet's compo-
sitional consciousness under certain guises. Words and phrases may
have, and at the same time may not have, *definite* meanings. There is
a strange neutrality in the words; meanings flow in and out of them.

In a sense, none of the words appearing in a text can claim to be
totally new and independent. The appearance of any word entails
double, triple, and even multiple associations. When I say, "This is
black," you will automatically and simultaneously think of "white" to
make the concept "black" possible, even though the statement points
to black, and black alone. If the object of my reference is not an
absolute black — there is no such thing as an absolute black in
nature — you will think of other shades of color aside from white. The
moment you hesitate, saying "Is this truly black?", many other con-
tending voices will instantaneously emerge in your consciousness.

The situation of doubling, tripling, and multiplying associations in
a literary text is even more complicated; the spaces and times into
which a text might lead are far and wide. What we have rehearsed
here is only a small part of the entire echoing phenomenon.

Let us first finish going through Ssu-k'ung Tu's poem. In *Hsiung-
hun* (雄 渾, masculine whole), *Hsiung* immediately evokes echoes
from the *I Ching*. In line 4, Ssu-k'ung T'u says, "Amass power (*Chien,*

健) to become masculine," (*Hsiung,* 雄), which echoes, and (appropriately) is echoed by this line from the first hexagram, *Ch'ien* (乾): "Heaven moves with power (*Chien,* 健); the superior man strengthens himself tirelessly." With this added echo, the tenor of "stretching proudly across Space" is even clearer. Our first impression of "True Body" (眞體) is that it is Buddhist, as indeed it can be, in the way that it was used by Prince Hsiao T'ung of Liang (501–531) in his exegesis of the meaning of "Two-Sacca"[9] as "not separated from True Body." But because of the echo of "Heaven moves with power," another clear voice emerges. It is the voice of art critic, monk Yen Tsung (ca. 627–649), of the T'ang Dynasty: "Chiang Chi's brush work is strong and powerful, his flair and spirit crisp. When he depicts mountains and rivers, he brings out their true bodies." This voice, in turn, closely echoes another poem from *The Twenty-four Orders of Poetry* titled "Strong and Powerful" (勁健):

> Spirit moves like the vast space.
> Breath moves like a rainbow.
> The Wu Gorges, deep, thousands of feet.
> Clouds run, bringing along winds.
> Sip the true, nourish the strong;
> Store the plain, keep to the inside.
> This, like the movement of power,
> Is called preserving the masculine.
> Sky and earth merge with it.
> Spirit and change function in it.
> Take it to actualize.
> Master it to complete.
>
> Poem No. 8

This poem within the series seems to be the best supplementary footnote to the word *chien* (健, power). Interestingly, the idea of "true" or "real" in this echo points us directly back to the Taoist Lao-tzu's notion of *P'u* (樸, Uncarved Block) and "the empty within"; this, in turn, means that the idea of "power," which comes from the *I Ching,* now also has the parameters of the Taoists—in particular, the dependence on "achieving masculinity" by "guarding femininity" (存雄, 守雌). This interdependence, no doubt, resounds with the "non-discrimination of opposites" to arrive at the center of the ring and the natural balance achieved by traveling two courses simultaneously. The echoes and correspondences come full circle and continue to expand—doubling, tripling—as they permutate into patterns of meanings.

"Masculine whole" is the *first order* in the twenty-four orders of poetry. In this, we find a distinctive echo of the fact that the hexagram *Ch'ien*, the first of the sixty-four hexagrams of the *I Ching*, leads the other sixty-three hexagrams. Likewise, "Masculine Whole" leads the other twenty-three orders of poetry. As will become clear in subsequent pages, the structural activity of *The Twenty-four Orders of Poetry* in many ways resembles that of the hexagrams of the *I Ching*.

I will next talk about internal correspondence. By external correspondence, we normally mean voices occurring outside the text, but here I want it to mean voices of other people evoked by the text and to reserve the term "internal correspondence" to mean echoes within the author's own corpus of works, either (1) within a specific text, or group of texts, or (2) in the author's other writings. The correspondence of the poem "Strong and Powerful" to the phrase "True Body" of the first poem is a clear example of the first type. The phrase *"Hsiang-wai"* (象 外, beyond form or shape) no doubt echoes the different levels of the meaning of form in the word "hexagram" (in Chinese the word *"Hsiang,"* 象, is often attached to the word "Kua," 卦, translated now as hexagram) and also echoes Liang Wu-ti's (464–549) use of the term in the lines: "Open the auspicious trace in the heavens; flash the spiritual meaning from beyond the visible form"[10] (a term used in connection with the discussion of things Buddhist). But more relevant is the internal echo from Ssu-k'ung T'u's own prose:

> Tai Jung-chou said, "The *scene* of poets, like 'the warm sun in the blue fields,' and 'smoke engendered from pearls,' is visible but not placeable before the eyes." *Form beyond form, scene beyond scene*: it is not speakable.[11]

In another place, Ssu-k'ung T'u compares the ability to write good poetry to that of distinguishing extremely subtle differences in tastes and flavors, and only with this ability can one arrive at what he calls *"taste beyond taste"* and *"the finest reach beyond rhythm."*[12]

The internal echoes and correspondences can be seen as the birthing and branching activities of a main growth — one gives rise to two, two to four, four to eight, and so forth. They form a kind of back-and-forth talk about an idea, an aside, or an extension of an idea. In the *I Ching*, not only can the first hexagram give rise to other hexagrams, but other hexagrams can give rise to each other; indeed, all hexagrams are interconnected and interrelated. We will examine the full working of this system in the second and third parts of this essay.

The internal echoes in *The Twenty-four Orders of Poetry* work in many ways, like those in the *I Ching*. For example, "Return to void" in the poem gives rise to the second poem in the series, "Thinning Out," and "What comes this way comes without end" is picked up by the tenth poem, "Naturalness." Indeed, a careful examination of the twenty-four poems will reveal a surprising branching and connecting web at work, as has been cogently argued by Yang Ting-tzu.[13]

Part of the reason for my proposing the activities of "secret echoes and complementary correspondences" as central to our understanding of the making and unmaking of a text is to point out the fact that Chinese literary theory and criticism from the very beginning has always been inclined to favor the total activity that occurs *outside* the word and phrases of a text. What we read is not one poem but a fabric of many poems, the concerto and symphony comprised of many other poems and voices. The mode of interlinear commentary so widely practiced in classical Chinese text editing is not a kind of mechanical source-hunting exercise, as it has generally been viewed, but an effort to re-create the symphony of voices, images, and poetic forms that the editor-reader of the texts heard and noted outside the text or believed must have originally occurred in the wide horizon of the author's consciousness. Let me use this mode of interlinear commentary to orchestrate an apparently simple poem on departure by Li Po (701–762) of the T'ang Dynasty:

Taking Leave of a Friend

Green mountains lie across the north wall.
White water winds the east city.

from *The Songs of the South*
    Up the mountains, down the rivers,
    See friends home.

Li Ling (B.C.?–74): "Parting from Su Wu"
    Hand in hand up the bridge over the river.

Ying Yang (died 236): "Farewell"
    Wide and far the water of the long river
    Nine turns toward the northeast. . . .
    Faraway into the road of a million miles.
    No means to return.

Lu Chi (261–303): "Parting"
    Riding out to the east city,
    I see you off to the brim of the winding river.

Yin Chung-wen (?–407): "Parting"
    Before the water about to see you off.

Here once we part
Lone tumbleweed, a million miles to travel.

from *Nineteen Old Poems*
    Tumbleweed, cut off from roots,
    Blown about, fearful of long winds.

Ts'ao Chih (192–232): "Woe indeed!"
    Tumbleweed, cut off from roots,
    Blown up and down scurrying with long winds.

Ssu-ma Piao (?–306): "Parting"
    Autumn tumbleweed; alone, who would pity?
    Blown up and down, turning with winds. . . .
    Into the distance, no means to return.

Pao Chao (421–465): "Rhymeprose on Wu-cheng"
    A lone tumbleweed trembles all alone,
    Startled sands fly from their seats.

Wu Yün (469–520): "Parting"
    Flow and turn, let loose like a flying tumbleweed.

Wang Pao (513?–76?): "Parting"
    Blown sand is like a canopy,
    Rolling tumbleweed, a turning wheel.

Floating clouds, a wanderer's mood.
Setting sun, an old friend's feelings.
We wave hands, you go away from here.
Neigh, neigh goes the horse at parting.

From *Nineteen Old Poems*
    Walk on again walk on.
    From you, separated alive.
    Between us, a million odd miles,
    Each at one end of the sky
    The roads are difficult and long.
    . . . .

To meet: where, how, and when?
Floating clouds veil the white sun.
The wanderer: no thought of return.
Thinking of you makes me old
Months, years: all of a sudden: dusk.

Li Ling: "For Su Wu"
Oh, the thought of you!
Sun dusks, but I will not lower the blind. . . .
Hesitating and not to return —
Floating clouds, a thousand miles a day
Who knows my heart is sad? . . .

Li Ling: "Another Poem for Su Wu"
Looking up to see floating clouds speed.
Almost instantly, we crossed each other . . .
and each of us at separate ends of the sky.

Hsü Kan (171–218): "Parting"
Floating clouds, how vast, how vast!
Would that through them I could see my tidings
They drift and drift, and none can be sent.
And it is vain to linger here and pine.
Others part but reunite:
Only for you there is no date of return . . .

Liu Shuo (431–453): "Restrain Tears to Go on the Road"
Sad winds blow up floating clouds.
Bleak! a million miles of separation!

Shen Yo (441–513): "Parting from a Friend"
Floating clouds, one south, one north . . .
Stars of *Ts'an* and *Shang* never to meet

Chiang Yen (444–505): "After Ancient Miscellaneous Poem
Yellow clouds covering a thousand miles
Wanderer: when will you return?

Hsiao Shen (479–529): "Parting"
Setting sun: we hold the reins
And make separation at the river-bank.

So much for the echo of motifs and images, now an echo in form and stylistic accent:

Yü Hsin (513–581): "Parting from Chou Hung-cheng"
North of Fu feng, at the Stone Bridge.

> Before Han-ku, the ancient Pass.
> Once we part here,
> To meet again? How many years?
> Yellow geese look back, flying.
> They linger, heart-smitten, dejected.
> I know no end to sorrow.
> In vain, to abate the strings of the lute.

The interlinear commentator is, of course, still limited in re-creating the voices that originally occur within the wide field of the poet's consciousness. In the case of Li Po's "Taking Leave of a Friend," more than a thousand poems must have traversed the poet's consciousness. But, even with this limited array of possible voices, we can still see that, when a classical Chinese poet writes a poem, he wants to talk, with these voices, to his friend (clearly, a friend who also knows most of the sources of these voices) and to invite him to move together into the spaces and the times in which these voices occurred. In this way, he can more fully communicate to him what he feels, which is not a simple form of sadness but the total sum of the different accents of sadness other poets have experienced and ex-pressed. To write a poem is not simply to leave a note: "I am leaving. Please don't forget me!" Words and phrases in the poem are spring-boards into larger spaces and deeper times. A poem is never locked within a text but is a conversation across historical space and time.

Some Chinese readers might notice that my interlinear com-mentary has made considerable use of the Chinese *lei-shu* (類書, a kind of topical encyclopedia). The intention of both the interlinear commentary and the *lei-shu* is precisely to help us re-create the com-plex conversational moment described above. When a poet writes down a line, he is already active in historical space. When we speak a word, we have already disclosed our historical roots. But we also know that the words or phrases of a poem are not closures of mean-ings but are an activity of meanings as old and new voices blend and weave, double and change, playing themselves out in an open "field" outside the text—a complex, multivocalic, thick-textured musical composition.

Liu Hsieh and the I Ching

The first theorist who discoursed on the aesthetic activity of "secret echoes and complementary correspondences" was Liu Hsieh of the fifth century. His model is the *I Ching*. In a chapter entitled "The

Hidden and the Manifest" in his *The Dragon-Carving of the Literary Mind*, he says:

> The movement of the mind's craft is distant indeed! And profound is the change of literature's pulsations. With deep sources to feed the tributaries and strong roots to support lush leaves, the growth of literature has both the manifest and hidden levels. What is meant by "the hidden" is its doubling of motifs; what is meant by "the manifest" is the prominently unique in a piece of writing. The hidden excel in incremental "senses"; the manifest show skillfulness in being matchless. . . . The body of "the hidden" actualizes itself in having meanings growing outside of the text, with secret echoes and complementary correspondences, with latent colors emerging from the deep, the way the change of lines in the hexagrams gives rise to nuclear trigrams. . . . Therefore, nuclear trigrams and line changes to complete the transformations of four forms.

This passage, which has been taken as expressing the seminal theory of the Chinese aesthetic concept of *han-hsü* (涵蓄, implication, suggestiveness, holding back or containing more than it appears), is clear and needs no further elaboration. The notions of "meanings growing outside the text" and "secret echoes and complementary correspondences" are also self-explanatory after the exposition in the first part of this essay. Since the phrase "secret echoes and complementary correspondences" was deeply implicated within the working dynamics of the *I Ching*, it is necessary to trace the exact sources and meanings of "complementary correspondences" (旁通, *p'ang-t'ung*) and those of two other terms, "line changes [in the hexagram] and nuclear trigrams" (互體爻變, *hu-t'i yao-pien*) and "four forms" (四象, *ssu-hsiang*).

The first two are topics that were current in Han Dynasty (206 B.C.– A.D. 220) studies of the *I Ching*; the latter is first found in the *Appended Judgments* (繫辭, *Hsi-tz'u*). A critic active in the Six Dynasties, Liu Hsieh easily made use of topics current in the recent past. In this case, one may ask, what kind of structural activity and aesthetic implications did Liu Hsieh derive from the system of the *I Ching* that lent support to the morphology of a text? I will review these topics briefly before examining the roles they play in the total system.

P'ang-t'ung, "complementary correspondences," began with Yü Fan (虞翻, 170–239) of the Han Dynasty. According to Yü, for every hexagram there is always a complementary or corresponding hexagram implied by the inherent possibility of changing *yang* lines to *yin* lines, or vice versa. For example, *Pi* (比, Holding Together [Union]) ䷇ complements/corresponds to *Ta Yu* (大有, Possession in Great Measure) ䷍, and *Fu* (復, Return [The Turning Point]) ䷗ complements/corresponds to *Kou* (姤, Coming to Meet) ䷫. Even in this simplified description, we can see that no object exists independently and in isolation, because its appearance always calls up or leads to another one closely related to it. This can also be said of the situation in regard to words or phrases in a text.

Hu-t'i yao-pien (nuclear trigrams and change of lines): The term *hu-t'i* (interrelated trigrams or nuclear trigrams) began with Ching Fang (京房, 77–37 B.C.) of the Han Dynasty. It means that within one hexagram there are four trigrams: the upper trigram, lower trigram, inner nuclear trigram, and outer nuclear trigram. In the hexagram *Wu Wang* (无妄, Innocent [the Unexpected]) ䷘, for example, the upper trigram is *Ch'ien* (乾, the creative) ☰; the lower trigram is *Chen* (震, the Arousing) ☳; the inner nuclear trigram—that is, lines 2 to 4 from bottom—is *Ken* (艮, Keeping Still) ☶; and the outer nuclear trigram—lines 3 to 5 from bottom—is *Sun* (巽, the Gentle) ☴. When Yü Fan took over the idea, he mixed these divisions with the principle of hexagram change (developed from suggestions in ancient writings in *Kuo-yü* and *Tso-chüan*)[14] and counted in also the first and the sixth lines as well as half lines, giving rise to countless hexagram changes. What is significant for us here is that each hexagram already contains inherent nuclear trigrams as well as numerous hexagram change possibilities. Thus, "secret echoes and complementary correspondences," as Liu Hsieh uses it, refers to the simultaneous responses, opposites, complementarities, and changes inherently occurring in each word or phrase, in much the same way as in each hexagram. Take the hexagram *T'ai* (泰, Peace) as an example:

Gram	*Complementary gram*
䷊ 泰 (*T'ai*, Peace)	䷋ 否 (*P'i*, Standstill [Stagnation])
☷ above; 坤 (*K'un*, the Receptive)	☰ above; 乾 (*Ch'ien*, the Creative)
☰ below; 乾 (*Ch'ien*, the Creative)	☷ below; 坤 (*K'un*, the Receptive)
☱ inner nuclear trigram; 兌 (*Tui*, the Joyous)	☶ inner nuclear trigram; 艮 (*Ken*, Keeping Still)
☳ outer nuclear trigram; 震 (*Chen*, the Arousing)	☴ outer nuclear trigram; 巽 (*Sun*, the Gentle)

Hexagram contained in T'ai

䷡ 歸妹 (*Kuei Mei*, the Marrying Maid);
above: ☳ (*Chen*); below: ☱ (*Tui*)

Complementary hexagram in P'i

䷴ 漸 (*Chien*, Development
[Gradual Progress]); above:
☴ (*Sun*); below: ☶ (*Ken*)

Changes through the lines in T'ai

change in 1st line;
升 (*Sheng*, Pushing Upward)

change in 2nd line;
明夷 (*Ming I*, Darkening of the
Light)

change in 3rd line;
臨 (*Lin*, Approach)

change in 4th line;
大壯 (*Ta Chuang*, the Power of
the Great)

change in 5th line;
需 (*Hsü*, Waiting for
Nourishment)

change in 6th line;
大畜 (*Ta Ch'u*, Taming Power of
the Great)

Complementary changes in P'i

change in 1st line;
无妄 (*Wu Wang*, Innocence
[the Unexpected])

change in 2nd line;
訟 (*Sung*, Conflict)

change in 3rd line;
遯 (*Tun*, Retreat)

change in 4th line;
觀 (*Kuan*, Contemplation
[View])

change in 5th line;
晉 (*Chin*, Progress)

change in 6th line;
萃 (*Ts'ui*, Gathering
Together [Massing])

From this chart, we can see that one hexagram (in fact, any hexagram) always simultaneously points toward, evokes, or contains other hexagrams, which, in turn, help to define and modify the hexagram in question. Through complementary correspondences, line changes, and nuclear trigrams, all the hexagrams become interconnected, a structuring activity with interpointing, interdefining, and interresponding as its dynamics. In looking back on *The Twenty-four Orders of Poetry*, we find these same dynamics at work both in the act of creation and in the act of reading.

Ssu-hsiang (Four Forms): According to the *Appended Judgments*, Part I, it is said that "The *I* (Change) began with the Primeval One, which gives rise to the Parent Two, which, in turn gives rise to the Four Forms." This is based upon the combination and permutation of *Yin* and *Yang*, which continue on to produce the eight trigrams and sixty-four hexagrams (Fig. 3). The process of tributary or branching changes from One, to Two, to Four Forms, to eight trigrams, and, by doubling the eight trigrams, to sixty-four hexagrams, is the beginning of the Chinese numerological philosophy that became a sophis-

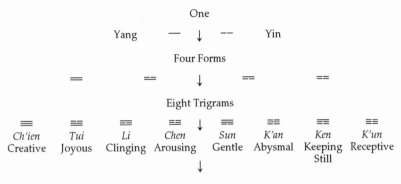

Figure 3. Formative process of hexagrams

ticated mathematical system in itself. When Liu Hsieh uses the term *ssu-hsiang*, he is clearly comparing this geometric progression and growth as represented by this term to a similar activity in a text. Other explanations have been advanced for this term. These include (1) seeing it as representing four of the five cosmic forces—metal, wood, water, fire—with the fifth, earth, occupying the center; or (2) to stand for *Yang*, *Yin*, strong, soft; or (3), in a much later stage of development, to mean old *Yang*, young *Yang*, old *Yin*, young *Yin*. All these associated meanings have no doubt affected conceptions of structure in Chinese literature. The term has also been taken to mean the real, the false or substitute, the ideational, and the functional. For example, for the hexagram *Ch'ien* (the Creative), the real is sky, its extension (thus false or substitute) is father, the ideational is the commentary "*Ch'ien* is powerful," and the functional is the four virtues: Primal, Unblocked, Advantageous, Just. This last explanation greatly conditioned the Chinese system of symbolic and semiotic activity. But these four explanations are not our concern here; they need to be treated separately within the context of hermeneutic philosophy. What is clear is the fact that the birthing and branching activity contained in the term *ssu-hsiang* again corresponds to the working dynamics of the text as proposed by Liu Hsieh.

I must hasten to add that, while the analogy between the activity of the text/s and that of the hexagram/s is clear, we must not see this concept of structuring activity as originating first from a set of arbitrary mathematical formulas or abstract semiotic systems and procedures that were then imposed upon constantly changing existential experiences. On the contrary, the whole hexagrammatic system was originally modeled after nature.

The Hexagrams and the Permutations of Nature

The *Book of Change* (*I*, 易) has also been called the *Book of the Easy-Simple-Plain* (*I*, 易), in spite of the fact that a good percentage of this ancient text is difficult to decipher. We need not go too far to notice the hexagrammatic principles at work. Let us begin with the easy, simple, and plain experiences.

Take, for example, the following natural phenomenon. On one side of a terrain is a windblown, pounding ocean beside which is a mountain reaching to the sky. We notice that much rain might fall along the coastal area, and, upon the slopes of the mountain, lush and dense vegetation might be stunted and bent by constant strong winds. But because the mountain serves as a buffer, we might find a desert with few or no trees on the other side of this imposing mountain. Occasionally, because of the change of air currents, some storms might come and vegetation might emerge, but the desert never quite becomes lush. Instead, the dry, sandy mountainside might be sculpted into a variety of strange forms. And, if there is underground water, an oasis might be formed. Suddenly, however, this oasis might also disappear because the inhabitants have overdrawn its water, or because the water source was disrupted by geological change, or because of human destruction brought about by mining. Thus, the coming together and separation of the elements in nature play out incessantly before us in countless phenomena. The formation of each phenomenon depends upon certain chance elements. We also notice that each phenomenon that we see as *formed* is actually *constantly changing*; every minute there are new elements coming into and going out of the formed phenomenon before us, making it impossible for that given phenomenon to remain unchanged, though the change might be incrementally slow and, indeed, almost indiscernable at any one moment. We also notice the following characteristics of this process: the position of a natural phenomenon is quite often stationary (such as a tree or a mountain), but the change-causing elements are often active (such as the change of climate). Change has regularity (such as the recurrent seasonal changes) but also irregularity (such as certain unexpected, natural catastrophes). No natural phenomenon can in a strict sense become what it is independently; it needs assistance or stimulation from other phenomena (such as trees needing sunshine, water, and soil). Location is important for a natural object to become what it is (water weeds cannot be grown on land, for example), as is time and season (e.g., many vegetables cannot be grown in winter; fertile soil is totally helpless in this case).

All growth is brought about by the relative push and pull of movement and stillness and the interaction of different natural elements, in which we find regularities and irregularities. Regularity is measure; irregularity is chance. This easy, simple, and plain working of nature is the very essence of the *I Ching*, the process of change.

Turning to the *I Ching*, we can say that after long observation of the cooperation, correspondence, and opposition between and among natural elements, the ancient Chinese came up with sixty-four major situations, represented by the sixty-four combinations of the eight trigrams:

Ch'ien	K'un	K'an	Li	Ken	Tui	Sun	Chen
sky	earth	water	fire	mountain	lake	wind	thunder

It was the convergence and divergence of different potentials inherent in each element or phenomenon that gave rise to the sixty-four natural situations (the patterning of which also points toward human situations). Before we trace the possible ways in which the hexagrams developed from the simple *yang* lines and *yin* lines, it is important to examine the structuring implications of hexagrams.

Hexagrams, as we have already explained, are formed from the coupling of two trigrams. But this formation must not be understood as combination (i.e., something static and closed) but *permutation* (i.e., something continually changing and open). This is to say that there are more than sixty-four situations, cosmic or human. Within each permutation, the possibility of change is continuous and never terminal; there is change occurring every moment within each given hexagram. This, in a way, is why each hexagram is given to continuous line change that leads to newer permutational possibilities. It is important to remember the continuously changing nature inherent in the word *permutation*, particularly in connection with the Chinese concept of structuralism. The Chinese form of structuralism is not only binary (*yin–yang*) but also both contrastive and complementary, oppositional and cooperative; it is not closed but open for constant change and revision, for it at once contains regularities (measure) and irregularities (chance).

As for the formation of the primary eight trigrams, it is said that they were developed from the *yang* (—) and *yin* (--) lines. The process begins with undifferentiated oneness, leads to the primeval pair (—, --), to the four forms (≡, ≡, ≡, ≡), and to the primary eight trigrams (*Ch'ien* ≡, *Tui* ≡, *Li* ≡, *Chen* ≡, *Sun* ≡, *K'an* ≡, *Ken* ≡, and *K'un* ≡). Legend has it that the *yang* and *yin* lines were based upon real experiences. One theory postulates that in our observation of things in the world, we easily notice odd and even numbers in almost all forms of life, hence —, --. Another theory asserts that they actually represent male and female, with the explanation that the most prominent sexual symbol for male is — and that for the female is --. Advocates of the second theory often cite, for their support, the statement that the marriage of *yin* and *yang* gives rise to the million things. (Thus, it is said that *Ch'ien* is father, *K'un*, mother.) The history of how certain lines came to represent what they represent is very complex. We have no absolute certainty about the ways in which the embryonic form of the *I Ching* derived from divination through cracked lines upon burned tortoise shells. It has been speculated that a few trigrams might have come directly from the cracked lines. But one thing seems to be clear; these line representations were most probably modeled after nature and were not purely abstract inventions. This can be seen from the trigram *K'an* ☵, which is exactly the same as the pictogram of the character for water ⺡ found in oracle bone inscriptions.[15] We can safely say, therefore, that the sixty-four hexagrams are not abstract, mathematical permutations but are permutations from the interactions between eight primary "real phenomena," verifiable from our experiences. Thus, each linear hexagram in the *I Ching* is also spoken of in terms of real phenomena. Here are some examples:

蒙	*meng*	youthful folly	䷃	above *Ken* below *K'an*	fountain from below mountain
復	*fu*	return	䷗	above *K'un* below *Chen*	thunder inside earth
大壯	*ta chuang*	power of the great	䷡	above *Chen* below *Ch'ien*	thunder above in the sky
解	*hsieh*	deliverance	䷧	above *Chen* below *K'an*	thunder and rain working together
既濟	*chi chi*	after completion	䷾	above *K'an* below *Li*	water over fire
未濟	*wei chi*	before completion	䷿	above *Li* below *K'an*	fire over water

We must observe that in the juxtaposition of two natural phenomena, the inventor/s of the hexagrams did not determine linear or causal explanations of how one phenomenon affects or conditions the other (how in the case of *meng*, for instance, the mountain is to be, or has been, affected by water), for there is more than one kind of interactive possibility. Thus, to explain *meng* as a condition of instability because of water under the mountain and, by extension, translating it as "youthful folly" (as the English translator has opted to do) is to decide on only *one* possible meaning at the exclusion of many others. The possibility of other kinds of interaction must be kept open. On this level, the structure of the hexagrams is like the structure of Chinese characters. For example, the Chinese character for time, *shih* (時), discussed in chapter 2, is a composite of two visual events juxtaposed, not an abstraction. The awareness of time in ancient China was of an activity consisting of real objects, phenomena, or events, a full ambience in which human beings could move about and participate. Similarly, what appears to be abstract, mathematical formations in the hexagrams turns out to be real phenomena in active interaction, disclosing themselves in concrete situations. Their meanings are not linear-causal but multiple-variable. In philosophy, this refusal to be tied down to one interpretation has been designated *aporia* (a word consisting of *apo*, to derive from, and *horos*, margin or brim), a condition that we might call trembling at the edge of discourse without committing oneself to determinable interpretation. The mode of presentation in the *I Ching* is congruent with that of poetic discourse defying the abstracting and unraveling procedures of prose. This realization is significant in our reading of the *I Ching*.

In the *I Ching*, the hexagrams, the judgments, and the expositions of individual lines are the urtext, and the "Ten Wings" are explanatory notes added at a later stage by scholars of the feudal Chou Dynasty and possibly by scholars with a Confucian orientation. A comparison between the two portions will reveal that the former disclose themselves with the poetic activity of indeterminacy, or *aporia*, while the latter is characterized by a clear-cut value-abstracting, judicial discursiveness. Let us take the first portion of the hexagram *Ch'ien* as an example:

☰ *Ch'ien* 乾

Ch'ien, primal, unblocked, advantageous, just.
Nine* in the first place:
    Hidden dragon. No function or don't function.
Nine in the second place:
    Dragon appears in the field: advantageous to
        meet the Great One.

Nine in the third place:
    Superior man creatively active whole day.
    Sundown: still vigilant as ever.
    Precarious — no blame.
Nine in the fourth place:
    Perhaps leaping from the deep. No blame.
Nine in the fifth place:
    Flying dragons in the sky: advantageous to meet
        the Great One.
Nine at the top place:
    Dragons exceeding limits — cause to repent.
The use of all nines:
    All dragons, no one to lead — auspicious.

*Nine is the number for *yang* lines, and six is for *yin* lines.

From its inception as divination, through its second stage as philosophical system, to its later numerological development, the *I Ching* discloses permutations of activities that can apply equally to both natural phenomena and human situations. This in part explains why the term "four forms" has been invested with the meanings of the real, the substitute, the ideational, and the functional. Between the real and the substitute, however, is not a simple relationship in which the signifier equals the signified but a morphological process with multiple-variable possibilities of correspondences. In the present instance, the dragon image is used, not only because it symbolizes "power" derived from "heaven (sky)" and "sun" (the etymological roots of *Ch'ien* being "sun's rays") but, more important, because of its suggestive logical possibilities in terms of time (i.e., timeliness), position, condition, and influence.

At the risk of oversimplification, let us dwell on the six stages involved in the morphological process of the represented image. The six stages are "hidden," "appearance in the field," "hesitation" (as revealed in the word "vigilant"), "leaping," "flying," and "exceeding limits." The time, position, condition, and influence of each of the six stages refer not only to the phenomenon in the sky (sunup to sundown) but also to the animal, the vegetable, and human worlds. "Hidden dragon. No function or don't function": Before an animal is born, before a plant sprouts, when a baby is in the embryonic stage, or before a practical matter matures from its initial conception, the limits of timeliness, position, condition ("hidden"), and influence (not ready to "function," although the influence is potentially there) are already set. If we ignore these four spheres and function ahead of time, regardless of the limits of position and condition, and tap the potential influence of each of the above-outlined situations, we are bound to fail and meet danger. Hence, "No function or don't function." Similarly, "Dragon exceeding limits — cause to repent" is also morphologically true of animals, plants, humans, as well as human affairs.

What the hexagrams and images signify is therefore not an abstracted meaning but morphological traces, or *wen* (文, a word now used to denote literature), traces that have correspondences simultaneously with all levels of phenomena. The inventors of the hexagrams, images, and lines modeled them after real objects or phenomena in their changing morphological situations and achieved a concept of structure that preserves the multiple, radiating indeterminacy of the moment and allows one to stand at the boundary, *aporia*, not knowing what meaning to choose but at the same time becoming fully aware of the multiple meanings in action. This is, of course, nothing less than the activity of poetry itself.

Returning to Liu Hsieh's adoption of "complementary correspondences," "line changes and nuclear trigrams," and "four forms" from the *I Ching* to explain the activity of the text, it must be clear by now that he was not referring to abstract and arbitrary mathematical permutations but to morphological permutations of real phenomena and their interpointing, interdefining, and intermodifying activities. The following explanation of "nuclear trigrams" by a recent *I Ching* scholar, Kao Huai-min, is instructive:

> The so-called hexagrams are nothing but a few linear signs
> designed to subsume all the affairs, all the things, all the
> patterns, visible and invisible affairs, visible and invisible
> things, visible and invisible patterns in the cosmos. It is natural
> that in the subsequent years of studies on the *I Ching*, people
> have come up, in time, with finer and finer extensions of earlier
> conceptions. The invention of nuclear trigrams is nothing but
> disclosing the fact that within each visible hexagram there are
> hidden hexagrams, to inform us that the hexagrams are not
> surface forms easily exhaustible, but built in within them cubist
> doubling-tripling through which one can detect hexagrams
> within hexagrams, from one to multiple.[16]

This can be seen, quite literally, as a footnote to Liu Hsieh's theory of "Secret Echoes and Complementary Correspondences."

At the end of the first section of this essay, I said that words or phrases of a poem constitute an activity of meanings, as old and new voices blend and weave, double and change, playing themselves out in an open field outside the text. When writing a poem a poet wants to disclose to the reader the mental image of an experience the poet has had, but in fact the total existential dimensions and activities of this image cannot be enclosed in words. This is comparable to the workings of the hexagrams. Each hexagram evolves into a series of permutations through complementary correspondences, line changes, and nuclear trigrams, implying that the permutations in the heavens, on earth, and among human beings are the major permutations observable from real phenomena (the manifest measures), within which there are still countless continuously changing permutations (the hidden chances), which are already contained in the manifest hexagrams. That each hexagram can do this depends upon the intermodifying, intersuggesting activities between real phenomena and upon preserving the *aporia* — that is, not arbitrarily determining one line of explanation. Thus, in the *Appended Judgments* we find such phrases as "The alternation between closing and opening, they call change. The going forward and backward without ceasing, they called penetration," and "Writing cannot express words completely. Words cannot express meanings completely." It is interesting that this last statement is in perfect harmony with those of the Taoist Lao-tzu, as in such statements as "The Tao, told, is not the Constant Tao," and "He who speaks does not know; he who knows does not speak." The Taoists and the Confucians in the *I Ching* can echo each other so closely because central to their concern over the question of whether language can authenticate the activities of phenomena is their recognition of the enclosing nature of language itself. This recognition led to the priority they gave to the entire activity outside language and text. "Meanings growing outside the text" (義生文外), "When you get the meanings, you are to forget the words" (得意忘言), "Text has no fixed (closed) meanings" (文辭無定義). All these statements view the text as a door that opens toward symphonic activities reaching through the vast reaches of space and time.

Other Voices

Julia Kristeva

Bakhtin was one of the first to replace the static hewing out of texts with a model where literary structure does not simply *exist* but is generated in relation to *another* structure. What allows a dynamic dimension to structuralism is his conception of the "literary word" as an *intersection of textual surfaces* rather than a *point* (a fixed meaning), as a dialogue among several writings: that of the writer, the addressee (or the character), and the contemporary or earlier cultural context. . . . In Bakhtin's work, these two axes [horizontal axis — subject/addressee — and vertical axis — text, context], which he calls *dialogue* and *ambivalence*, are not clearly distinguished. Yet, what appears as a lack of rigor is in fact an insight first introduced into literary theory by Bakhtin: any text is constructed as a mosaic of quotations; any text is the absorption and transformation of another. The notion of *intertextuality* replaces that of intersubjectivity, and poetic language is read as at least *double*.[17]

Roland Barthes

I read the text. The statement . . . is not always true. The more plural the text, the less it is written before I read it; I do not make it undergo a predicative operation, consequent upon its being, an operation known as reading, and "I" is not an innocent subject, anterior to the text, one which will subsequently deal with the text as it would an object to dismantle or a site to occupy. The "I" which approaches the text is already itself a plurality of other texts, of codes which are infinite or, more precisely, lost (whose origin is lost). . . . The meanings I find are established not by "me" or by others, but by their systematic mark: there is no other proof of reading than the quality and endurance of its systematics; in other words, than its functioning. . . . To read is to find meanings, and to find meanings is to name them; but named meanings are swept toward other names; names call to each other, reassemble, and their grouping calls for further meaning: I name, I unname, I rename: so the text passes; it is a nomination in the course of becoming.

Alongside each utterance, one might say that off stage voices can be heard: they are the codes: in their interweaving, these voices (whose origin is "lost" in the vast perspective of the *already-written*) de-originate the utterance: the convergence of the voices (of the odes) becomes *writing*, a stereographic space where the five codes, the five voices, intersect: the Voice of Empirics (the proairetisms), the Voice of the Person (the semes), the Voice of Science (the cultural codes), the Voice of Truth (the hermeneutics), the Voice of Symbol.[18]

M. M. Bakhtin

Any concrete discourse (utterance) finds the object at which it was directed already as it were overlain with qualifications, open to dispute, charged with value, already enveloped in an obscuring mist — or, on the contrary, by the "light" of alien words that have already been spoken about it. It is entangled, shot through with shared thoughts, points of view, alien value judgments and accents. The word, directed toward its object, enters a dialogically agitated environment of alien words, value judgments and accents, weaves in and out of complex interrelationships, merges with some, recoils from others, intersects with yet a third group: and all this may crucially shape discourse, may leave a trace in all its semantic layers, may complicate its expression and influence its entire stylistic profile.[19]

Harold Bloom

Poems are not things but only words that refer to other words, and *those* words refer to still other words, and so on into the densely over-populated world of literary language. Any poem is an inter-poem, and any reading of a poem is an inter-reading.[20]

6   Reflections on Historical Totality and the Study of Modern Chinese Literature

Obviously we must know accurately a great number of
minute facts about any subject if we are really to know it.
    —Ezra Pound, "I Gather the Limbs of Osiris"

The peculiar difficulty of dialectical writing lies indeed in
its holistic, "totalizing" character: as though you could not
say one thing until you had first said everything; as though
with each new idea you were bound to recapitulate the
entire system.
    —Fredric Jameson, "Toward Dialectical Criticism"

We are well informed by our common sense that historical totality is only a working concept and no intellectual formulation can ever expect to fully encompass it. We stop certain things in the flow of concrete history and lift them out of their forever changing environments for scrutiny and analysis; meanwhile, the flow goes on its continuous totalizing process, invalidating any claim of wholeness. Historical completeness, which requires comprehensive coverage of all spatial and temporal extensions, and historical objectivity, which presupposes verifiability with the sum total of concrete events, can never be authentically achieved. Invariably, *each history* comes to us as *a version*, a mere version, incomplete and always partial, because only certain facts, believed to be significant, are chosen and highlighted as if they can, indeed, represent the entirety of history. Thus, Pound, speaking of a "new method of scholarship" or "the Method of Luminous Detail," says:

> Any fact is, in a sense, "significant." Any fact may be "symp-
> tomatic," but certain facts give one a sudden insight into
> circumjacent conditions, into their causes, their effect, into
> sequence, and law. . . . In the history of development of

civilization or literature, we come upon such interpretating detail. A few dozen facts of this nature give us intelligence of a period — a kind of intelligence not to be gathered from a great array of facts of the other sort.[1]

Fredric Jameson, a totally different kind of critic, also emphasizes that any analysis must first isolate certain "dominant categories" that, seen as phenomena in dialectical interrelationship, will allow us "to see what something is through the simultaneous awareness of what it is not." The final moment must then deliver this abstraction back to the concrete world, "to abolish itself as an illusion of autonomy, and to redissolve into history, offering as it does so some momentary glimpse of reality as a concrete whole."[2]

To juxtapose Jameson, a dialectical critic, with Pound, whose historical consciousness is at best eclectic, is not to suggest that they share in any way the same philosophy of history. Rather, I want to point out this: In spite of their obviously different senses of hierarchy, they nonetheless have to come to grips with the same initial paradox in treating history: simultaneous admission of the limitation of thought before historical totality and their assertive desire to reach out and perceive, each in his own way, some semblance of wholeness through selected details.

It is clear that all historical studies must be considered provisional, inconclusive, and open for revision. It is this sense of seeing all efforts of historical formulations as provisional that will keep us in constant touch with the forever changing totalizing process. This sense of provisionality is thus linked with the full awareness of totality. When human beings lose sight of this sense, they are likely to gloss over totality and take partiality for wholeness. So, many large claims have been continuously pounded into our heads: Such-and-such a work is *the* "touchstone" of *the* spirit of the time, *the most significant* reinvention of tradition, and by tradition it is often meant that of the high culture, where, of course, the "artifice of eternity" and "absolute value" are supposed to be found. In certain cases, what is meant by "significant," "absolute," "mind of the first degree," all highly hierarchical terms, is to be verified by a set of standards put forth by some ancient authority of a particular culture. However, when applied anachronistically to another culture, such a set of standards is likely to prove quite arbitrary. This last statement is, of course, the central theme of my essay on the problems of the use of models.

But deeply ingrained in our consciousness is the danger of having already formed a set of prejudgments; and these prejudgments, pre-clusive in nature, are somewhat ordained, as it were, by authorities of the past, who, themselves grounded in specific time and space, had abstracted from the totalizing process of all phenomena certain models of experiences that were then proclaimed as universally valid for *all* times. Whether we want to admit it or not, examples of pre-judgments resulting from the lack of awareness of totality occur quite frequently.

Take the case of the history of Chinese literature. It designates only *a* history of Chinese literature produced mainly by "cultured" writers whose taste, sense of order, techniques, and aesthetic judg-ments have been conditioned by the system in which they find them-selves. Very few of them view folk literature as serious literary "art." And when it should happen that some of the works of folk origins are included in the forest of literature, they are either "co-opted" or "culturized," valued according to the degree of their assimilation into the literary imagination of the cultured writers and critics. Although the imaginative formulation of the cultured writers originally might have been a refinement (often by an eclectic process of selection) of the embryonic folk mode of expression, many important aspects of the compositional reality of oral tradition indigenous to the spon-taneous expressiveness of this so-called lower culture have been adulterated in the process.

In one sense, this is unavoidable. Culture is inevitably a process of filtering. The question is what this filtering process has done to wholeness itself. For even among studies of cultured works, this process has revealed some rather delimiting eclecticism. A ready example is T. S. Eliot's historical sense and his concept of tradition. We are told to embrace within our consciousness the entire body of literature since Homer, against which we can best judge our own work and see how and whether it will readjust the total order. Here, we are not to blame Eliot for not having included the Oriental hori-zons (Indian and Chinese, the existence of both of which he knew well enough before he made such a statement); for me, the total order (of cultured literary works) must at least include these two areas. Yet even within the Greco-Roman or European totality, Eliot's tradition is also extremely selective: only Dante, certain Elizabethan dramatists, metaphysical poets, and certain symbolist and post-symbolist practitioners are included.

What happens here is, of course, that when we are dealing with a poet-critic like Eliot, or, for that matter, any poet-critic at any historical juncture of time, we are looking at *one perception* of a total order, *one appropriation*, and one set of conditions governing how this appropriation is conditioned and, to a large extent, determined by all the historical factors with which the poet-critic has to negotiate to establish individual talent. To criticize Eliot, we must have a sense of this still larger totality to fully understand the limitation of the wholeness he claims.

The sense of totality allows us to know that what has been omitted by a critic or critics of a certain class is not necessarily something of no importance; it was omitted because the dominant ideology had excluded it, or, to put it another way, it was excluded by a special interpretation of history. Yet a new interpretation of history at a different juncture of time might permit these omitted elements to resurface as dominant categories.

As we can see now, while documentation of the sum total of concrete history is impossible (leaving aside the fact that mere quantification of historical data rarely can pass for history in a qualitative sense of the term), awareness of totality is indispensable if we are to claim any kind of significance at all for the details we select as the most important moments in the total historical stretch and flow. Awareness of totality, coupled with a sense of one's view as provisional, will guard against the arrogance of taking the partial for the whole, of claiming completeness when only isolated phenomena have been dealt with. There is also this to be understood: We know all literary studies must be placed within historical time, but discussion of all related phenomena (social, economic, etc.) need not remain within that constraint, and, in fact, true understanding of the compositional reality of literary history must always move beyond a particular time, for all the phenomena that have come to us are results of growth from the past and contain seeds for their growth in the future. This is how tradition must be seen. The emergence or actualization of a traditional aspect in the midst of a new web of socioeconomic changes involves, necessarily, a study of its transformation — from its source strength as it had operated in the past to its current manifestation as it operates in the present. From a practical point of view, all literary studies must start with only a few sequences (as opposed to *all* sequences), since our minds can register just so much at one time. But the selected sequences must reflect the fact that they are selected *only after* they have been related in our awareness (not always in a fully articulated manner) to all the phenomena available to us, including those inside and outside the particular historical period.

When we turn our attention to the studies of modern Chinese literature — works produced since the May 4th Movement — it is doubly important for us to possess, at all times, this sense of historical totality as understood above. The period since the May 4th Movement is one in which the conflict and negotiation between the Chinese and Western cultural models has been most intriguingly complex and in which the confrontation between them has deeply disturbed the native sensibility and its sense of order and value. In order to maintain their own *raison d'être*, the native intellectuals, playing the role of the oppressed, struggled and continue to struggle either to seek parallels in the imported models or to militantly assert the primacy of their indigenous mental horizon. Indeed, the confrontation of the two cultural models is a process of the interpenetration of past, present, native, and alien cultures, each of which has varying degrees of attraction or repulsiveness in the eyes of the Chinese people of today. Clearly, this complex process of becoming demands that we perceive each moment against the simultaneous sequences of historical events that have occasioned the dynamic and drastic changes in the midst of a somewhat blurred but stubbornly powerful native resistance.

Specifically, the search for a new cultural rationale, characterized by a radical rejection of the political-ethical-aesthetic order of the past and a large-scale transplantation of Euro-American ideologies and literary theories, was originally an attempt to free the Chinese people from domination both by the imperialistic foreign powers and by despotic native traditions and institutions. The scenario of this search consists of the following:[3] First, there appear highly emotional iconoclastic attacks on the Confucian autocratic monarchy, on the uncreative economy run by the gentry class (which had totally alienated the poverty-stricken peasantry), on feudal familial and societal customs and forms as well as on the classical language, literature, and thoughts that had once brought the Middle Kingdom supreme glory — all this in hopes of reestablishing China through institutional and social reforms (K'ang Yu-wei, Sun Yat-sen, Hu Shih, Ch'en Tu-hsiu, et al.) and in the name of a "renovation of the Chinese people" (Liang Ch'i-ch'ao, Hu Shih, Ch'en Tu-hsiu, Lu Hsün, Mao Tse-tung, et al.). Second, early attempts are made to provide surrogates for the deposed culture by promoting Western knowledge (practical, technological, and military) and scientific studies and, later, simultaneous transplantation (often indiscriminately) of liberalism, utilitarianism, pragmatism, individualism, Darwinism, Ibsenism (emancipation of women, in particular), socialism, Marxism, neoclassicism, romanticism, symbolism, aestheticism, naturalism, realism, futurism, expressionism, dadaism, revolutionary literature, proletarian literature, and so on. Third, the conflicts and debates rage over the questions of "Chinese spirit" and "Western substance"; the relationship of self to society and later to the party; and the significance of the scientific method; the doctrines of socialism, proletarian art, national form, and the suitability of socialist realism over critical realism. Fourth, running through these drastic changes were inbred violent events: the rapid destruction and unprecedented humiliation of the once inviolable China (unequal treaties, loss of territorial, economic, jurisdictional, and other rights) brought on by the gunboats of the Western aggressors, causing the Chinese to lose their national confidence, which seemed (and still seems to many now) to be irrecoverable; the ineffectual national resistance to the Western powers (from the Opium War to the Boxer Uprising) resulting in bloodbaths and national disgrace, pushing China to the brink of demise; a series of self-awakening revolutions (political, cultural, and literary) uniting the intelligentsia (urban intellectuals), students, and workers in street demonstrations and strikes (May 4, May 30) that successfully reversed the tides of foreign domination; and the revolutionary spirit born in these demonstrations, a spirit that finally helped the Chinese people carry through the fight against warlordism and against the Japanese invasion from the 1920s to the 1940s. Finally, in the midst of all these interpenetrating historical events and changes in consciousness, modern Chinese intellectuals have been caught in a love–hate relationship with both traditional and Western cultural modes.

Brief and oversimplified as it is, this scenario clearly shows that no single phenomenon from this complex process should be studied in isolation. The inseparability of historical consciousness and cultural-aesthetic forms necessarily calls for the study of a given phenomenon by comparing it with the total historical environment from which it emerges and within which it interacts with other constituents in some sort of tensional relationship.

Presently I will examine aspects of this morphological process, but first a few words about the difficulties created by contemporary Chinese politics. The internecine war between the Nationalist and the Communist parties led to all kinds of wilful disinformation. For example, until very recently, for almost thirty-five years, there was no flow of books between mainland China and Taiwan. But for the intelligence agencies in these two areas, almost all the books published on one side were not available to the other. Worst of all, many key literary works and documents produced between 1919 and 1949 were either banned and destroyed on ideological grounds, as in mainland China, especially during the Cultural Revolution, or simply locked up, as in Taiwan. Ironically, only in the British Colony of Hong Kong was the situation slightly better, at least for those scholars deeply committed to reconstructing an effective historical sense of modern Chinese literature, for books published in both places after 1949 *could* sometimes be found there. But works produced between 1919 and 1949 were still scarce. This distress was partially relieved by the reprinting enterprise undertaken sporadically in the 1960s and 1970s by a few small bookstores. Again due to the self-imposed walls created by both the Nationalists and the Communists, these reprints rarely traveled between mainland China and Taiwan.

Stopping the flow of Chinese books and journals from the mainland, including those produced in Hong Kong, into Taiwan on the pretext of possible ideological infiltration was further complicated by the Nationalists' cultural program. The authorities there, wary until very recently of the iconoclastic spirit of the May 4th heritage, downplayed the significance of the New Culture Movement and remained indifferent to the new literature. Their decision had the following consequences.[4] There was no department of modern Chinese literature in universities and no library holding of documents of this phase. In fact, books of the 1930s and 1940s were not seen anywhere except in a few guarded, locked-up libraries; even materials from the 1920s were scarce, and those available to the public had been carefully filtered. This is also true in the case of anthologies.[5] The various literary and ideological debates since 1919 were hardly known to college students, let alone the public, and the requests made by some intellectuals to the authorities to lift the ban on the works of the 1930s (condemned as being leftist) were repeatedly rejected. This resultant lack of effective historical consciousness has its sequelae. Thus, since the long overdue thaw came in 1987,[6] when for a few years pre-1949 books were reprinted (but by no means systematically) and books by current mainland Chinese writers were allowed into Taiwan, the responses have been anachronistically off-balance and off-mark. These works have been judged not within their proper historical contexts but according to local hermeneutical habits developed within a specific historicity cut off from the larger fabric of modern Chinese literature. It will take many years before a fuller, more effective, and more comprehensive historical consciousness can be reconstructed in Taiwan.

Sequelae of a different sort, but equally distortive, occur in mainland China. Mao Tse-tung's straitjacket literary program, as spelled out in his famous 1942 Yenan Talks and his two earlier essays "The May 4th Movement" (1939) and "The Culture of New Democracy" (1940),[7] continues to possess writers and critics alike long after his demise.

Let us first look at Mao's streamlining of the writing of modern Chinese literary histories. Besides stipulating that all writers should write from the standpoint of workers, peasants, and party cadres and abandon all residual individualism and subjectivity of the urban petit bourgeoisie, he further insisted that the May 4th Movement is a "proletarian-led, anti-imperialist and anti-feudal culture of the broad masses." These dictates predisposed the narratives of almost all the literary historians after him. The official literary history by Ting I, for example, adhered most loyally to this argument. Ting found no room for the urban intellectuals such as Hu Shih and his friends, the entire Crescent Society and many theorists who contributed to the fermentation of the New Culture Movement, for they were, according to Mao, "traitor" writers. To institute Mao's directives, an orthodox format was worked out in 1951 by a committee consisting of Lao She, Ts'ai I, Wang Yao, and Li Ho-lin in a small book entitled *Summaries for a History of Modern Chinese Literature for Teachers*.[8] But when Wang Yao, one of the drafters of this program, tried in 1953 to make room in his big book, *Chung-kuo Hsin-wen-hsueh shih-kao* (Drafts for a History of Modern Chinese Literature), for Hu Shih, Hsü Chih-mo, and others, attempting, no doubt, to reach out for some form of historical totality, he was severely scathed. The charges included these: that he departed from Mao's directives and assigned a leading role to such urban petit bourgeoisie as Hu Shih and Ts'ai Yuan-pei and gave undue praises to Hsü Chih-mo and Lin Yu-tang without understanding that literature is a product of class struggle rather than of individual talents, failing, therefore, to portray the final defeat of the bourgeoisie by the proletariat; that he, by implication, did not subscribe to the view that literature exists to serve political struggle and that, by stating that "formulaism in art comes from formulaism in life," he dared to criticize "party-mindedness" as well as question the foundation of Marxism-Leninism as being abstract and dogmatic; and that he condoned the subjectivism of Hu Feng and his gang.[9]

These views reflect the general tenor of most of the Chinese Communist critical studies; and Mao's insistence upon the proletariat as the true makers of literary history has colored the approaches of many Western literary historians, such as Huang Sung-k'ang and J. Prusek, in spite of their claims to scientific objectivity. Mao's strictures have also affected poetry anthologies. A good example is Tsang K'o-chia's *Chung-kuo Hsin-shih-hsuan 1919–1949* (New Poetry in China, 1919–1949 [i.e., poems written before the creation of the Peoples' Republic of China], 1956), in which the omissions are, as expected, almost all the Crescent poets. Wen I-to, who had the strongest influence on Tsang, has only one minor poem included. Indeed, the works of many of the poets writing in the period 1930–1950, works that represent the best tensional dialogues emerging from the confrontation between native sensibility and intruding alien ideologies, had been buried by this trend. Only a few insignificant poems by the poets of the 1930s were included in the literary histories and critical notices written after 1949, and almost none of the creative and critical efforts by the poets of the 1940s were given a chance to voice themselves. The commitment of these poets to the making of individual styles and to the refinement of language as an art made it impossible for historians and critics in Communist China to mention their names without being severely criticized by the party.

In the realm of critical studies, Wang Hsi-yen's study of Lu Hsün, *Lun Ah Q ho t'a-ti pei-chü* (On Ah Q and His Tragedy, 1957), is quite typical. Wang must seek answers to three sets of questions to justify seeing Lu Hsün in Marxist-Leninist terms, although Lu Hsün's early stories were written before he leaned toward communism. The questions were (1) In Lu Hsün's stories of the May 4th period, are there elements of socialist realism? If there are, in what are these to be found? (2) From his collections from *Outcry* to *Hesitation*, is there any advancement in thought and in art? What is it? (3) Is there any national character in his polemic essays? What is the source of this national character? Wang finds in Lu Hsün a fighter who attacks the man-eating feudal systems. Although he also recognizes the early Lu Hsün as evolutionist, individualistic, lacking in party-mindedness, and without a scientific Marxist view, yet he must consider these early works as containing the necessary "seeds" of communist ideas.

With the second set of questions, Wang thinks Lu Hsün has begun to advance from identification with his petit bourgeois class to solidarity with the mass movement of workers and peasants, but the stories show that this is not true. To the third set of questions, Wang answers that Lu Hsün's essays are rooted in the Chinese soil.[10] Thus, we find that the complexity of Lu Hsün, a soul-searching individualist caught between public commitment (to progress, to science) and private vision (the search for meaning in a crisis of identity) and between his advocacy of the new and his deep-rooted love for the classical world, has been reduced to a mere ideological code. The Chinese Communist critics bypassed all the possibilities of dialectical complexity in the Marxist aesthetic and submitted themselves to a reductionist, conformist, and formulist approach, which is diametrically opposed to the historical consciousness of totality so central to Marxist criticism in the hands of its most enlightened practitioners.

This master narrative dominated and continued to dominate mainland Chinese critical opinion. For over thirty-five years, writers and readers alike have been directed and redirected by a party-guarded parent consciousness to a single mode of apprehending reality and a single mode of expression. This mode asks the writers to represent reality, in particular the external manifestations of the lives of workers, peasants, and soldiers, *not as it actually is* but as it ought to be, that is, according to the party's vision of a yet-to-be-realized socialist state, in which no form of darkness, fear, hesitation, and agony are supposed to exist. Consequently, there was only a monotone "singing" and a monotone of "critical voices." Indeed, even now, except for the enlightened few, many writers and critics have internalized this mode without seriously questioning it. This can be seen on many levels. But for our purpose here, let us look at three instances.

Many years into the post-Mao era, critics are still using the same rhetorical strategies. Typically, they would begin an essay by quoting Mao, aided perhaps by Marx, often out of context or half-understood, and would drone on for several pages, rehearsing many familiar party-ordained positions, before they would discuss some "real" issues. It is possible to distinguish two types of critics. The first type would attempt to assimilate new ideas into the orthodox Maoist-Marxist positions. ("Critic so-and-so's theory is not bad, but it should be substantiated by this or that aspect of Mao and Marx.") The second type is more shrewd. This type of critic either expands the Maoist-Marxist framework to such an extent that it can comprehend many hitherto tabooed critical perspectives or infiltrates Maoist-Marxist terms with new ideas and in doing so subtly redirects the readers away from the fetters of the vulgar Marxism of the Chinese Communist party writers. The tension created in reappropriating political and ideological clichés for new strengths is a subject beyond the scope of this chapter and must be reserved for another occasion.

When, in the wake of the fall of the Gang of Four, novelists (in what is now known as the "Literature of the Wounded") and poets (in what is now known as the "Misty [Obscure] Poetry") attempted to awaken the memories of the suppressed and indeed despised populace, including those of some of the darkest moments of their minds, of their living conditions, and of the retrieval of the critical spirit as well as of self-awareness of the May 4th heritage, they encountered a huge barrage of criticism. Although these novels and poems survived and, together with the reissuance of the more art-oriented poets of the 1940s, have successfully retrieved for the public a larger arena for imaginative exploration, they have not been condoned by the party whose power of censorship is still at work, as can be witnessed by a series of controls instituted after the T'ien-an-men tragedy in 1989.

Some time after the fall of the Gang of Four, a few centers were established in designated provinces to study the literature of Taiwan and Hong Kong. In many of the studies and anthologies, especially the earlier ones, the same internalized censorship is operating. Critics unconsciously tried to frame the works from these two places in formulas prevalent in China. Consistently, they sought out those works that are closer to "the literature of peasants, workers and soldiers" and, following the vulgar Marxists' mechanical explanation of base and superstructure, dismissed all modernist attempts as decadent, formalistic, and typical of capitalist societies, without coming to grips with the historical specificity of Taiwan—a historical situation that has led to these kinds of works, not as replicas of Western modernist models but as a counterdiscourse to the then repressive atmosphere of the Nationalists.

We must admit, however, that the Chinese Communist or pro-Communist critics are historical, though perhaps biased and eclectic. It is their refusal to see their interpretation of history as provisional that has blurred their vision of totality. By the same token, those who claim to be ahistorical often turn out to be antihistorical also. Here, let us turn to the famous argument between Prusek and C. T. Hsia.[11] On the surface, it is a debate between a leftist and a rightist, but a closer examination would reveal that it is a debate between historical and ahistorical approaches, although the historical stance repre- sented by Prusek has pitfalls similar to those of the Chinese Commu- nist line, as C. T. Hsia rightly pointed out. From Prusek's charges and C. T. Hsia's own confession, we can have some idea of the latter's ahistorical position:

> There are certain tasks properly belonging to the literary historian which I could have undertaken were I not mainly concerned with what seems to me the basic task—a critical examination of the major and the representative writers of the period. . . . Thus, I have not systematically studied the relations between modern experiments in fiction and the native tradition. Thus, though I have ventured many remarks concerning the impact of Western literature upon modern Chinese fiction, I have made no systematic study of that impact. I have indeed cited many Western works in a comparative fashion, but primarily as an aid to define more precisely a work under examination and not as an attempt to establish lineage and influence. . . . I also have not attempted a broad comparative study of the normative technique employed by Chinese writers of fiction, though such studies . . . can be of definite value in assisting the task of evaluation. . . . [My] primary task is . . . discrimination and evaluation.[12]

Rejecting the thesis that the meaning or form of a literary work has its grounding in a historical base, Hsia proceeds to examine liter- ary works as if, once created, they possessed some sort of autonomous status free from historical time. Like the New Critics who influenced him, he begins with a set of aesthetic assumptions that are supposed to be unquestionably universal: What is true of the great works in the West must also be true of the native products of China. We find him conjuring up the names of James Joyce, Hemingway, Matthew Arnold, Horace, Ben Jonson, and Aldous Huxley as suitable for com- parison with Lu Hsün without examining, in each case, the historical condition from which certain characteristics of style, form, genre, and aesthetic assumptions emerged, without considering whether and in what exact manner they can be so compared.[13] Throughout his book, Hsia cites other names from Western literature as suitable compari- sons for Chinese authors: for Yeh Shao-chün (Dr. Johnson's *Rasselas* and Chekhov—59, 66); for Yü Ta-fu (Baudelaire and Joyce—108-9); for Lao She (Joyce and Fielding—173, 180); for Shen Tsung-wen (Yeats, Wordsworth, and Faulkner—190, 202, 203, 204); and for Eileen

Chang (Mansfield, Porter, Welty, McCullers, and Austen—389, 392). Here are some typical one-sentence comparisons: "The story [Lu Hsün's "K'ung I-ch'i"] has an economy and restraint characteristic of some of Hemingway's Nick Adams stories" (34); "the slow movement, the stylized language [of Yeh Shao-chün] and the pervasive cast of melancholy remind one . . . of Johnson's *Rasselas*" (59); "[In Lao She's *Two Mas*], the elder Ma is also something of a Leopold Bloom . . . his son is the counterpart of Stephan Dedalus" (173). Indeed, we are asked to read these Chinese writers, whose historical concerns and personal obsessions are obviously different from those of their Western counterparts, through the filtering lens of the entire Western tradition. Anybody familiar with the historical development of these Chinese writers will find that the convergence of aesthetic elements in Chinese and Western writers, when they occur in a given work, came about and exist in a much more complex way than given in these passing hints and remarks.

Behind Hsia's approach is another assumption, endorsed by many scholars of modern Chinese literature, namely that, since a certain given work has imitated a transplanted model, we can proceed to examine the native Chinese product from the cultural assumptions of the Western model as if what is true of the source model must also be true of its derivative product. The fact is that there has never been such a thing as total acceptance of an alien model, in spite of the enthusiastic rhetoric with which modern intellectuals spelled out their advocacy of complete Westernization. In the consciousnesses of these advocates there were always native elements that conditioned the process of transplantation. We must ask these questions: what were the historical and social changes that prompted the rejection of the traditional past and the acceptance of a certain alien ideology? In the course of the acceptance, what native ideological aesthetic models were resorted to (albeit unconsciously) for support or justification? What kind of modification was being made to localize an alien model so that native acceptance could be gained? What intellectual or aesthetic obsessions in the native world view, including theory of history and mental habits, conditioned the rejection of certain dimensions of an imported theory? We should also observe that the notion of a consistent literary model in Western literature is itself questionable; the so-called "Western model" employed by these poets and critics is itself a distortion of Western literature.

Take the example of Romanticism so feverishly embraced by Chinese writers of the 1920s and 1930s. These writers highlighted only the emotional side of Romanticism (often in the extreme form of sentimentalism) and hardly understood the activities of imagination so central to the Romantics. Overwhelmed by the imposing stature of science recently deified, they did not understand that it was in reacting against the rising threat of science itself—especially as conceived in the seventeenth century, when it was believed that everything, including the mind, operates passively, according to certain physical laws—that the Romantics affirmed the importance of Imagination as an organizing agent, through which they embarked upon an agonized metaphysical quest into the noumenal. This aspect of the epistemological quest so central in Coleridge, Wordsworth, Goethe, Novalis, and others was hardly understood by the early Chinese "Romantics." Thus, it is appropriate to ask a question of this sort: To what extent had the choice of emotional Romanticism over epistemological Romanticism been conditioned by a native brand of emotionalism, such as the emphasis upon the impulsive as found in certain neo-Taoists of the third and fourth centuries (the Recluses of the Bamboo Groves, etc.) and in the poetic celebration of this emphasis as in the work of Li Po? To what extent had the more central concern of seeing nature as it is, self-complete, promoted by the philosophical Taoists, induced the Chinese writers to refrain from participating in the self-made agony of the metaphysical search?

Similarly, the Chinese symbolists were more attuned to the interplay of color, light, and sound in the nuances of Verlaine's *Art poetique* than to the metaphysical complexities of Mallarmé. They knew very little about Mallarmé's "flower" that is not to be found in the plant world but arises musically from words divine, absolute, privileged, and self-referential, nor did they understand the sophistication of his reversed Platonic scheme. For example, one may ask: What kind of aesthetic parallel did Liang Tsung-tai abstract from Baudelaire's "Correspondances," inducing him to speak of Bashō's frog *haiku* and Lin P'u's couplet as prime examples of symbolist poetry, in spite of their obviously divergent philosophical and aesthetic assumptions?[14] One may continue to ask what native philosophical and aesthetic obsessions conditioned the Chinese Marxists to denounce the Hegelian system, so pivotal to Marxist philosophy, as merely idealistic?

The answers to these and many other questions require us to be simultaneously aware of the scope and operation of both cultural systems in the total scheme of things. The entire process of a cultural phenomenon's growth cannot be fully grasped by merely comparing and contrasting two works from two cultures in abstraction from their relationship to the historical moments in question. The morphology of many of the ideological and aesthetic positions in modern China must be grounded in the total fabric of the economic, historic, sociological, and cultural complex. The historical factors leading to the rise of Romanticism in Europe were very different from those that prompted its sudden rise in China. For example, the side-by-side transplantation of science and Romanticism in China must be considered as having many ambiguous ramifications. European classicism, which occurred centuries before Romanticism, and realism, which occurred after, as well as many other transplanted ideologies and theories—all had their specific socio-historical origins, each occupying different spatial and temporal extensions and many of them being clearly mutually antagonistic. It is intriguing that all these ideologies and literary movements appeared in their transplanted forms almost simultaneously (sometimes all merged in one writer)—in a matter of ten to twenty years. However, merely to point up the difference begs the question of how one can explain adequately this composite phenomenon (let us call it superstructure, to follow temporarily the Marxist argument) as a result of its economic base.

Thus, if we proceed only from the socio-cultural assumptions of Western models (Marxism being only one of them), what we get would be some abstract conceptions cut off from the total, historically determined complex of concrete reality. We must try to understand the "inner necessity" that led Chinese writers to accept (and accept simultaneously) all these ideologies. What kind of historical relevance did Chinese writers find in these ideologies? How much of this relevance was determined by historical events and how much by the subjective consciousness operating within the interweaving web of these events? I use the word "relevance" with no implication that the Chinese intellectuals had, at that historical juncture, any kind of root understanding of certain imported ideologies. They often did not. As a matter of fact, if they had understood fully the extreme form of egoistic individualism implied in Romanticism, if they had understood fully the racist and selfish attitude partially implied in Darwin's "natural selection" and "survival of the fittest" (Spencer's term later adopted by Darwin) and understood that these views are at the root in opposition to the Chinese emphasis upon the Taoist "equality of things" and upon the Confucian "Great Unity," they would have rejected them immediately.

Therefore, we must understand the complex way in which an

ideology enters into the historical consciousness of the Chinese. The part of the ideology accepted by the intellectuals might not even be the essential part. Rather, it is the part that happens to be relevant to the historical-sociological changes at that particular juncture of time. Thus, we have to further distinguish this part from the transplanted model's cultural aspects that are conducive to the consolidation of the Chinese tradition in the process of innovation. To do this, we must first have a full grasp of the essential Chinese quality of the traditional cultural and aesthetic horizon and its source strength as it operated in the past. We must then investigate the Western ideology in question, including its source strength in its own spatio-temporal environment, before we can distinguish the possibilities and impossibilities of its convergence with and cross-fertilization of the Chinese tradition. Only then can we tell what exactly has been iconoclastically rejected in the process, what remains unaltered, and how this unaltered part has helped to mediate those elements from the West to effect a synthesis that would consolidate and enrich, but not substantively change, the native intellectual horizon.

Here, I must hasten to say that not all the intellectuals were clear about the choice they made. For example, those in the early phase of the May 4th Movement indiscriminately embraced Western ideas. It was not exactly blind worship. It was originally born out of a need for revenge, a need to strike back with the same weapons the aggressors used against the Chinese. The threat of total destruction by the Western powers and the consequent national humiliation drove them to this action. The intellectuals felt, as never before, that China had reached the end. There was no time to think through both systems to carefully work out a politico-socio-cultural framework best suited to the indigenous temperament. Caught up in revolutionary zeal, what they saw was the potential of salvation that these Western ideologies, collectively, seemed to promise, as if all of them, at root, were Promethean and Faustean, capable of instantly saving and transforming a China in crisis. These interpretations dominated their process of appropriation. The minds of almost all the intellectuals were colored by such an explosive emotionalism that the May 4th Movement can hardly be called a Chinese Renaissance. As one Chinese historian aptly observed, the intellectuals did nothing to revive traditional Chinese culture or to establish knowledgeably the Western tradition. What they did was to reenact more than two hundred years of Western cultural changes in a matter of ten to twenty years.[15] Hence, rather than judging the intellectuals abstractly against either a Chinese or Western mode of thinking, we must understand their *perception* of culture and history and their *appropriation* of foreign culture as a function of their anxiety and of their attempt to come to grips with the chaos of their own times as they searched for some possibility of totality. Thus, their works should not be viewed from a strict aesthetic perspective, cut off from concrete history. They must be projected into the arena where life-process and art-process, being one and inseparable, became the final composition of true meaning.

Let us dwell here, for a moment, on the process of cultural *appropriation*, which holds a sort of pivotal position in all these changes. Cultural appropriation can be seen either in an individual act by an artist, as, for example, in Lu Hsün's use of Gogol in his "A Madman's Diary," or in a larger cultural whole, as, for example, the appropriation of democracy and science or what has been characterized as the spirit of Enlightenment in the Chinese cultural milieu. Like Eliot's eclectic vision of tradition discussed in the first part of this essay, each appropriation must be worked into some traditional scheme so as to take root. An instructive parallel can be found in the neo-Confucianists' appropriations from Taoism and Buddhism. In order to rival the metaphysical and transcendent dimensions of Buddhism, a popular and powerful religion, the early neo-Confucianists turned to the *I Ching* and came up with the idea of *T'ai Chi* (太極, the Great Ultimate) as the source of all physical phenomena. The *T'ai Chi*, often explained as *hsü* (虛, the Great Void), echoes the Buddhist *Sunyata* (空, *k'ung*, emptiness) and the Taoist *wu* (無, nothingness); it is infinite, unlimited, and absolute, but, unlike the Buddhist or Taoist terms, it is the basis of ethics. From this ultimate principle, two cosmological aspects can be distinguished: *li* (理, pattern, laws of the universe) and *ch'i* (氣, material force), which give rise to all phenomena. And this cosmic principle, which satisfied the intellectuals' hunger for a metaphysical understanding of the world, was anchored solidly within the Confucian framework.

Moving from appropriation to synthesis, neo-Confucianism not only overturned the dominant Buddhism but also emerged as a new, leading source of intellectual power for centuries to come. But the process of appropriation and synthesis in modern China has been more complicated and, as time has now shown, more difficult. The confrontation and negotiation between Chinese and Western cultural models has been going on for almost seven decades, and there still exists the impression of misfits and mismatches—of what the

Chinese call *sui-t'u pu-fu* (水土不服, climate and body do not agree). Part of the reason is that the confrontation has been more drastic than that between neo-Confucianism and Buddhism. There are at least three reasons for the success of neo-Confucianism. First, it was hardly shaken the way the traditional system was in the troubled years prior to the Republic. Second, it had not lost ground; it still occupied a pivotal position among the ruling hierarchy as well as among intellectuals who often were statesmen at the same time. Third, Buddhism was no longer an alien model. When Buddhism tried to conquer the Chinese intellectual world during the Han and post-Han Dynasties, it, too, appropriated concepts from Chinese philosophy, such as the Taoist *wu* to explain *k'ung*. In other words, it had already acclimatized itself to the Chinese mode of thinking. These factors helped to facilitate the process of synthesis in the early Sung Dynasty. The complex process of appropriation, negotiation, and synthesis in modern China, however, has taken place without the benefit of any earlier acclimatization, and this requires us to delve deeper into the historical moment to locate what has obstructed an authentic cross-fertilization that will consolidate and enrich the Chinese indigenous model. Before we attempt any tentative thesis on this still-evolving drama, however, let us look at a few cases of appropriation.

The so-called denunciation of tradition was often a surface gesture. The education of all these intellectuals, Hu Shih, Lu Hsün, Kuo Mo-jo, Hsü Chih-mo, Wen I-to, and others was in the Chinese classics. Therefore, when they expressed themselves in creative works or meditated on societal forms, the traditional aesthetic sense and cultural ideals submerged below their consciousness would still, like a ghost behind the arras, affect their choices. Take, for example, the early Kuo Mo-jo, whose poetry is often characterized by an explosive celebration of the self in a bombardment of apostrophes that proclaimed him an all-out iconoclast. And yet, as he endorsed Western concepts of freedom, unconsciously he would usher in the Taoist concept as the Chinese counterpart. When he celebrated revolution, he would resort to the myth of Kung-Kung as an unstated justification for his acceptance of the Western source of inspiration. Even more interesting is "Nirvana of the Phoenix," a poem on the rejuvenation of China from dead ashes. The poem is prefaced by both the Western and the Chinese myths of the phoenix; then there is a middle section, which is almost a direct paraphrase of Ch'ü Yüan's "T'ien Wen" (天問, "Questions Addressed to Heaven"), which, in turn, is an emergence song or song of the creation myth. Here, as in many similar examples in Hsü Chih-mo, Wen I-to, Lu Hsün, and others, there is an unconscious attempt to give the appropriation of a foreign cultural motif a traditional footing, so to speak, even though, as we will see, these links may be only contingently relevant. From our point of view, Chuang-tzu's "depending on nothing" (無 待), which has been constantly referred to as the prime example of absolute freedom, must be seen together with his emphasis on "equality of thing" (齊 物), which precludes the possibility of the dominating, self-centered individualism of the West. The same position, which sees humankind as only a component in the cooperative design of the total composition of things, a position also endorsed by the Confucians, in part aided the same intellectuals in the 1930s when they proclaimed the death of individualism. This went along, of course, with the inspiration of "Western" socialist ideals.

Is there a way to modernize China without substantively changing her intellectual horizon? To this question, I have no satisfactory answers. It is clear, however, that many of the assumptions in the transplanted models go against the Chinese grain. The close examination of this fact would move well beyond the scope of this essay. But let me offer at least one perspective in the hope that it will stimulate thought in this much-contested area of debate.

The May 4th Movement has been called by the Chinese critic Li Ch'ang-chih a Chinese Enlightenment characterized by a primacy of rational thinking, skepticism, the critical spirit, verifiable scientific truth, mathematical precision, and pragmatic instrumentalism.[16] These were indeed new dimensions to the Chinese intellectual horizon of the early twentieth century. They spurred intellectuals to back away from traditional dogmas and seek out new vistas. In this sense, we must consider them a real contribution to historical change. And yet, these same elements have now taken on the dimension of myths and have disturbed the native sensibility the most, creating a constant feeling of alienation and separation. What is most intriguing is the fact that these same elements, which have played a key role in the West (in spite of periods of resistance to them), have recently been put in question. One such view may be an important oblique footnote to the yet-to-be-articulated phenomenon in China. Max Horkheimer, in a series of books — *The Dialectic of Enlightenment* (with Theodor W. Adorno), *Eclipse of Reason*, and *Critique of Instrumental Reason* — takes Western rational humankind to task for manipulating, dominating, and consequently alienating the natural world, turning it into a mere object.[17] The process has not only alienated nature but made humankind into an object as well:

> The program of the Enlightenment was the disenchantment of the world. . . . What man wants to learn from nature is how to use it in order wholly to dominate it and other men. . . . For the Enlightenment, whatever does not conform to the rule of computation and utility is suspect. . . . Men pay for the increase of their power with alienation from that over which they exercise their power. Enlightenment behaves toward things as a dictator toward men. He knows them in so far as he can manipulate them. . . . Thinking objectifies itself to become an automatic, self-activating process; an impersonation of the machine that it produces itself so that ultimately the machine can replace it. . . . Mathematical procedure became, so to speak, the ritual of thinking. . . . It turns thought into a thing, an instrument. . . . World domination over nature turns against the thinking subject himself. . . . Subject and object are both rendered ineffectual.[18]

> The principle of domination has become the idol to which everything is sacrificed. The history of man's efforts to subjugate nature is also the history of man's subjugation by man. . . . As the principle of the self endeavoring to win in the fight against nature in general, against other people in particular, and against its own impulses, the ego is felt to be related to the functions of domination, command, and organization. Mathematics, crystal-clear, imperturbable, and self-sufficient, the classical instrument of formalized reason, best exemplifies the working of this austere agency. . . . The ego dominates nature.[19]

In the process of appropriation from the West, to what degree were the Chinese intellectuals aware of the consequences of this development, which clearly goes against the much-cherished Chinese position that sees human beings as cooperative partners of nature, not exploiters? Both the Taoist and Confucian philosophies urge humans to model themselves after nature. As human beings are members of the cooperative design of the total composition of things, they must also be cooperative members of a community, a community that emphasizes giving rather than taking and in which the tacit understanding is to forgo the primacy of the ego in order to complete a larger unity in society and with nature. In this united community human beings can function to their maximum without distorting the original potentials of others. In such a cooperative framework, to which most traditional Chinese intellectuals commit themselves, the principle of domination and manipulation is out of place. Is it the threat of the dehumanizing and denaturizing effects of the Western ideologies upon this Chinese temperament that has occasioned the almost ceaseless series of antagonistic literary debates from the May 4th Movement to the present? How has this clash between two cultural positions informed us about the debates between the iconoclasts and the traditionalists, between the Creationists and the Society of Literary Studies, between the Creation-Sun Societies and the Crescent poets over revolutionary literature as well as those various debates over the issues of nationalism, proletariat literature, popularization, national form, and so forth?

The answer to this is not simple. The attitudes behind the Chinese intellectuals' appropriation of Western ideas and their negotiation between models are at best ambivalent. We must remember that it was initially to combat foreign domination that they turned away from tradition, but they in actuality embraced a world view the implied practice of which would eventually bring them under another form of domination. Even more intriguing is the fact that it was not only foreign domination they were up against; they were also trying to free themselves from a native form of domination, namely, despotic autocratic rule that derived, paradoxically, from the same ideology that supposedly condemns such despotism. The ideal state of the Confucianists asks that each member of society fulfill his or her natural endowment by functioning according to a series of norms based upon a thorough understanding of the nature of things as they are (*tao, hsing, li*). Ideally, the ruler should obtain this natural measure by investigating the original states of things, making himself sincere at heart, rectifying his character accordingly, and thus regulating, always in step with the natural measure of things, his family and his state. But in the actual process of governing, the ruler would proclaim himself to be following the "mandate of Heaven" and would establish and centralize his absolute rule with the aid of a landlord-gentry class that would manipulate and exploit the peasant masses.

Thus, we find that the total fabric of the modern Chinese intellectuals' negotiation between native and alien cultural models is rife with ambivalence. Almost all the Chinese intellectuals vacillated between the promise of democratization and the threat of the commodification of humanity in the transplanted models, between the rejection and affirmation of the native ideology. Liang Ch'i-ch'ao is a case in point. Liang, whose "The Renovation of the People" of 1902 paved the way for the later intellectuals' acclamation of Western democracy and whose journal *Hsin-min t'ung-pao* (*A Miscellaneous Journal for New People*) has been considered the semantic source for many of the new democratic (*hsin-min-chu*) claims of later decades, was also one of the first to impugn Western culture. In his "Impressions of Europe," he abhors Europe's overreliance on science and material culture, a dependency that he believes would lead to the destruction of Chinese cultural traits. Indeed, he considers the scientific inventions of the West to be based upon greed, manipulation, and warfare.

Any study of this period must begin with a recognition of the complex ambivalence in the processes of appropriation and negotiation between Chinese and Western cultural models. To fully understand the interpenetration of the planes and surfaces of past and present and native and alien cultures that have been in a constant double state of attraction and repulsion, we must possess a clear awareness of historical totality, an awareness that will require us to step out of single, monocultural perspectives to witness the simultaneous sequences of dynamic growth and change of cultural traits in the torrential flow of concrete history.

Epilogue
The Framing of Critical Theories
in Cross-cultural Context

Interreflection

A true theorist should always be fully aware of the double edges of his proposal: At the moment he insists upon the centrality of his theoretical claims, he has already exposed his negativity. His theory, being only one among a thousand others formulated, can never claim to be absolute, authoritative and final. Eventually, it will be seen only as a working notion, a hypothesis even, based upon *one* orientation toward the total aesthetic sphere. For, what are we to understand from centuries and centuries of reformulations or redefinitions if they are not acts of shifting from one center of significance to another, if they are not attempts to replace certain dominant forms with those once regarded as marginal?

A little reflection would further disclose to us that our existential experiences in the phenomenal world and in our contact with other human beings are endless and protean. As such, they will forever defy any human attempt to encase them in definitive forms. They are often filtered through language with preconceived rubrics such as those that might be summed up in Althusser's two phrases "mechanistic causality" (a transitive, analytical effectivity) and "expressive causality" (which involves isolating and privileging one element among many in order to achieve the so-called sense of unity).[1] For these rubrics to be operative, certain inevitable procedures of selection, discrimination, and closure are preferred in which the so-called relevant are differentiated from the irrelevant; these are then connected according to some predetermined relationships into definable shapes, which, in turn, are promulgated as absolute or complete. But are they?

We need only a moment to realize that these orders, systems, or critical frameworks are nothing but partial truths or presences and that the extent of their meaning has to depend upon the simultaneous presence of other orders or systems excluded by historical accidents or wilful neglect. To put it bluntly, all theories are provisional because none can unhesitatingly claim to have authenticated existential experiences, which are ongoing and forever changing. All theories are culturally and historically restricted, and thus their universal applicability is never beyond doubt.

Immediately, these questions are apt to arise: Can there be a "common poetics" underlying all literatures? If yes, how are we to establish the common aesthetic grounds upon which we can proceed with a fair degree of certainty to discuss literatures from different cultural systems? These are, no doubt, central questions in comparative literature, in particular in East–West studies and comparative studies of written and oral literatures, but these should also be central questions for all proponents of critical theories, since critical theories are models by which writers and readers alike have been consciously and unconsciously directed or conditioned. To seek some grounds for constructing a workable common poetics, we must, therefore, first recognize the impossibility of arriving at such common grounds if we restrict ourselves to only one cultural model. As I have argued in chapter 1, we must avoid privileging a monocultural perspective. To take the aesthetic assumptions of one cultural model as universally valid and indiscriminately applicable to any other is to behave like the fish in the fable. When the fish heard the frog describe the man, the bird, and the car he had seen on land, the fish imagined them in the form of a fish having a hat and a stick, wings, or four wheels. For decades, either in literary or cultural studies, critics and scholars have too often imposed the cultural-aesthetic assumptions and values of one system upon the literature of another, without realizing that they have significantly changed and distorted the perceptual horizon of the other culture.

As we now look back upon the translations and comparative studies done between Eastern and Western literatures and between oral and written traditions, examples of gross distortions abound. I have pointed out in chapters 2 and 6 a whole array of unforgivable misfits and mismatches both in Western approaches to Chinese literature and in Chinese studies of Western literary and cultural problems.

The grossest of these misfits is found in many translations of Chinese poetry in which, as I have detailed in chapter 2, the paratactic and coextensive mode of presentation in the originals have been destroyed by being recast in unnecessarily discursive, analytical, and syntactical structures.

Similar distortions are found in the translation of Chinese novels. Take *The Dream of the Red Chamber*. All the earlier translations have omitted the myth portion and a few other incidents before we come to the so-called main story to fit in with the so-called logic of relevance. Almost all of them have decided to forgo the some 200 poems therein. In doing so, they have turned the largely lifelike non-matrixed novel into consciously matrixed and goal-directed presentation, paring off the so-called irrelevant incidents without knowing that a peony (i.e., the protagonist's story) needs green leaves (i.e., all the surrounding stories and incidents) to bring out its true-to-life total existence, without knowing that the exchanges in poems are not embellishments but essential markers of the speakers' actual life activities and their various personal and social temperaments. Only very recently do we find this novel vindicated by David Hawkes's full translation. There is also this for us to ponder: the tyranny of written poetics over oral compositions.

Non-Western cultures such as those of American Indians, Africans, and Oceanic peoples, a great number of which still retain their oral format and charm, have suffered no insignificant loss in the process of being recorded or translated into written form by early anthropologists and poets, all of whom came to them with preoccupations and preconceptions totally alien to the indigenous outlooks and aesthetic functions of the people they studied. The early anthropologists quite often ignored the total oral event and abstracted from it only a "message" to the exclusion of a whole spectrum of expressive strategies and priorities uniquely inherent in the oral act. These oral strategies, as disclosed in a homogeneous ritualistic event in which singing, clapping, miming, dancing, drumming, and "sounded" words (with an extended vocal horizon or incantatory dimensions) help to accentuate and complement one another, are not to be viewed as *mere* embellishments to some major messages in a closed system of written words; they are themselves primary form as well as substance, all aspects interpenetrated, indivisible, inseparable. The poets and literary scholars have often come to these events of recorded materials with creative concerns and theoretical models based on *written* poetics, and, as a result, they have not been able to view the sounding of the voice, the improvisational function, the nonclosure of text, and so on properly and have tended to see them as peripheral, marginal, and even irrelevant. As revealed in translations, a long two-day ritualistic event with choric arrangements and incantatory expletives has often been grossly reduced to a simple poem of only a few lines divested of all the repetitions; only a few so-called major motifs are retained, and these are then restrung according to a model of linear development typical of the mechanistic or expressive effectivity of Western poetics.[2]

Thus, to avoid this kind of unwarranted reductionism and distortion of native aesthetic horizons, or, to put it in more precise terms, to break the monocultural perpetuation of certain critical and theoretical hypotheses as being the sole authority on the subject of literature, we must philosophically question the bases of theories from different cultural systems, understand how and from where they evolved, and try to understand their potentialities and limitations as well as their ramifications in monocultural and cross-cultural contexts, before working out a series of methodological guidelines toward the possibility of constructing a common poetics.

This investigation, which must involve comparing and contrasting several different cultural models from their indigenous sources, attempts to achieve what might be called an interillumination or inter-recognition to replace the principle of dominance currently used by many cross-cultural comparatists and monocultural theorists. It will allow Western readers to be aware of the fact that there are millions of literary works in the world that *do not* proceed from the aesthetic assumptions of the Platonic-Aristotelian constructs. It will also allow Oriental readers to realize that outside the Confucian-Taoist-Buddhist frameworks, there are many *other* perceptual modes and judgmental perspectives equally sensible within their indigenous systems. The true meaning of the interflow of cultures is, and must be, a mutually expanding, mutually adjusting, and mutually containing activity, an effort to push the boundary of our understanding toward a wider circumference.

Am I suggesting, then, a different idea of totality? The answer cannot be a yes, a no, or an either-or. The word "totality" belongs to the rhetoric of power employed to perpetuate a certain type of expressive priority, a certain type of ideological center that excludes other types of activity. For me, totality is an impossible concept. As I have argued in chapter 6, we stop certain things in the flow of concrete history and lift them out of their forever changing environments for scrutiny and analysis. Meanwhile, the flow goes on in its continuous, total-izing process, invalidating any claim of wholeness. Totality, which is often treated in terms of serial orders broken away from millions of disjointed, dispersed, untidy, ill-adjusted fields of actual experience (e.g., historical periods, literary movements, etc.), always comes to us prepackaged. As such, each of these claims invariably comes to us as a *version*, merely a version, incomplete and always partial, because only certain facts, believed to be significant, are chosen and high-lighted as if they could, indeed, represent the entirety of history and culture. This concept of totality is restrictive, not only in the sense that it does not comprehend all aspects of actual experience but also in the way in which it is packaged within one dominant ideology only.

My proposal to proceed simultaneously with two or three cultural models will immediately break this myth, revealing and confirming the simple fact, stated earlier, that all forms of "presences" and all the "models" we are working with are, in the final analysis, provisional, inconclusive, and open for revision. It is only in this sense of seeing all such formulations as provisional that we can keep in constant touch with the forever changing totality, for totality is a circle with-out circumference. It is also through this open consciousness that we can understand better the recent efforts to unseat the deep-rooted circling and centering activities of the West. The challenge comes from both the creative and the theoretical camps. This is no place to enumerate all the creative efforts that have been made over the last century. The list is very long. For my purpose, two passages will be adequate. First, Jean Dubuffet:

> If there is a tree in the country, I don't bring it into my labora-tory to look at it under my microscope. Because the wind which blows through its leaves is necessary for the knowledge of the tree . . . also the birds . . . in the branches . . . the song of these birds. My turn of mind is to join with the tree always more things surrounding the tree, and further, always more of the things which surround the things which surround the tree.[3]

Like many of his contemporaries, Dubuffet challenges the centrality of reason, logic, and analysis in the deliverance of experience. He advocates nonintervention so as to allow elements to imprint their traces immediately upon us in their preinterpretation modes.[4] This attitude comes directly from the distrust of the circling and centering activities of the West; hence his attempt to diffuse the center by not defining the circumference.

In a similar manner, the postmodernist American poet Robert Duncan, in calling for a "Symposium of the Whole" to reinclude those orders excluded by a dominant ideology, also appeals to the metaphor of center by not defining the circumference. He says in his "Rites of Participation" that Western society has lost

> the ambience in which all things of our world speak to us and in which we in turn answer, the secret allegiances of the world of play. . . . It was not only the Poet, but Mother and Father also that Plato would exclude from his Republic. In the extreme of the rationalist presumption, the nursery is not the nursery of an eternal child, but a grownup, a rational man. Common sense and good sense exist in an armed citadel surrounded by the threatening countryside of fantasy, childishness, madness, irrationality, irresponsibility, — an exiled and despised humanity. In that city where Reason has preserved itself by retreating from the totality of self, infants must play not with things of imagination, nor entertain the lies of the poets, but play house, government, business, philosophy or war.[5]

Duncan calls for a reactivation of those aspects of aesthetic activities that are still prominent in those oral and other non-Western cultures that do not proceed with the same form of exclusion.

Not to reach out from a preordained center but to disperse it into several points; to travel along the circumference, the endlessly stretching circumference, occasionally glimpsing the not always certain center; and, together with this orientation, to resurrect the enigmatic and the *aporia*, which leaves the reader-viewer trembling, as it were, at the boundary of meanings — these have been some of the strategies attempted by such modernists and postmodernists as Pound, Williams, Borges, and Guillén, to name just a few. The so-called marginal or supplementary cultures or points of view are not just the *other*; the other is the indispensable partner of the proclaimed normative *this*.

In the realm of philosophical and critical explorations, the deconstructionists and poststructuralists, following Kierkegaard, Nietzsche, Heidegger, and Merleau-Ponty, attempt to overturn and displace existing centers and presences. The movement is well known and is still going strong in the Euro-American scene. While I am not necessarily championing their cause, this must be said: Deconstruction and poststructuralist thinking began precisely by philosophically questioning the bases of the models according to which circling processes were made. But the unburdening of traditional systems, like the birth throes of postmodernist poetry, has to take the form of "displacements" that, like a maze, are often twisting, tortuous, and extremely intertwining, and in the process of which traces in multifarious webbing overwhelm the attempt at erasures.

The investigation of the bases of our critical models, if it proceeds from comparison and contrast between two or three cultural systems in the way I have mentioned, will perhaps help us bypass this painful labyrinth. Take one issue among many as an illustration: the question of text. A text is never an enclosed entity with definable meanings, self-sufficient, self-present, but a constantly changing activity, infiltrated by a mirage of other texts and voices with infinite traces. But this polyphonic activity outside the text has always been emphasized in ancient Chinese poetics (as, for example, in Liu Hsieh's theory of secret echoes and complementary correspondences, developed from the ancient text of the *I Ching*)[6] and in oral poetics in which the text is often the springboard of a much larger aesthetic activity.

I must hasten to add here, however, that by saying this I have no intention of equating deconstruction and poststructuralism with everything Oriental and oral poetics have to offer, for the act of equivalence is also an act of power or dominance that must be avoided. At root, we will find many differences between them, in both Derridean senses, and these differences can only become illuminated by a comparative examination of the grounding of each of these systems. To juxtapose the Oriental or the oral with traditional Western aesthetic systems in an interilluminating, interdefining, interrecognizing manner will give us a larger circumference whereby we can view better the contributions and limitations of deconstructive and poststructuralist criticism.

Interreflection is indeed the key for resolving some of the major critical issues because it allows us to raise questions that monocultural theorists are not inclined to ask. Take, for example, the literary genre called tragedy. It is interesting to note that certain dominant features that have been used to define tragedy (e.g., the hero's courage in facing an overpowering challenge and the hubris that causes the hero's inevitable defeat) are found to be either absent or neglected in Chinese counterparts. We might want to ask: Do the

Chinese have the kind of tragedy prescribed by Aristotle? If not, why not? Could it be that the Chinese emphasis on humanity's well-tuned correspondence with nature and their view of undifferentiated time help to eschew the linear, antagonistic relationship with reality that underlines the making of the tragic hero of the West? Is heroism possible in China, or rather, what is the Chinese concept of heroism?[7] How do the facts that traditional China did not have epics and that drama as a significant literary form did not emerge in China until the thirteenth century, after many centuries of brilliant flowering of the lyric, compare with the fact that, in the West, drama almost began as the primeval genre and that epic was the first dominant poetic form? While the ancient texts in China, such as the oracle bone inscriptions, reveal that ancient China, like the West and other cultures, had her share of ritualistic activities, we must then ask: What cultural or philosophical occurrences had taken place to have deterred rituals from developing into full-fledged dramas? What socio-cultural factors accounted for the absence of epics or long narratives that celebrated heroes' will to power? Lacking dramas and epics as genres for theoretical elaboration the way ancient Greek plays had furnished models for Aristotle's *Poetics*, ancient China had concentrated her theorizing on the lyric form. How much has this historical phenomenon conditioned the critical temperament of the Chinese, and what role did it play when, for example, they turned toward the genres of the novel and the drama? Or, to reverse the question, how has Aristotle's *Poetics*, which was founded heavily upon dramatic—mainly diachronic—structure, set certain straitjackets upon the conception of the lyric from which later theorists have been trying, not without difficulty, to liberate themselves?

Or consider the interrelatedness of language and perception, discussed in chapter 2. There I raised questions about how a language of rigid syntactical rules (such as Indo-European languages) could successfully approximate a mode of presentation whose success depends upon freedom from syntax and how an epistemological world view developed from Platonic and Aristotelian metaphysics—which emphasize the ego in search of knowledge of the nonego and attempt to classify being in concepts, propositions, and ordered structures—how such a world view could turn around to endorse a medium that belies the function and process of epistemological elaboration.[8]

The dialogue should not stop here. For example, we should continue to ask: What philosophical or cultural conditions led the ancient Greek thinkers to proceed the way they did? What *other*

orientations did the ancient Chinese provide both in terms of percep-
tion and in terms of expression? To investigate both simultaneously
with equal attention is what we must do. But the full investigation of
the trajectories of both cannot be undertaken here.[9] Here I will focus
on one key point in the question of perceptual priorities.

We open our eyes; we see things, or things offer themselves to our
eyes, transparent, concrete, real, complete in themselves. They do not
need our explanations to be what they are. And yet, these questions
have been constantly asked: Who are we (i.e., the perceiver)? What is
seeing (the perceiving act)? What are things (the perceived)? When
these questions were asked, they implied that the inquirers (the
sophisticated men) did not trust their primary intuitions of (their
natural responses to) things as they are. The asking, in fact, raised
this question: Under what conditions does reliable knowledge occur?
From Plato to Kant to many post-Hegelian thinkers, all kinds of
answers have been advanced through a series of reinspections,
redefinitions, and reformulations of the originally transparent
notions, and in doing so these philosophers or critics have each
created new verbal substitutes for the concrete objects. This process,
in turn, has affirmed the centrality of (1) the perceiver as the agent of
order, the knower of truth; (2) reason and logic as the reliable tools;
(3) *a priori* synthesizing principles (Platonic intelligence; Kantian
transcendental ego) possessed by the subject; (4) serial order and
dialectical movement toward a higher absolute; and (5) abstract
system over concrete existence.

The ancient Chinese, in particular the Taoists, accepted the natural
perception of things as they are but questioned instead the act of
questioning itself as well as the subsequent acts of naming, classifi-
cation, and categorization; they also rejected the premises that
language (as intellectual conceptions and linguistic formulations) can
adequately represent reality and that humankind is the primary para-
digm of orders. The questioning, then, leads to the Taoist proposal to
retrieve the prepredicative moment of the given by using "words that
are not words," by leaving them in an "engaging-disengaging" rela-
tionship with the reader, and by having the poet retreat immediately
after presenting the vibrating objects so as to let the reader directly
witness the workings of these objects and participate in completing
the aesthetic moment.

These philosophical and aesthetic positions resulted from different
steps taken toward the same ground. Once we recognize this fact, it
will be possible for the West to endorse the position of the other, as

Heidegger and others have done. I am not suggesting that phenome-
nology parallels Taoism in every aspect, but this interreflection makes
it possible for us to identify at least one important line of conver-
gence, namely, their questioning of previous acts of questioning the
givenness of things in the original, real-life world.

In this way, interreflection promotes an open dialogue between
and among cultures. In this way, different critical and aesthetic posi-
tions will have a chance to look at each other frankly, to recognize
among themselves potential areas of convergence and divergence as
well as their possibilities and limitations as isolated theories and as
cooperative projects to extend each other. Thus, when we turn to the
numerous existing theoretical perspectives or orientations, such as
some of those outlined in Figure 4[10], a similar set of inquiries will
arise to force us to reexamine the historical morphology of each of
these positions and to mark afresh the ways in which the contours of
their applicability have been drawn. Whether they are pre/text the-
ories related to perceptual positions and activities that include modes
of apprehending reality, choices of "object/s" for artistic re/presenta-
tion (real objects, fictive objects, language as "world," subjectivity as
objectivity, etc.), or an author's psychological archive and horizons of
imaginative activities; whether they are theories related to the
actualization of the text (the question of art versus nature; modes of
selection from experience; genre theories; technical considerations;
language strategies, etc.); whether they are theories related to the
contact and contract with the text (theories of communication: func-
tion, effect, social and linguistic contract, rhetoric, hermeneutics,
reader's perception); or whether they are theories of seeing the liter-
ary work as an autonomous system or seeing language as a complete
communicative machine with an elaborate system of signs—under
the interreflective scheme, we must conduct bilateral or multilateral
investigations into the triple complex of language, history, and cul-
ture (the center portion in the chart) of two or three systems. It is with
this complex that an author begins his or her perceptual-expressive
activities; it is through this complex that a literary work achieves its
existence; and it is upon this complex that readers construct, recon-
struct, or deconstruct their understanding of the literary work. As we
look back on the development of literary histories of different cultural
systems, we find many discrepancies between the given and the
perceived, between the perceived and the expressed, between the
expressed and the received. These discrepancies already occur fre-
quently within a monocultural system; this is due to the fact that the

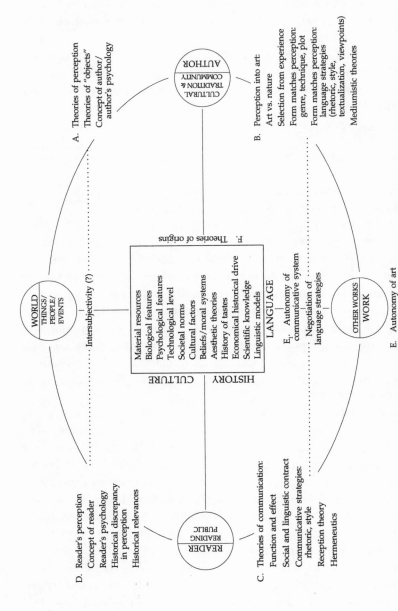

A. Theories of perception
   Theories of "objects"
   Concept of author/
   author's psychology

B. Perception into art:
   Art vs. nature
   Selection from experience
   Form matches perception:
   genre, technique, plot
   Form matches perception:
   language strategies
   (rhetoric, style,
   textualization, viewpoints)
   Mediumistic theories

WORLD
THINGS/
PEOPLE/
EVENTS

AUTHOR
CULTURAL
TRADITION &
COMMUNITY

Intersubjectivity (?)

F. Theories of origins

Material resources
Biological features
Psychological features
Technological level
Societal norms
Cultural factors
Beliefs/moral systems
Aesthetic theories
History of tastes
Economical historical drive
Scientific knowledge
Linguistic models

CULTURE   HISTORY

LANGUAGE

E. Autonomy of
   communicative system
   Negotiation of
   language strategies

WORK
OTHER WORKS

D. Reader's perception
   Concept of reader
   Reader's psychology
   Historical discrepancy
   in perception
   Historical relevances

C. Theories of communication:
   Function and effect
   Social and linguistic contract
   Communicative strategies:
   rhetoric, style
   Reception theory
   Hermeneutics

READER
READING
PUBLIC

E. Autonomy of art

Figure 4.   Scheme for a multicultural discussion of critical theories. I am indebted to suggestions in M. H. Abrams's *The Mirror and the Lamp* and Arnold Berleant's *The Aesthetic Field* for some of the items in this scheme.

addresser and the addressees are both locked inside different hermeneutical domains rooted in specific socio-cultural milieus. They always miss each other's centers, so to speak. This kind of mutual crossing is infinitely greater between or among different cultures. Therefore, intercognition of the indigenous ways in which each of these historic-linguistic cultural complexes provides for different modes of perception, expression, and recognition should be promoted as the primary road to reconsidering the framing or deframing of critical theories.

A Possible "Narrative"

It is clear that the scope of this paper cannot accommodate a full exposition of all the theoretical orientations listed in the chart. What I can do is to focus on the various trajectories of the perceptual object and follow their critical implications in broad outline.[11] We can begin by asking this: How would a perceiver choose from all natural phenomena, the events and human beings to (re)present? What are some of the consequences of these choices? The choices will, no doubt, be as many and varied as the perceivers, but, for the sake of illustration, I will limit them to seven. The perceiver can focus aesthetic attention upon (1) natural phenomena as they are; (2) human beings in harmony with natural phenomena; (3) human beings at odds with natural phenomena; (4) humans in harmonious relationship with society (or other humans); (5) humans at odds with society; (6) the individual as a self-sufficient entity; and (7) language as an autonomous world.

In the first case—that is, viewing natural phenomena as they are, as concrete particulars, as self-generating, self-transforming, self-regulating, self-conditioning, and self-sufficient forms of being—the avoidance of intellectual interferences is immediately called for because natural phenomena, by definition, need no human supervision or explanation to be what they are. Each form of being has its own nature, its own place and rhythmic activity and has existed independently as it is outside conceptual and linguistic territorializations. The transparence of this simply given condition of things will necessarily put language and thinking into question. This we find in Taoist philosophy and aesthetics; this we also find in parts of Heidegger, Merleau-Ponty, William James, and A. N. Whitehead.[12] Several modern and postmodern poets (e.g., William Carlos Williams, Gary Snyder) have approached this orientation *when* they attempt to resurrect the immanence of things as the grounding for truth.[13]

Understanding that language is always dangerous in the sense that its use (under the pretexts of naming, defining, and clarifying) always comes with a certain form of eclipsing that which is given to us, both the Taoists and Western philosophers and poets concerned with this perceptual priority are forced to give language only a provisional function (Lao-tzu: "I willy-nilly call it Tao"; Chuang-tzu: "Get the fish and forget the fish-trap; get the sense-of-things and forget the words"; Ch'an Buddhist advice: "To sweep away [words] immediately after [they are] spoken"; Heidegger: "destruction"; Derrida, with a twist: "erasure"[14]) and attempt to find ways to diffuse language's normal functions. Likewise, poets who want to return to "a natural measure" with things in their prepredicative condition, consciously or unconsciously, have to adjust their syntactical structures, creating empty spaces as revolving entrances into the indeterminate, multiple relationships implicit in the prepredicative condition of things as things.[15]

We must not consider this moment of convergence of two cultures a simple form of identity. The overlapping segment of two circles of culture is only part of the story; we must investigate the historical trajectories that have led each culture to this awareness. When Plato and Aristotle were privileging an artificially created eternal outline to centralize and rationalize everything, at the expense of the so-called irrational elements in the mind, and proposed verbal surrogates to replace the so-called illusory appearances, Lao-tzu and Chuang-tzu proclaimed the inadequacy of humans and their language, exposing the tyrannical nature of humankind's conceptual and linguistic formulations. In the West, it was in reaction against centuries of heavy doses of Platonic-Aristotelian discourses that Heidegger and others proposed a rethinking of language and knowledge. The questions that need to be asked here are: Why had Plato and Aristotle taken such a turn? Why were the Taoists questioning thinking and language at such an early date? Were they reacting against a form of tyranny, similar to that of the West, in Chou or pre-Chou dynasties? If so, what was it and in what way or on what level can that form be claimed to parallel, if at all, discourses rooted in or prepared by Plato and Aristotle? Most scholars would agree, though, that whatever it was that had provoked Lao-tzu and Chuang-tzu to preach the priority of natural phenomena as well as the natural self, it was quite different from the cultural condition and form in which we find Plato and Aristotle. What are we to make of this fact? Later, we will have occasion to briefly suggest a way of looking at this curiously complex cultural interchange. For the time being, it is important to remember: Convergence points toward possible new syntheses, but both its trajectories and current relevances may be very different.

When the perceiver turns with wonderment toward the harmonious, cooperative design in the total compositional activities of natural phenomena, humankind is seen as a component in this grand design, and the perceiver's expressions attempt to reenact this relationship. These expressions range from a simple, apostrophic "Ah!" to a ritualistic reenactment of the phenomena at work, direct, dramatic, and concrete, in which music, dance, song, and gestures interpenetrate one another as one homogeneous form.

As we can see, much early oral poetry began as a fully integrated, performance-oriented activity in an attempt to emulate, as well as to participate in, the (w)holistic lifeworld as it unfolds itself. In this perceptual priority, human beings as the orderers of things have no place, nor has the soul cry of the individual; instead, the ego is diffused with the nonego. In this perceptual priority, goal-directed historical time is submerged into, or subsumed by, mythic time, or "dream-time."[16] In a sense, this position has also privileged the mythic origin as the final blueprint of all our present actions, making it a utopian schema against which all presumably deviant courses and discourses can be measured.

Many philosophers and poets have been obsessed with this mythic origin and have attempted to pinpoint the so-called Great Break. The Taoists blamed it on the system of naming, as though to say that as soon as language was invented, Tao was destroyed. For the West, the most common themes have been, of course, the Fall of Eden and the Tower of Babel, after which the human race is doomed to be separated permanently from its original harmony.

Many other projects pointing toward a cultural coherence vaguely recalling that of the mythic origin have also been advanced by modern artists and philosophers: the intensive manifold of T. E. Hulme, the "radiant world where one thought cuts through another . . . a world of moving energies" of Ezra Pound, the Dantean world of unified sensibility of T. S. Eliot,[17] the pre-Socratic world of Heidegger, and many others.[18] None of these projects has produced working dynamics comparable to those we find in the performance poetics of the early oral traditions; after all, their ideal cultural moments — Renaissance, the medieval world, or even the pre-Socratics — are still far removed from the so-called mythic origin. And yet, the sense of the increasing threat of disintegration of an originally interweaving, interdependent, and interdefining manifold of things into countless separated, individualized, and mutually exclusive disciplines or self-referential orders has led postmodern poets and artists to search in oral traditions for a semblance of (w)holistic feeling. I am referring to the different sets of mock performance strategies advocated in post-Happening multimedia and multisensory art events and lifelike activities. These artistic activities attempt to evoke a sense of connectedness to a sacramental lifeworld suppressed by centuries and centuries of instrumental reductionism and rationalism.

Having said this, I must mention the fact that the assumed harmony between human beings and natural phenomena is at root mythic in nature, and thus all versions of this mythic harmony will remain rooted in the ideology and historical necessity of the period in which a certain project is proposed. Again, the case of convergences and divergences must be critically and dialectically differentiated.

When attention is turned toward the conflict between humankind and natural phenomena, such as when humans doubt and fear the catastrophic powers of nature, two obvious choices can be made. Human beings can mythologize these powers and turn them into objects of idolatry, which in turn would become power-wielding instruments for rulers. Fearing natural phenomena, humans can also attempt to control them and bring them into some manageable form of order according to their interests. Under this perceptual orientation, what humans want to learn from nature is how to use it to wholly dominate it, to make the various phenomena serve their purposes and values rather than seeing them in their self-so-ness. Distrusting the innate completeness and adequacy of things as things, and seeing them as illusory and without permanent values as such, humans first set themselves apart from them and then, with the rationalizing processes of naming, definition, classification, and clarification, they privilege one form of being as more paradigmatic (humans), one form of consciousness as more significant (reason, logic), and one locus as more correctly the seat of truth (the logos, the metaphysical abstract realm). This prioritization not only alienates humankind from nature but has also territorialized nature according to the subjective interests of humankind and thus has further alienated things in nature from themselves as things. Ignoring the richness of things in their multiplicity, humans sort them out according to their use and order them into various serial sequences before proclaiming these artificially demarcated orders as independent, complete, and even autonomous. As William James commented on this perceptual orientation, "[we ignore the real order] which we break . . . into histories . . . into arts . . . into sciences. . . . We make ten thousand separate serial orders of it, and on any one of these we react as though the others did not exist."[19]

I hardly need to point out here that this perceptual orientation is diametrically opposed to the first position in which the real world is taken as *real* and *concrete* in its indeterminate multiplicity, in which linguistic formulations are seen as provisional and humankind as only a component of the totalizing composition of things. By affirming an abstract system over concrete existence, by continually validating notions of truth as absolute truths (i.e., verbal surrogates in place of "appearances"), this perceptual priority often indulges in the territorializations of language activities and thus becomes removed from the "inalienable presence" of things as things.

A Ch'an Buddhist story may be illuminating here. "On one full moon night, an old man called the children to the courtyard and pointed his finger at the moon. Some children saw the moon and not the finger, but some children saw only the finger and not the moon." In an extreme form of this perceptual orientation under discussion, many theorists in the West have indulged themselves in the finger (verbal surrogates or signifiers) rather than in the moon (the signified, which has recently been pronounced either dead or never existing).[20]

Now, the perceiver can also focus on the relationships between human beings, in particular, upon the events involving the relationship between self and society. Two schemes parallel to the harmony and the conflict between human beings and natural phenomena emerge.

Like the search for mythic origin, the harmony sought in the relationship between human beings is also utopian in color. The kind of utopian society advocated may be either modeled after the cooperative design in nature or of human design. Either utopia demands the loss of self into a larger communal purpose very much the way the individualistic voice is replaced by the communal voice in early tribal poetry. There is also a preference for mythic time over historical time, although quite often this mythic time is placed in the future rather than in the past. Indeed, most social reforms and revolutions are made by appealing to a golden future that will presumably reinscribe all the features of the mythic golden past. The rhetoric used in such campaigns is, like the ecstatic poetry of celebration, apostrophic and prospective, being immersed in the belief that a utopia is realizable in the future. Like the various projects advanced to approximate the lost harmony discussed earlier, utopias prescribed both in literature and in revolutionary movements are, in the final analysis, also responses to specific historical conditions; they cannot be seen as identical to one another except that they always appeal to a feeling of the (w)holistic qualities of the mythic past. This is true of utopias both in the West and in the East. The so-called golden age is hardly a master model that can explain all the narratives for all the utopias. It is evoked only because of some imminent socio-historical crisis. Thus, the mythic past is nothing but inscriptions from contemporary social needs. Quite often, we would find a utopia reminiscent of the society the proponent sets out to abandon. (Robinson Crusoe's Island contains rules that are mostly England's.) Thus, all utopias must be studied, not by matching them with some master blueprint, but by grounding them within the dialectical tensions found in each respective historical moment.

If the utopia proposed in society is a refraction of the natural measure sought by human beings, the conflict between self and society emerges as a parallel to humankind's pose against nature. The principle of domination is now transferred to the human realm, where human beings are gauged, not according to the potentials of their natural selves, but according to use value, or, as in postindustrialized period, production potentials. In this way, certain aspects of humanity are territorialized as norms and paradigms at the expense of distorting the total self.

In delineating the conflicts between self and society, both the portrayal of characters and the depiction of events often follow the tension between the oppressing class (whose aggressive acts are directly evolved from the desire to protect and consolidate its special privileges) and the oppressed. But the tension is not a flat confrontation between two classes as such but comes out of something much deeper.

What is at stake eventually is how the natural or impulsive self is constantly being distorted by social institutions. As we can now see, the narrative centered on the conflict between self and society is not exactly free from utopian color, for to judge and criticize the destructive powers of social institutions, to mark out the stratifications of society as forms of tyranny over the self, one must first have some sense of an ideal relationship between self and society, some utopian vision, however vague it may be. When I say that the tension is not a flat confrontation between classes, I also mean this: We must avoid black and white depiction of fictional characters, depiction such as that proposed by the following statement: "If you tell me his material possessions, I can tell you his thoughts and actions." The truth often is that "the natural self" can surface from the oppressor just as "destructive powers" are found in the oppressed. The oppressor is not born an oppressor; his actions have been framed for him by a whole web of institutional codes. Likewise, the oppressed. The suppressed memories of an oppressor's own "natural self" may be awakened through a series of unusual events. To ignore this possibility is to submit oneself to the falsifying influence of types and formulas.

All the above perceptual orientations are directed outward, although events in nature or in society are often invested with the subjective interests of the perceiver. But we also find human beings turning their backs on nature and on society, embarking on an inward journey, seeking, searching, questing, and questioning. This often happens when people are driven into some form of existential extremity or crisis, such as when they are in exile, finding themselves cut off from a center of coherence, lost among shattered pieces, hesitating between the disintegrated past and the uncertain future. Solitary, anxious, and nostalgic, overwhelmed by a sense of futility and desperation, human beings turn inward to seek for a new *raison d'être* by attempting, through creativity, to come up with a new world (even if it were only aesthetic!) of coherence. An extreme case is found in the modern, industrialized era, when humanity, under the accelerated fragmentation and reification that has broken knowledge into numerous isolated self-referential "worlds," finds itself in double jeopardy: the existence of human beings' natural selves is in danger, as is the authenticity of their language. Writing now becomes an odyssey through the senses, the only mechanism, as it were, with which he can reclaim his *felt* existence or resurrect that which culture, now an industry aided by new myths of technocracy and commercialism, has completely shattered. Writing now becomes an odyssey through language with full attention on language as it is, because language, now stripped of all the holistic correspondences it once had, must reclaim itself, albeit in a tour-de-force manner, by freeing itself from its instrumental characteristics.

Perhaps it is time to question the "narratives" thus far presented and ask in what way they can operate as modes of discourses for intercultural reflection. More than once, as we journey through these highly abbreviated "narratives," we sense a clear polarization between the choices made by Eastern and Western poets and philosophers, although we also see convergences of sorts resonating across time and space.

Both East and West have been seeking a new master code or grand narrative, a new sense of unification, so to speak, to explain the incompatible and slippery diversity. (In this sense, both East and West have been driven—by different forces—into a profound cultural crisis.) But is such a master code or grand narrative possible? It is intriguing, for example, to find that in breaking away from Platonic and Aristotelian discourses, modern Anglo-American poets have promoted a syntactical structure resembling that of classical Chinese poetry. If expression and culture are inseparable, how is this possible? If the asyntactical structures found in classical Chinese poetry and in certain Anglo-American poetry represent projection into some common aesthetic ideal, what would be their shared cultural specifics? Suddenly, the convergence or commonality threatens to break down. But perhaps we are coming to this phenomenon with a "narrative" embedded in an already pre-determined set of expectations framed within a special kind of poetic economy.

I would like to propose a different or, rather, an alternative "narrative," within the language I have been using, without resorting to some externally imposed metalanguage. This possible "narrative" has no claim of becoming a master code. It will be like any "narrative," except that it attempts to open up spaces or gaps through which different cultures can move about to look at each other's similarities and dissimilarities. To do this, I will begin with a paraphrase of some "recent" voices about language.

Recently, critics argue that all verbal artifacts are forms of interpretations, which in turn become forms of rewriting. As such, they are grounded in specific cultural conditions and framed by specific ideologies as hidden structures of power. In other words, all discourses are power-wielding, and all aesthetic facts must, in the final round of negotiations, be realigned with their political underpinnings.[21] In regard to the linking of language to power, it might be profitable to unfold a "narrative" suggested by Lao-tzu's Taoist project.

Most of us are by now aware of the Taoist distrust of language—the gist of which can be briefly summarized as follows: No conceptions or linguistic formulations will be able to comprehend the totalizing process of the Great Composition of things in Phenomenon, which is changing and ongoing; all conscious efforts to name, to generalize, to classify, and to order this process will necessarily result in some form of restriction, reduction, and distortion. But the Taoist distrust goes deeper and can be traced to its clearly historically grounded response to the territorializations of power in the naming activities of the feudalistic Chou Dynasty. As Lao-tzu puts it: "With the beginning of Institution, there emerge Names."[22]

Since I have two long Chinese essays on this subject, I will present here only a broad outline of its implications.[23] A quick illustration of the territorialization of power in language use can be seen in the attempt to name the Chinese emperor the "Son of Heaven" and the medieval adoption in the West of the geocentric conception of the universe, by which Christianity laid the hermeneutical foundation of its hierarchical structures.

In the Chou Dynasty before the rise of Taoism, names or norms were invented to delineate hermeneutical structure and activity out of the need and desire to legitimitize and solidify a power structure by separating out determinable attributes such as privileges and duties. In order to facilitate feudalistic rule, the clan system was rationalized according to various class stratifications with well-defined duties and rights; hence the concept of the "Son of Heaven," various orders of dukes, relationships between lords and subjects, fathers and sons, husbands and wives, the investment of special privileges in first males, whose power over other males, not to mention females, came in complex forms and matrices as well as clearly demarcated sets of rituals and directives. The system of names or norms was invented as the cement that held the feudalistic power structure together. As a result, the birthrights of humans as natural beings were restricted and distorted. Lao-tzu began his project with full awareness of this restrictive and distortive activity of names and words and their power-wielding violence. It was this awareness that opened up the Taoist reconsiderations of language and power, both an aesthetic and a political project. By questioning the limits of language, the Taoists suggested a decreative–creative dialectic as part of an aesthetic project for repossessing the prepredicative concrete world by dispossessing the partial and reduced forms the process of abstract thinking has heaped upon us. A series of strategies was advanced, including asyntactical structures, the diffusion of distances, negative space as departure for retrieval of the undifferentiated, and the use of paradox and other off-norm words, phrases, or events.

But these aesthetic strategies have also political implications. When Lao-tzu said, "Tao, told, is not the Constant Tao. Name, named, is not the Constant Name" and proposed to return to the *Su P'u* (Uncarved Block) or the "Great Undivided Institution," he intended to implode the so-called kingly Tao, the heavenly Tao, as well as the naming system of the feudalistic ideology of the Chou Dynasty, so that memories of the repressed, exiled, and alienated natural self could be fully reawakened. The Taoist project, from the point of view of the naming system, is a negating, abandoning, and even escapist act; but from the point of view of "no naming" (that is, before the territorializations of power) and that of the Uncarved Block, it helps to break the myth of the reductive and distortive naming activities, affirm the concrete total world that is free from and unrestricted by concepts, and move toward reclaiming the natural self as well as Nature as it is. Thus, we can say that the Taoist project is a counterdiscourse to the territorialization of power, an act to disarm the tyranny of language; it is not, as most superficial readers believe, a passive philosophy.

At this point, a possible "narrative" seems to have emerged. The dialectical relationship between language and power, as understood in the above sense, is clearly working at the core of both Eastern and Western cultures. Perceptual priorities traced out earlier can be seen as being made by various philosophers and poets in direct proportion to the degree of their commitment or resistance to the ideology inscribed in the territorializing functions of language. The so-called closed and open systems, predicative and prepredicative views of the world, or noetic and noematic strategies can also be measured against this spectrum. It is interesting to find, for example, that at about the time Lao-tzu and Chuang-tzu were questioning names, Plato, through the mouth of Cratylus, affirmed the importance of names and the myth of the connectedness of words to things. While this affirmation did not lead immediately to feudalistic ideology, the dominatory, exclusionary, and repressive functions of language ordained by Plato and Aristotle, together with the latter's logically deducted model of the universe, had prepared for medieval Christianity's cosmology, leading to hierarchical structures of power, very much the way the Confucian System of Rectification of Names had prepared for Tung Chung-shu of the Han Dynasty (ca. 179–104 B.C.) to use the same functions of language to territorialize a whole cosmic system of correspondences that served, at root, to legitimitize existing power hierarchies.

It is clear that for East–West comparative studies, the concept of periodization must be radically revised, even abandoned, for periodization makes sense only within each respective cultural paradigm and cannot be used across all cultures. The responses to the dominatory and exclusionary functions of language occurred at very different junctures of history for the West and for the East. The major challenge to the territorializations of power in the West came with Copernican and Galilean discoveries (for which Galileo was put on trial precisely because his affirmation of Copernicus's heliocentric premises threatened to shatter the power hierarchy cemented by the hermeneutical justifications—the Great Chain of Being, etc.—of medieval cosmology). Thus, John Donne said, "All coherence gone . . . all relation: Prince, subject, father, son." It is intriguing to find that both cultures used almost identical modes of legitimatizing the hierarchies of power (the doctrine of the God-ordained ruler in medieval and Elizabethan ideology and that of the Son of Heaven in ancient China; the concept of the Great Chain of Being in hierarchical orders and body politics and Tung Chung-shu's notions of the "Institution Modeled after Heaven" and "Men Correspond to the Measure of Heaven"), in spite of the different religious or mystical projections of each culture. Although these modes of legitimizing the hierarchies of power occurred at quite different periods of time (almost thirteen centuries apart), they emerged in manners in which similar curves and patterns can be identified. Indeed, when considered in this light, the coding activities in the caste system in India and the shogunate system in Japan disclose rather similar curves and patterns.

There is also this to consider: how the timing of the said implosions in each respective culture have affected the complexity of its morphological traces. While Taoism did not literally overturn the Confucian orthodoxy as it was deified in the Han Dynasty, as a counterdiscourse at such an early date, it continually challenged the orthodoxy to question and modify itself, where possible, to become a cultural force with new syntheses from the Taoist project. Indeed, the Taoist counterdiscourse, which continues to resist the divisive functions of language so as to evoke the return to the Uncarved Block, has been playing a pivotal role in balancing the dominatory and exclusionary activities of the dominant ideology. We see a continuous readjustment and expansion of Confucian positions in the ancient classics—from the Appendices to the *Book of Change* and others such as *Chung Yung*, to the neo-Confucianism of the Sung and Ming Dynasties (which was in response to the challenges of Taoism, as well as Buddhism, particularly Ch'an Buddhism, which had incorporated within it major premises of Taoism). In Chinese aesthetics and poetics, Taoism assumed a primary rather than secondary role as it played off the Confucian-dominated institutions. Most interesting of all is the fact that almost all the scholar-statesmen in China assumed two roles simultaneously: A Confucian statesman and a Taoist poet converge into one person, who keeps the two roles apart and together at the same time, allowing one to define the other.

Although the Platonic-Aristotelian discourses had been challenged and revised before the Copernican revolution (by critics such as Longinus, Plotinus, and Lucretius), these challenges had not seriously questioned the tyrannical activities of the Platonic and Aristotelian hermeneutical models. Even after the Copernican revolution, sediments of their abstract systems, including the systematic theology of the Middle Ages, rational concepts, standardized methods of scientific experimentation, a rational sense of balance, symmetry, and restraint in art and music, bureaucratic conduct of organized spheres, as well as pursuit of economics dictated by instrumental reason, continued to have a strong grip upon Western intellectuals. Although one witnesses the rise of a new search for knowledge (as seen in Shaftesbury and others) to come up with a new framework to explain the world, to rechart humankind's relationship to nature, and to question the authenticity of language (in other words, to move out from a closed system to an open system), the search has taken perhaps the most complex, most tortuous, and one of the longest courses. Modern and postmodern attempts to break away from and to deconstruct the now proverbial logocentric thinking are one of the most agonizing and labyrinthine, because most philosophers and poets are still haunted by the "ghosts" of texts of the past. Thus, although we find many echoes of other non-Western cultures in modern literature and art, they are still not speaking the same language, for as William Carlos Williams has said, "Unless there is/a new mind there cannot be a new/line." But it is precisely this awareness, shared by many contemporary philosophers and poets, that will make the inscription of a new mind, or shall we say, the creation of a new line, possible.

Notes

1. Wai-lim Yip, "The Chinese Poem: A Different Mode of Representation," *Delos* 3 (1960): 62–79.

2. In the post-Mao era in China, there suddenly appeared a flurry of comparative literary studies, but, in their eagerness to appropriate Western theories, most of them, with a few notable exceptions, remain superficial and demonstrate no understanding of the historicity or of the aesthetic grounding of the theories they adopted.

3. Fredric Jameson, "Transcoding Gadamer," paper presented at the Symposium on Culture, Literature, and History, July 15–28, 1987, National Tsing-hua University, Taipei. My own reading of this aspect of Gadamer can be seen in my Chinese article, "Dialogue with the Work: Aspects of Hermeneutics," *Unitas* 22 (August 1986): 148–99. The relevant part reads: "In the third mode must be preserved an openness supported by an effective historical consciousness. Only in this openness can real human relationship occur, which should always include mutual listening and mutual expression of different and dissenting opinions."

4. See also chapter 3, in which I compare James to the Taoist discussion of language and its distortion of the total composition of things.

5. William James, *The Will to Believe and Other Essays* (London: Longmans, Green and Co., 1905), 118–19.

6. In addition to chapter 3 and the Epilogue, please see also my essay "The Daoist [Taoist] Theory of Knowledge," in *Poetics East and West*, Toronto Semiotic Monograph Series, no. 4 (Toronto: Toronto Semiotic Circle, 1988–89), 55–74, and my article in Chinese "The Framing of Meaning and Power," in my book *Li-shih, Ch'uan-shih, Mei-*

hsueh [History, Hermeneutics, Aesthetics] (Taipei: Tung-tai, 1988), 209–50.

7. *Ch'i-ch'eng-chuan-ho* or "beginning-following-turning-closing" in the Chinese rhetorical tradition is not unlike that of the West, but it is not always observed, and, when applied to the discussion of the structure of a poem, it can come in quite a range of sophisticated variations.

8. For further discussion of this, see my "Brief Discussion on Methods in Chinese Criticism," in *Yin-chih T'ai-ho* (Taipei: Shih-pao, 1980), 85–100.

1. THE USE OF "MODELS" IN EAST–WEST COMPARATIVE LITERATURE

1. Claudio Guillén, *Literature as System* (Princeton: Princeton University Press, 1971), 109, 119.

2. William Warbuton, *The Works of the Rev. William Warbuton*, ed. R. Hurd, 7 vols. (London, 1788) 3:404.

3. *Boswell's Life of Johnson*, ed. G. B. Hill and L. F. Powell (New York: Harper and Bros., 1889), 3:339.

4. For examples of the structural dynamics of the Chinese character, see chapter 2.

5. Wai-lim Yip, "The Chinese Poem: A Different Mode of Representation," *Delos* 3 (1960): 62–79; *Ezra Pound's "Cathay"* (Princeton: Princeton University Press, 1969); "Aesthetic Perception in Classical Chinese Poetry: A Comparative Approach," *Chung-hua Wen-hua Fu-hsing Yueh-k'an* 4, no. 5 (May 1971): 1–6; "Classical Chinese Poetry and Anglo-American Poetry: Convergence of Languages and Poetry," *Comparative Literature Studies* 11, no. 1 (March 1974): 21–47. The last article has been rewritten and now forms part of chapter 2 of this book.

6. Yip, "The Chinese Poem," 62.

7. Yip, "Classical Chinese and Anglo-American Poetry," 26.

8. For Jean Dubuffet, *Anticultural Positions*, see appendix in Wylie Sypher, *Loss of the Self in Modern Literature and Art* (New York: Vintage Books, 1962).

9. Charles Olson, "Human Universe," in *Selected Writings* (New York: New Directions, 1950), 54–55.

10. Robert Duncan, "Rites of Participation: Parts I & II," in *A Caterpillar Anthology*, ed. Clayton Eshleman (New York: Anchor, 1971), 29.

11. Claude Lévi-Strauss, *Structural Anthropology* (New York: Anchor Edition, 1963), 21.

12. For more systematic criticism, including E. R. Leach's 1969 critique of Lévi-Strauss, see George Steiner, *Language and Silence* (Harmondsworth, Middlesex, England: Penguin Books, 1969), 239–50.

13. Martin Heidegger, *On the Way to Language*, trans. Peter D. Hertz (New York: Harper and Row, 1971), 4–5.

14. I do not question, however, the computer's predictive power in matters of scientifically explainable physical properties.

15. See n 5 and chapter 2.

16. Benjamin Lee Whorf, *Language, Thought, and Reality*, ed. J. B. Corroll (Cambridge, Mass.: MIT Press, 1956), 57–60.

17. It is interesting that the Chinese character *hsin* 心 for heart also means mind. This makes it impossible to translate into English. "Mind" is too intellectual and "heart" is too emotional. *Hsin* is both heart and mind, the total activity of consciousness, at once intuitive and intellectual.

18. Whorf, *Language, Thought, and Reality*, 60.

19. See chapter 4.

20. Ulrich Weisstein, *Comparative Literature and Literary Theory* (Bloomington: Indiana University Press, 1973), 7–8.

21. C. T. Hsia, *The Classic Chinese Novel: A Critical Introduction* (New York: Columbia University Press, 1968), 6.

22. Charles Witke, "Comparative Literature and the Classics: East and West," *Tamkang Review* 2, no. 2, and 3, no. 1 (October 1971–April 1972): 15.

23. Pound's statement prepared for Eliot's famous "historical sense."

24. See my Chinese book *History, Hermeneutics, Aesthetics* (歷史 · 傳釋 · 美學) (Taipei: Tung-tai, 1988), 155–208.

25. Lily Winters, "Ch'ü Yüan, Fourth-Century Poet Viewed from the Western Romantic Tradition," *Tamkang Review* 2, no. 2, and 3, no. 1 (October 1971–April 1972): 222.

26. Arnold Hauser, *The Social History of Art*, trans. Stanley Godman (New York: Vintage Books, 1957), 2:172.

27. See, in particular, R. Wittkower, *Art and Architecture in Italy: 1600 to 1750* (Baltimore: Penguin Books, 1958), and L. Venturi and L. Salerno, Introduction, *Il Seicento Europo*, Exhibition (Rome: 1956). I am indebted to Julius S. Held and Donald Posner for this information; see their *Seventeenth and Eighteenth Century Art* (Englewood Cliffs, N. J.: Prentice-Hall, n.d.), 12.

28. See Hauser, *Social History of Art*, Chaps. 9 and 10; W. Weisbach, *Barock und Kunst de Gegenreformation* (Berlin: P. Cassirer, 1921); and E. Male, *L'Art religieux après le Concile de Trente* (Paris: A Colin, 1951).

29. Hauser, *Social History of Art*, 174.

30. See, for example, Frank Warke, *Versions of Baroque: European Literature in the Seventeenth Century* (New Haven: Yale University Press, 1972); Helmut Hatzfeld, "A Critical Survey of Recent Baroque Theories," *Boletin del Intituto Caso y Cuervo* 4 (1948): 46–91; Helmut

Hatzfeld, "The Baroque of Cervantes and the Baroque of Góngora, Exemplified by the Motif 'Las Boclas,'" *Anales Cervantes* 3 (1953): 87–119; Mario Praz, "The Flaming Heart: Richard Crashaw and the Baroque," in *The Flaming Heart* (New York: Doubleday, 1958).

31. John Donne, "An Anatomie of the World," in *The Complete Poetry and Selected Prose of John Donne*, ed. Charles M. Coffin (New York: Modern Library, 1952), 191.

32. Hauser, *Social History of Art*, 182.

33. James Liu, *The Poetry of Li Shang-yin: Ninth-Century Baroque Chinese Poet* (Chicago: University of Chicago Press, 1969), 253.

34. Ibid., 254.

35. For a critique of various attempts to apply the term "baroque" to Chinese works, see Tak-wai Wong, "Toward Defining Chinese Baroque Poetry," *Tamkang Review* 8, no. 1 (April 1977): 25–72.

36. For a detailed discussion of the problems in the study of modern Chinese literature, see chapter 6 and my "Modernism in Cross-cultural Context," in *Proceedings of the XIIth Congress of the ICLA*, ed. A. Owen Aldridge, vol. 3 (Munich: 1988), 379–89.

37. For my attempt in this respect, see chapter 2.

2. SYNTAX AND HORIZON OF REPRESENTATION IN
CLASSICAL CHINESE AND MODERN AMERICAN POETRY

1. There is no attempt here to equate the syntactic freedom of the palindrome poem to that found in all classical Chinese poems. But the syntactic flexibility revealed in the palindrome poem and the horizon of representation constituted therein can be used as a yardstick to measure the degree of freedom and the aesthetic functions in other classical Chinese lines.

2. Kuo Hsi, quoted in Lin Yu-tang, *The Chinese Theory of Art* (London: William Heiemann, 1967), 75.

3. Most of these phrases are taken from Tu Fu (712–770), with the exception of the last line, which is from Li Po (701–762). Word for word, the lines from which these phrases are taken run as follows:

1. 岸　　花　　飛　　送　　客
bank / flower / fly / see off / guest

2. 檣　　燕　　語　　留　　人
mast / swallow / word / stay / person (guest, friend)

3. 樓　　雪　　融　　城　　濕
tower / snow / melt / city / wet

4. 宮　　雲　　去　　殿　　低
palace / cloud / go / hall / low

5. 樓　　雲　　籠　　樹　　小
tower / cloud / shroud / tree / (seem) small

6. 湖　　日　　落　　船　　明
　　lake / sun /set / boat / bright(en)
7. 風　　林　　纖　　月　　落
　　wind / forest / slender / moon / set
8. 溪　　午　　不　　聞　　鐘
　　stream / noon / not / hear / bell

4. I am fully aware of the fact that this poem is a *yüeh-fu* (ballad-songs, a genre named after the Music Bureau, Yüeh Fu, of the Han Dynasty) and that it must also be read intertextually with early models of the same title. (See my chapter on polyphonic reading, "Secret Echoes and Complementary Correspondences — A Chinese Theory of Reading.") The intertexts of this poem do not change the initial perceptual activity described here.

5. That is, phenomena as a whole; the singular form is used here to avoid thinking of totality as consisting of differentiated units.

6. Chuang-tzu, *Complete Works of Chuang-tzu*, trans. by Burton Watson (New York: Columbia University Press, 1964), 19.

7. Ralph Stephenson and Jean R. Debrix, *The Cinema as Art* (Baltimore: Penguin Books, 1968), 107.

8. Ibid., 100.

9. The examples are from five different sources, cited here in order. Herbert Giles and Arthur Waley, trans., *Selected Chinese Verses* (Shanghai: The Commercial Press, 1934), 22 (this book has two parts, translations by Giles and those by Waley, and offers a good comparison of the styles of these two early translators); W. J. B. Fletcher, *More Gems of Chinese Poetry* (Shanghai: 1919), 150; Witter Bynner, *The Jade Mountain* (New York: Anchor, 1964), 85; Arthur Christy, *Images in Jade* (New York: E. P. Dutton, 1929), 74; Soame Jenyns, *A Further Selection from the Three Hundred Poems of the T'ang Dynasty* (London: John Murray, 1944), 76.

10. Bynner, *The Jade Mountain*, 122; Cyril Birch, ed., *Anthology of Chinese Literature* (New York: Grove, 1965), 238–39.

11. Bynner, *The Jade Mountain*, 153.

12. Sergei Eisenstein, *Film Form and Film Sense*, trans. Jay Leyda (New York: Harcourt, Brace and World, 1942), 29.

13. Wai-lim Yip, *Ezra Pound's "Cathay"* (Princeton: Princeton University Press, 1969), 22. The quotation is from Eisenstein, *Film Form and Film Sense*, 7.

14. Bynner, *The Jade Mountain*, 119.

15. See discussion in the next chapter.

16. The philosophical rationalization of the subject has been closely examined by Wylie Sypher in *Loss of the Self in Modern Literature and Art* (New York: Vintage Books, 1962).

17. Walter Pater, *The Renaissance* (London: Macmillan, 1922), 236–37.

18. Walter Pater, *Appreciations* (London: Macmillan, 1924), 66–68.

19. T. E. Hulme, *Further Speculations*, ed Sam Haynes (Lincoln: University of Nebraska Press, 1955), 70–71.

20. Ibid., 134.

21. Ibid., 73.

22. More specifically, "Explanation means *ex plane*, that is to say, the opening out of things on a plain surface . . . the process of explanation is always a process of unfolding. A tangled mass is unfolded flat so that you can see all its parts separated out, and any tangle which can be separated out in this way must of course be an extensive manifold" (Ibid., 177).

23. Ezra Pound, "I Gather the Limbs of Osiris," *New Age* 10, no. 6 (December 7, 1911): 130.

24. Ezra Pound, "Chinese Poetry," *Today* 3 (1918): 54.

25. Ezra Pound, *The Letters of Ezra Pound*, ed. D. D. Paige (New York: Harcourt, Brace and World, 1950), 90–91.

26. The part I refer to runs:

I will sing of the white birds
In the blue waters of heaven,
The clouds that are sprays to its sea.

When one first encounters "the white birds," one "sees" white birds on a mental screen. With the juxtaposition of "blue waters of heaven," the white birds are now both "waves" and "clouds." On the reader's mental screen appear simultaneously "water" and "sky," and, as a result, the birds are at once clouds and sprays. This effect, achieved by superimposition, can be seen as a footnote to Hulme, although this part was written long before Hulme formulated his theory. It is important to note that the similarity between or among the various objects involved is evoked, not stated, and is noticed *after* the reader's mental vision moves back and forth between the sea and the sky, allowing one visual image superimpose itself upon another. H. D.'s "Oread" works in a very similar fashion.

27. William Carlos Williams, *Paterson* (New York: New Directions, 1946), 6.

28. William Carlos Williams, *Selected Essays* (New York: New Directions, 1954), 196, 213.

29. Kenneth Burke, "Heaven's First Law," *Dial* 72 (1922): 197–200.

30. Williams, *Selected Essays*, 5.

31. Charles Olson and Robert Creeley, "Projective Verse," in Charles Olson, *Selected Writings* (New York: New Directions, 1966), 20.

32. In spite of some stylistic resemblances, Mallarmé is, at root, dif-

ferent from the Chinese aesthetic position, which seldom deals with an artificially created world that has no reference to physical reality. See the next chapter for further discussion.

33. See Arthur Symons, *The Symbolist Movement in Literature* (New York: Dutton, 1958), 197–98. See also Frank Kermode, *The Romantic Image* (New York: Vintage, 1957), "Symons," and my *Ezra Pound's "Cathay,"* 48ff.

34. Ezra Pound, "Vorticism," *Fortnightly Review* 96 (1914): 471. Reprinted in Pound's *Gaudier-Brzeska* (New York: New Directions, 1961), 94–109.

35. For discussion of the origin of this poem and other related aesthetic questions, see my *Ezra Pound's "Cathay,"* 56–60.

36. See my *Ezra Pound's "Cathay,"* particularly the part subtitled "Graphic Ironical Play" (143ff.) for full treatment of this technique. Discussion of the line in question is on pp. 125–28.

37. It was through the good offices of Hugh Kenner that I saw a copy of this crib.

38. Wai-lim Yip, *Ezra Pound's "Cathay,"* 161–62.

39. For Williams's relationship to the Armory Show, see Bram Dijkstra's *The Hieroglyphics of a New Speech* (Princeton: Princeton University Press, 1969).

40. See her account in "A Transatlantic Interview, 1946," in *A Primer for Gradual Understanding of Gertrude Stein*, ed. Robert Bartlett Haas (Santa Barbara: Black Sparrow Press, 1976), 15–35.

41. Ibid., 15–18.

42. See quotation, ibid., 15.

43. *Selected Writings of Gertrude Stein*, ed. Carl Van Vechten (New York: Vintage Books, 1972), 495.

44. Williams, *Selected Essays*, 114.

45. Olson, *Selected Writings*, 17.

46. The early version was first published in *Poetry* 43:3, 4 (1933) and was later included in *The Collected Earlier Poems* (New York: New Directions, 1951), 94. The later version is conveniently included in *The Selected Poems of William Carlos Williams* (New York: New Directions, 1963), 42.

47. Robert Creeley, "Notes Apropos 'Free Verse,'" in *Naked Poetry*, ed. Stephen Berg and Robert Mezey (Indianapolis and New York: Bobbs-Merrill, 1969), 185.

48. Robert Creeley, Preface to *For Love: Poems, 1950–1960* (New York: Charles Scribner's, 1962).

49. We must add here e. e. cummings, whose graphic arrangements of language into gestures to reflect the ritualistic procedures of a moment, as in "In-Just," make him one of the forerunners of concrete poetry.

50. *Phi Theta Annual* (Papers of the Oriental Languages Honor Society, University of California), vol. 5 (1954–55), 12.

51. Michael McClure, *Scratching the Beat Surface* (San Francisco: North Point Press, 1982), 102–3 [emphasis added]. The two versions read as follows:

Tune: "Immortal by the River"

night   drink   East   Slope   wake   again   drunk
return   —   it-seems   third   watch
home   boy   nose-breath   already   thundering   —
knock   door   all   no   response
lean   staff   listen   river   sound
long   regret   this   body   not   my   possession
when   —   forget   —   busy-buzz
night   deep   wind   quiet   waves   —   smooth
small   boat   from   here   gone/drift
river   sea   entrust   rest-of-life

Drinking into deep night at East Slope, sober then drunk.
I return home perhaps at small hours,
My page-boy's snoring already like thunder.
No answer to my knocking at the door,
I lean on my staff to listen to the river rushing.
I grieve forever that this body, no body of mine.
When can I forget this buzzing life?
Night now still, wind quiet, waves calm and smooth,
A little boat to drift from here.
On the river, on the sea, my remaining years.

52. Robert Duncan, *Bending the Bow* (New York: New Directions, 1968), 40, 45.

3. LANGUAGE AND THE REAL-LIFE WORLD

1. William Carlos Williams, *Paterson* (New York: New Directions, 1946), 50.

2. The phrase is borrowed from Fredric Jameson's book on Russian formalism, *The Prison-house of Language* (Princeton: Princeton University Press, 1972), but my use here is also related to Heidegger. See chapter 1, n. 13.

3. Jerome Chen and Michael Bullock, *Poems of Solitude* (London and New York: Abelard-Schuman, 1960), 73.

4. G. W. Robinson, trans., *Poems of Wang Wei* (Harmondsworth, England: Penguin, 1973), 31.

5. H. C. Chang, *Chinese Literature: Nature Poetry* (Edinburgh: Edinburgh University Press, 1977), 76.

6. Chang Yin-nan and Lewis C. Walmsley, *Poems of Wang Wei* (Rutland, Vermont, and Tokyo: Tuttle, 1958), 42.

7. All quotations from Lao-tzu's *Tao-te-ching* (abbreviated as Lao) will be indicated by chapter. Those from *Chuang-tzu* and Kuo Hsiang's annotation follow Kuo Ch'ing-fan's 郭慶藩 edition of *Chuang-tzu chi-shih* 莊子集釋 (Taipei: Ho Le, 1974), abbreviated as Chuang. Translations of *Chuang-tzu* in the text are primarily Fung Yu-lan's (1933; reprint, New York: Paragon, 1964), although I have modified them for stylistic cogency. When feasible, one or two phrases from Burton Watson's *Complete Works of Chuang-tzu* (New York: Columbia University Press, 1964) will be adopted. For the political dimension of the Taoist project, see my Epilogue.

8. Martin Heidegger, *Introduction to Metaphysics*, trans. Ralph Manheim (New Haven: Yale University Press, 1959), 5.

9. William James, *The Will to Believe and Other Essays* (London: Longmans, Green, and Co., 1905), 118–20.

10. Alfred North Whitehead, *The Aims of Education* (New York: Macmillan, 1967), 157–58.

11. This chapter, believed to be written by later Taoists, is fully in keeping with Lao-tzu and Chuang-tzu's teachings. It is a direct extension of Chuang's passage on "ancient men" and Lao's idea of *su p'u*: "Constant instinctive virtue now full, one returns to the Unhewn" (Lao, 28).

12. Heidegger, *Introduction to Metaphysics*, 14. More will be said about this concept in the second part of this chapter.

13. Wai-lim Yip, *Hiding the Universe: Poems of Wang Wei* (New York and Tokyo: Mushinsha-Grossman, 1972); "Aesthetic Consciousness of Landscape and Anglo-American Poetry," *Comparative Literature Studies* 15 (1978): 211–41, the rewritten form of which appears as chapter 4 of this book; "The Morphology of Aesthetic Consciousness and Perimeter of Meaning in the Example of Pre-Romantic Concept of Nature" can be found in my Chinese book, *History, Hermeneutics, Aesthetics* (Taipei: Tung-tai, 1988), 155–208.

14. Henri Brémond, *Prayer and Poetry*, trans. Algar Thorold (London: Folcroft, 1927), 108ff.

15. Ibid., 147, 116.

16. William James, *The Varieties of Religious Experience* (New York: New American Library, 1958), 61.

17. Lu Chi, "Wen-fu," in *Lu Shih-heng Wen-chi* 陸士衡文集 (*Ssu-pu-ts'ung-k'an*; reprint, Taipei: Shang-wu, 1965), 33:1, p. 2.

18. Liu Hsieh, "Shen-ssu," in *Wen-hsin Tiao-lung* 文心雕龍, annot. Huang Shih-lin (1738; reprint, Taipei: Kai-ming, 1959), 6.

19. Chang Yen-yüan, *Li-tai ming-hua chi* 歷代名畫記, annot. Yu Chien-hua (Hong Kong: Nan-t'ung, 1973), 35–36, 40–41.

20. Ssu-k'ung T'u, *Shih-p'in chi-chieh* 詩品集解, annot. Kuo Shao-yu (Hong Kong: Shang-wu, 1965), 5.

21. Su Tung-p'o, *Chi-chu fen-lei Tung-p'o hsien-sheng shih* 集註分類東坡先生詩 (*SPTK* ed.) 21, p. 391.

22. Yen Yü, *Ts'ang-lang shih-hua chiao-shih* 滄浪詩話集釋, annot. Kuo Shao-yu (Peking: Jen-min wen-hsueh, 1961), 6, 24.

23. Wang Kuo-wei, *Jen-chien tzu-hua* 人間詞話, in *Wang Kuo-wei I-shu* 王國維遺書 (*Works of Late Wang Kuo-wei*) (Shanghai: Shanghai ku-chi, 1983), 15:1.

24. Ssu-k'ung T'u, *Shih-p'in chi-chieh*, 19.

25. Su Tung-p'o, *Ching-chin Tung-p'o wen-chi shih-lueh* 經進東坡文集事略 (*SPTK*, ed.) 46, 279.

26. Ibid., 57, 335.

27. See chapter 2.

28. Roland Barthes, *Writing Degree Zero*, trans. Annette Lavers and Colin Smith (New York: Jonathan Cape, 1968), 47–48, 49–50.

29. "Il s'agit de savoir si notre langue est mensonye ou verité" (Albert Camus, *Essais*, ed. by R. Quillot and L. Faucon [Paris: Gallimard, 1965], 1, 672).

30. Stephane Mallarmé, *Oeuvres complètes*, ed. Henri Mondor and G. Jean-Aubrey (Paris: Gallimard, 1945), 363.

31. Ibid., 368.

32. Ibid., 378.

33. Stephane Mallarmé, *Correspondence*, vol. 1, ed. Henri Mondor (Paris: Gallimard, 1959), 220.

34. Mallarmé, *Oeuvres Complètes*, ed. Henri Mondor and G. Jean-Aubrey (Paris: Gallimard, 1945), 67–68.

35. Francis Bacon, *The Works of Francis Bacon*, 14 vols., ed. James Spedding, Robert L. Ellis, and Douglas D. Heath (London: Longman and Co., 1857–59), 1:496: "artificialia a naturalibus non Form aut Essentia."

36. René Descartes, *Oeuvres de Descartes*, 2 vols., ed. Charles Adam Paul Tonnery and Le Centre National de la Recherche Scientifique. Liberairie philosophique. (Paris: J. Vrin, 1974), ix. p. 321.

37. T. S. Eliot, *Selected Essays* (New York: Harcourt, Brace, and World, 1950), 248.

38. T. E. Hulme, *Further Speculation*, ed. Sam Hynes (Lincoln: University of Nebraska Press, 1962), 70–71.

39. See chapter 2.

40. Soren Kierkegaard, *Concluding Unscientific Postscript* [1844], trans. Dorothy Swenson and Walter Lowrie (Princeton: Princeton University Press, 1941), 47, 267.

41. See chapter 2.

42. All quotations from this work are from the edition translated by Ralph Manheim (New Haven: Yale University Press, 1959). Except as indicated otherwise, all page numbers in the text refer to this edition.

43. Maurice Merleau-Ponty,"What Is Phenomenology?" (trans. Colin Smith), in *European Literary Theory and Practice*, ed. Vernon W. Gras (New York: Dell Publishing Company, 1973), 69.

44. Martin Heidegger, "Holderlin and the Essence of Poetry," in *European Literary Theory and Practice*, 27ff.

45. Merleau-Ponty, following this key, focuses on the primacy of vision.

46. Martin Heidegger, *Poetry, Language, and Thought*, trans. Albert Hofstadter (New York: Harper and Row, 1971), abbreviated as *PLT* in the text.

47. See the similar Taoist view in the first section of this chapter.

48. See J. Hillis Miller, *Poets of Reality* (Cambridge, Mass.: Belknap Press of Harvard University Press, 1966), 287–91.

49. This and other abbreviations in this section are Miller's. SL = *Selected Letters*, ed. John C. Thirlwall (New York: McDowell, Obolensky, 1957); P = *Poems* (Rutherford, N.J.: privately printed, 1909); SE = *Selected Essays* (New York: Random House, 1954); CEP = *The Collected Earlier Poems* (New York: New Directions, 1951); SA = *Spring and All* (Dijon: Contact, 1923).

4. AESTHETIC CONSCIOUSNESS OF LANDSCAPE
IN CHINESE AND ANGLO-AMERICAN POETRY

1. Harold Bloom, "The Internalization of Quest Romance," in *Romanticism and Consciousness*, ed. Harold Bloom (New York: W. W. Norton and Co., 1970), p. 9.

2. Abrams's famous essay, "Structure and Style in the Greater Romantic Lyric," which was first published in 1965, has been widely referred to by many critics. The most relevant part of this essay is the following: "The speaker begins with a description of the landscape; an aspect or change of aspect in the landscape evokes a varied but integral process of memory, thought, anticipation, and feeling which remains closely intervolved with the outer scene. In the course of this meditation the lyric speaker achieves an insight, faces up to a tragic loss, comes to a moral decision, or resolves an emotional problem. Often the poem rounds upon itself to end where it began, at the outer scene, but with an altered mood and the intervening meditation" (in *Romanticism and Consciousness*, 201). As will become clear later in my argument, the middle part here is alien to the Chinese counterpart.

3. For example, in a loose sense, we must call the following poem by Tiberianus of the Constantine Period a landscape poem:

Through the fields there went a river; down the airy glen it wound,
Smiling mid its radiant pebbles, decked with flowery plants around.
Dark-hued laurels waved above it close by myrtle greeneries,
Gently swaying to the whispers and caresses of the breeze.
Underneath grew velvet greensward with a wealth of bloom for
    dower,
And the ground, agleam with lilies, coloured 'neath the saffron-
    flower.
While the grove was full of fragrance and of breath from violets.
Mid such guerdons of spring-time, mid its jewelled coronets,
Shone the queen of all the perfumes, Star that loveliest colours
    shows,
Golden flame of fair Dione, passing every flower—the rose.
Dewspent trees rose firmly upright with the lush grass at their feet:
Here, as yonder, streamlets murmured trembling from each well-
    spring fleet.
Grottos had an inner binding made of moss and ivy green,
Where soft-flowing runlets glided with their drops of crystal sheen.
Through those shades each bird, more tuneful than belief could
    entertain,
Warbled loud her chant of spring-tide, warbled low her sweet
    refrain.
Here the prattling river's murmur to the leaves made harmony
As the Zephyr's airy music stirred them into melody
To a wanderer through the coppice, fair and filled with song and
    scent,
Bird and river, breeze and woodland, flower and shade brought
    ravishment.

from H. W. Gorrod, *The Oxford Book of Latin Verse*
(London, 1912), p. 372

But we should know that this poem was created out of a sort of rhetorical game of medieval times, involving such things as odd and even lines, rather than out of unconditional faith and love in landscape. As such, it falls short of the name of landscape poetry.

4. *Wu-teng Hui-yuan*, vol. 17 in *Ching-yin Wen-yuan-ke Ssu-k'u Chuan-shu Tzu-pu*, no. 359 (Taiwan: Shang-wu, 1983), 1053 che, p. 735.

5. All the Chinese landscape poems in this essay are my translations. They can be easily located in my *Hiding the Universe: Poems of Wang Wei* (New York: Grossman, 1972) and in my *Chinese Poetry: Major Modes and Genres* (Berkeley: University of California Press, 1976). Quotations from Chuang-tzu and Kuo Hsiang's annotations

follow Kuo Ch'ing-fan's edition of *Chuang-tzu Chi-shih* (Chuang-tzu: Collected Annotations) (Taipei: Ho Le, 1974), abbreviated as Chuang. All quotations from Wordsworth follow E. de Selincourt's edition of *The Poetical Works of William Wordsworth*, 5 vols. (London: The Clarendon Press, 1940–1949), abbreviated as *PW*. Those from *The Prelude* follow the Parallel Text, ed. J. C. Maxwell (Baltimore: Penguin, 1971).

6. See Geoffrey Hartman, *The Unmediated Vision* (New York: Harcourt, Brace, and World, 1966), 4.

7. Hartman, *Unmediated Vision*, 23.

8. See also Donald Wesling, *Wordsworth and the Adequacy of Landscape* (New York: Barnes and Noble, 1970).

9. In his "Excursion on Mount T'ien-t'ai: A Rhymeprose," Sun Cho said, "Tao, dissolving, becomes rivers; Tao, gathering, becomes mountains." The next phrase was originally from Chuang Tzu's "T'ien Tzu-fang," in which, using the mouthpiece of Confucius, Chuang Tzu said, "With such a man, what strikes your eyes is where the Way is. Little room there is for speech" (*Chuang*, 706). This phrase came into critical use beginning with the Sung Dynasty (960–1279). See Kuo Shao-yu's annotations of Yen Yu's *Ts'ang-lang Shih-hua chiao-shih* (Peking: Jen-min wen-hsueh, 1961), in particular pages 29–34.

The Taoist-oriented neo-Confucianist Shao Yung, in the introduction to his collection of poems "Beat the Earthen Chime," elaborated from Lao Tzu this view:

. . . the one: to view Human Nature through the Way
    Mind through Human Nature
    Body through Mind
    Things through Body
    (Control, yes, there is,
    But not free from harm)
is unlike
the other: to view the Way through the Way
    Human Nature through Human Nature
    Mind through Mind
    Body through Body
    Things through Things
    (Even if harm were intended,
    Can it be done?)

10. "The good man delights in mountains. The wise man delights in waters" (*The Confucian Analects*, 6:12).

11. Among important English works, see Richard Mather, "The Landscape Buddhism of the Fifth-century Poet Hsieh Ling-yün," *Journal of Asian Studies* 17, no. 1 (1958): 67–79; J. D. Frodsham, *The Murmuring Stream* (Kuala Lumpur: University of Malaysia Press, 1967),

"The Poetic Tradition," 86–105. For the synthesis of Taoist and Buddhist ideas, including the case of Chih Tun (314–366), who also annotated Chuang Tzu, see E. Zurcher, *The Buddhist Conquest of China*, 2 vols. (Leiden: E. J. Brill, 1959).

12. See chapter 3.

13. The possibility of writing nonmetaphorically will help throw light on the questioning of metaphor as an expressive device by contemporary philosophers and writers, as summarized in an important article by Beda Allemann, "Metaphor and Antimetaphor," in *Interpretation: The Poetry of Meaning*, ed. Stanley Romaine Hopper and David Miller (New York: Harcourt, Brace, and World, 1967). Thus, even though we begin with I. A. Richards's technical distinction, the question of metaphoric thinking is hermeneutical. I am fully aware of the fact that as a mere literary device, metaphor has never been excluded in Chinese poetry. (See further discussion on this in the second section of this essay.)

14. From the *I Ching*: "When heaven and earth deliver themselves, thunder and rain set in. When thunder and rain set in, the seed pods of all fruits, plants, trees break open" (Wilhelm/Baynes, Chap. 40).

15. Kuo Hsiang's commentary on change.

16. This and subsequent lines, in order, are from Pao Chao, "Ascend Lu-shan"; Hsieh Ling-yün, "Passing Hsi-ning Villa," "Ascend the Summit of Stone Gate," "Excursion to the Southern Pavilion," "Ascend a Lone Island in the River"; Hsieh T'iao (464–499), "To Hsün-ch'eng, past Hsin-lin-p'u, toward Pan-ch'iao," "Roaming the East Field"; Wang Chi, "Into the Jo-yeh Stream."

17. This refers to E. de Selincourt, ed., *The Letters of William and Dorothy Wordsworth* (Oxford: Oxford University Press, 1937).

18. Geoffrey Hartman, "Romanticism and Anti-Self-consciousness," in *Romanticism and Consciousness*, 51, 53.

19. Wesling, *Wordsworth and the Adequacy of Landscape*, 23.

20. Wordsworth's "When the light of sense goes out" is, in some way, comparable to the Taoist "loss of self."

21. Fred Randel, "The Mountaintops of English Romanticism," *Texas Studies in Literature and Language* 23 (1981): 294–323.

22. Marjorie Nicolson, *Mountain Gloom and Mountain Glory* (Ithaca, N. Y.: Cornell University Press, 1959), 50.

23. Randel, "Mountaintops of English Romanticism," 297.

24. Lin Wen-yueh, "Chung-kuo San-shui-shih ti t'e-chih" (The Unique Characteristics of Landscape Poetry), in *San-shui yü Ku-tien* (Taipei: Ch'un-wen-hsueh, 1976), 41.

25. See the historical treatment of this in Kenneth Clark's *Landscape into Art* (Boston: Beacon Press, 1961).

26. Allemann, "Metaphor and Antimetaphor," 108–15.

27. Franz Kafka, "Beschreibung eines Kampfes," in *Gesammelte Werke*, ed. Max Brod (New York and Frankfurt am Mein: 1954), 42, quoted in Allemann, "Metaphor and Antimetaphor," 111.

28. Ezra Pound, *The Literary Essays of Ezra Pound*, ed. T. S. Eliot (London: Faber and Faber, 1954), 9.

29. Alain Robbe-Grillet, "Nature, Humanism, Tragedy," in *For a New Novel* (New York: Grove Press, 1965), 52, 56, and 58.

30. Owen Barfield, *Saving the Appearances: A Study in Idolatry* (New York: Harcourt, Brace, and World, n.d.), 73–78.

31. This cartography has been fully explored by Marjorie Nicolson's two important books, *The Breaking of the Circle* (New York: Columbia University Press, 1960) and *Mountain Gloom and Mountain Glory* (New York: W. W. Norton, 1963). Read also Basil Willey's *The Seventeenth-Century Background* (New York: Anchor Books, 1953) and *The Eighteenth-Century Background* (Boston: Beacon Books, 1961).

32. For the so-called "decays," see Nicolson, *Mountain Gloom and Mountain Glory*, 111–12. Both *The Seventeenth-Century Background* and *The Eighteenth-Century Background* by Basil Willey have discussed in great detail the crisis of consciousness brought about by this shift of cosmological-hermeneutical paradigms. I am indebted to both Nicolson and Willey for this part of my summary.

33. Nicolson, *Mountain Gloom and Mountain Glory*, 291; and Willey, *The Eighteenth-Century Background*, 63.

34. Hegel's (w)holistic conception of the world speaks to this problem most clearly. I am indebted to Hartman for pointing out this incisive summary of his position. See Hartman's "Romanticism and Anti-Selfconsciousness" in Bloom, 49.

35. See chapter 2 for further discussion.

36. Kenneth Rexroth, interview with Cyrena N. Pondrom, in *The Contemporary Writer*, ed. L. S. Dembo and C. N. Pondrom (Madison: University of Wisconsin Press, 1972), 154–55.

37. Kenneth Rexroth, *The Collected Shorter Poems* (New York: New Directions, 1966), 248, 145 (emphasis added).

38. Wallace Stevens, *Collected Poems of Wallace Stevens* (New York: Knopf, 1954) (emphasis added); 403.

39. Ibid., 193–94.

40. John Crowe Ransom, "Poetry: A Note on Ontology," in *The World's Body* (New York: Charles Scribner's, 1938), 115–16.

41. See J. Hillis Miller, Introduction to *William Carlos Williams* (Englewood Cliffs, N.J.: Prentice-Hall, 1966).

42. See various statements made by contemporary American poets in the 1976 Conference on Chinese Poetry and American Imagination,

in *Ironwood* 17 (1981): 11–59. See also Charles Altieri, "From Symbolist Thought to Immanence: The Ground of Postmodern American Poetics," *Boundary 2* 1 (1973): 605–37.

43. Kenneth Rexroth, *An Autobiographical Novel* (New York: New Directions, 1969), 122, abbreviated here as *AAN*; Kenneth Rexroth Papers in the University of California, Los Angeles, Library, 175/2/ box 11 (I am indebted to Ling Chung's dissertation, "Kenneth Rexroth and Chinese Poetry: Translation, Imitation, and Adaptation," University of Wisconsin, 1972, for this information); *AAN*, 318–19.

44. Rexroth, *AAN*, 319.

45. Kenneth Rexroth, Introduction in *One Hundred Poems from the Chinese*, ed. Kenneth Rexroth (New York: New Directions, 1964), xi.

46. Rexroth, *AAN*, 319.

47. Kenneth Rexroth, *The Classics Revisited* (New York: New Directions, 1969), 131.

48. Kenneth Rexroth, "Science and Civilization in China," in *Assays* (New York: New Directions, 1961), 86.

49. See Ling Chung, "Kenneth Rexroth and Chinese Poetry," 164–66.

50. Rexroth, interview with Cyrena N. Pondrom, 159.

51. Ibid., 161 (emphasis added).

52. Ibid., 155.

53. Rexroth, *Collected Shorter Poems*, 221.

54. Rexroth, *Classics Revisited*, 130.

55. Kenneth Rexroth, *New Poems* (New York: New Directions, 1974), 20, 28.

56. Donald Davie, Introduction to Charles Tomlinson, *The Necklace* (New York: McDowell Obolensky, 1955), xiii.

57. Charles Tomlinson, *Seeing Is Believing* (New York: McDowell Obolensky, 1966), 11.

58. Charles Tomlinson, Introduction in *William Carlos Williams: Selected Poems*, ed. Charles Tomlinson (New York: New Directions, 1985), vii–viii.

59. Gary Snyder, *Regarding Waves* (New York: New Directions, 1970), 39, hereafter abbreviated as *RW*.

60. Gary Snyder, *Earth House Hold* (New York: New Directions, 1969), 101, hereafter abbreviated as *EHH*. Also in his *Turtle Island* (New York: New Directions, 1974), 106, hereafter abbreviated as *TI*.

61. *TI*, 106.

62. *EHH*, 123. Also in his *The Old Ways* (San Francisco: City Lights, 1977), 9, hereafter abbreviated as *OW*. For Snyder's relationship to Amerindian culture, aside from *The Old Ways*, read also his B.A. thesis he did at Reed College in 1951, now published as *He Who Hunted*

Birds in His Father's Village: The Dimensions of a Haida Myth (Bolinas, Calif.: Grey Fox Press, 1979), and my essay "Against Domination: Gary Snyder as an Apologist for Nature," in *The Chinese Text*, ed. Ying-hsiung Chou (Hong Kong: The Chinese University Press, 1986), 75–84.

63. Gary Snyder, *Riprap and Cold Mountain Poems* (San Francisco: Four Seasons Foundation, 1969), 1.

64. David Kherdian, *A Biographical Sketch and Descriptive Checklist of Gary Snyder* (Berkeley: Oyez, 1965), 13.

65. Snyder, *Riprap and Cold Mountain Poems*, 6.

66. Snyder, *TI*, 33, 34.

5. "SECRET ECHOES AND COMPLEMENTARY CORRESPONDENCES" —
A CHINESE THEORY OF READING

This chapter was developed from a Chinese version first published in *Chung-wai Literature* 13 (1984): 4–22. All translations of quotations from Chinese texts are mine. For examples from Taoism, I have followed Fung Yu-lan's *Chuang-tzu* (1933; reprint, New York: Paragon, 1964) with modifications, where necessary, for stylistic cogency. In the footnotes, it will be referred to as Fung. For the translation of the hexagrams of the *I Ching*, I have followed the easily available edition translated by Richard Wilhelm and Cary F. Baynes (Princeton: Princeton University Press, 1967). The interpretation of the various aspects of the *I Ching* and the translations are basically mine. For an overall understanding in English of the workings of the *I Ching*, read Hellmut Wilhelm, *Change: Eight Lectures on the I Ching* (Princeton: Princeton University Press, 1964) and Hu Shih, "The Confucian Logic and the Book of Change," in *The Development of the Logical Method in Ancient China* (Shanghai: Oriental Books, 1922; reprint New York: Paragon, 1963), abbreviated in the footnotes as Hu Shih.

1. The edition of Ssu-k'ung T'u's *The Twenty-four Orders of Poetry* I use here is *Shih P'in Chi Chieh* 詩品集解, annotated by Kuo Shao-yü (Hong Kong: Shang-wu, 1965), by far the most comprehensive in existence. It will be referred to hereafter as Kuo.

2. Fung, "The Human World," 88–89 (emphasis added).

3. Fung, 75–93.

4. Fung, "Mountain Tree," 93.

5. Fung, "The Happy Excursion," 38–39.

6. Fung, "On the Equality of Things," 50, 51–53.

7. Lu Chi, "Wen-fu," in *Lu Shih-heng Wen-chi* (*ssu-pu-tsung-k'an* ed.; reprint, Taipei: Shang-wu, 1965), 33:1, p. 2.

8. Liu Hsieh, "Shen-ssu," in *Wen-hsin Tiao-lung*, annot. Huang Shih-lin (1738; reprint, Taipei: Kai-ming, 1959), 6.

9. In Indian Buddhism, there is the concept of Aryasacca (also written as Aryasatyani), which means "Four Dogmas" or "Four Truths," involving the following stages: Everything in the world is a suffering (Dukha), the cause of which is the confluence of desires and actions in one's consciousness (Samadaya), which, in turn, must be "extinguished," leading to Nirvana (Nirodha). To achieve Nirodha, one has to cultivate the understanding of Truth (Marga). The concept of Two-Sacca—that is, Two Dogmas or Two Truths—has quite an elaborate development in China. Briefly put, they are "worldly" truth and "real" truth. "Worldly" truth means that the world is "being," when viewed phenomenally; but the world, in essence, is "empty" "without being," and this is the "real" truth.

10. Kuo, 4.

11. Kuo, "Letter to Chi-p'u on Poetry," 552 (emphasis added).

12. Kuo, "Letter to Master Li: Discourse on Poetry," 52 (emphasis added).

13. Kuo, 62.

14. See Tai Chun-jen, *T'an I* (*On I Ching*) (Taipei: Kai-ming, 1960), Chapter 9. For a good reevaluation of earlier studies of the *I Ching*, read *Ku-shih-pien*, ed. Ku Chieh-kang, vol. 3 (Peking, Pu she, 1931).

15. *Hu Shih, 30.*

16. Kao Huai-min, *Liang-han I-hsueh-shih* [*History of the* "Book of Change" *in the Two Han Dynasties*] (Taipei: Wen-chin, 1970), 165.

17. Julia Kristeva, "Bakhtine, le mot, le dialogue et le roman," *Critique* 239 (1967), reprinted in her *Semiotike* (Paris: Seuil, 1969), 145–46. The present translation is from *Desire in Language*, ed. Leon S. Roudiez, trans. Thomas Gora, Alice Jardine, and Leon S. Roudiez (New York: Columbia University Press, 1980), 64–65, 66.

18. Roland Barthes, *S/Z*, trans. Richard Miller (New York: Hill and Wang, 1974), 10–11, 21.

19. M. M. Bakhtin, *The Dialogic Imagination*, trans. Caryl Emerson and Michael Holquist (Austin: University of Texas Press, 1981), 276.

20. Harold Bloom, *Poetry and Repression* (New Haven: Yale University Press, 1975), 2–3.

6. REFLECTIONS ON HISTORICAL TOTALITY AND
THE STUDY OF MODERN CHINESE LITERATURE

1. Ezra Pound, "I Gather the Limbs of Osiris," *The New Age* 10, no. 6 (Dec. 7, 1911): 130–31. This essay is reprinted in *Ezra Pound: Selected Prose 1909–1965*, ed. William Cookson (New York: New Directions, 1975). See p. 23.

2. Fredric Jameson, "Toward Dialectical Criticism," in *Marxism and Form* (Princeton: Princeton University Press, 1971), 311–12.

3. I am fully aware of the fact that I am generalizing. The events summarized here, however, have been well rehearsed in many books on modern China, among them Chow Tse-tsung's *The May Fourth Movement* (Cambridge, Mass.: Harvard University Press, 1960). The condensed scenario is done to show the scope of complexity of modern Chinese history, not to account for all the details.

4. Chow Tse-tsung, in his *The May Fourth Movement,* traces this attitude to Chiang Kai-shek himself (p. 344). He quotes Chiang: "Let us see what the so-called new culture movement . . . means. . . . Does the new culture movement mean the advocacy of the vernacular literature? . . . the piecemeal introduction of Western literature? . . . the demand for individual emancipation and an ignorance of nation and society? . . . the destruction of all discipline and the expansion of individual freedom? . . . the blind worship of foreign countries and indiscriminate introduction and acceptance of foreign civilization? If it does, the new culture we seek is too simple, too cheap and too dangerous!"

5. For example, *Liu-shih-nien shih-ko-hsuan* (Poetry of the Recent Six Decades), ed. Wang Chih-chien et al. (Taipei, 1973), contains no selections from the Creation Society or the Sun Society, nothing from Wen I-to, Pien Chih-lin, or Ho Ch'i-fang, not to mention Tsang K'o-chia, Ai Ch'ing, and the other proletarian poets.

6. The thaw includes the establishment of the first opposition party, the Democratic Progressive Party, in 1986, the lift of the ban on visiting mainland China in 1987, the ending of the thirty-eight years of martial law, and many still evolving changes. These changes have led to a rather busy interflow between Taiwan and mainland China in areas of art, literature, and, above all, commerce.

7. Mao's Yenan Talks, which officialize Chü Ch'iu-pai's literature-for-the-masses thesis, is too well known to need elaboration here. All the essays can be easily located in Mao Tse-tung's *On Literature and Art* (Peking: Foreign Languages Press, 1967).

8. See Li Ho-lin, *Chung-Kuo Hsin-Wen-hsueh-shih Yen-chiu* (Peking: Hsin-chien-she, 1951).

9. These views were expressed by the students of the Lu Hsün Literary Society in Peking University. See the reprint edition of Wang's book, *Chung-kuo Hsin-wen hsueh shih-kao* (Hong Kong: Po Wen Bookstore, 1972), which includes thirteen anti-Wang Yao essays.

10. Wang Hsi-yen, *Lun Ah Q ho t'a-ti pei-chu* (Shanghai: Hsin-wen-i, 1957), 216–46.

11. J. Prusek, "Basic Problems of the History of Modern Chinese Literature," and C. T. Hsia, "A History of Modern Chinese Fiction," *T'oung Pao* 49 (1961): 357–404; C. T. Hsia, "On the Scientific Study of Modern Chinese Literature," *T'oung Pao* 50 (1963): 428–73.

12. C. T. Hsia, "On the Scientific Study of Modern Chinese Literature," 429–30.

13. Ibid.

14. See Liang Tsung-tai, "Symbolism," in his *Shih yü Chen* (Poetry and Truth) (Shanghai: Shang-wu, 1935), 75–105. Bashō: "Ancient pond/A frog jumps in/splash of water." Lin: "Sparse/shadows/aslant—/water/limpid and shallow; Dark/scent/floating—/moon/at-dusk."

15. Li Ch'ang-chih, *Yin Chung-kuo ti Wen-i Fu-hsing* (Welcome China's Renaissance) (Chungking: Shang-wu, 1944), 14–21.

16. Ibid., 15–16.

17. I fully understand that, to be fair, the Western literary tradition must also be treated in its multiplicity, in its totality. When I isolate here the rationalist tendency for discussion, I do not mean to see it as the only tendency. We can find many countertrends to the principle of domination in the evolution of the Western literary tradition. I highlight this significant tendency here to call attention to its ironic relationship to the Chinese intellectuals.

18. Max Horkheimer and Theodor W. Adorno, *Dialectic of Enlightenment* (New York: Herder and Herder, 1972), 3, 4, 6, 9, 25, 26.

19. Max Horkheimer, *Eclipse of Reason* (New York: Seabury Press, 1974), 105–7.

EPILOGUE: THE FRAMING OF CRITICAL THEORIES
IN CROSS-CULTURAL CONTEXT

1. Louis Althusser, et al., *Reading Capital*, trans. Ben Brewster (London: New Left Books, 1970), 186–89.

2. Compare, for example, William Brandon's translation of part of the Hako ceremony of the Pawnees in *The Magic World* (New York: Morrow, 1971), 68, to Alice C. Fletcher's full record of the ceremony in *The Hako: A Pawnee Ceremony*, 27th Annual Report of the Bureau of American Ethnology (Washington, D.C.: Smithsonian Institution, 1902), 123 in particular, and to Fletcher's own literary translation (223). Both Fletcher's literary translation and Brandon's substantially reduced version have ignored the oral expressive strategies and have greatly distorted the original aesthetic dimension.

3. Jean Dubuffet, "Anticultural Positions," in Wylie Sypher, *Loss of the Self in Modern Literature and Art* (New York: Vintage Books, 1962), 172–73.

4. Jean Dubuffet, "Empreintes," in *Theories of Modern Art*, ed. Herschel B. Chipp (Berkeley and Los Angeles: University of California Press, 1968), 615.

5. Robert Duncan, "Rites of Participation," in *Caterpillar Anthology*, ed. Clayton Eshleman (New York: Anchor, 1971), 29.

6. See chapter 5.

7. C. H. Wang, "Toward Defining a Chinese Heroism," *Journal of the American Oriental Society* 95 (1975): 25–35.

8. See chapter 2.

9. See chapters 2, 3, and 6.

10. The chart is only a rough working blueprint and should not be taken as final, complete, or clear-cut.

11. Here, I am fully aware of the danger of privileging one area of theoretical projections at the expense of the others. For a good view of other possible convergences, see the Introduction to my *Pi-chiao Shih-hsueh* (Comparative Poetics) (Taipei: Tung-tai, 1983), 12–13. The question of whether and how art can or cannot become nature finds treatment in both Chinese and Western theories, as does the question of the function of literature — to teach, to move, to please, to cleanse, to rectify, to regulate government, to contain the (moral) way, to beautify, to civilize — especially in Horace, Sidney, Shelley, and Arnold in the West and many Confucian-oriented critics in China.

12. See my discussion of James and Whitehead in chapter 3.

13. Aside from chapter 3, see also my essay on Gary Snyder, "Against Domination: Gary Snyder as an Apologist for Nature," in *The Chinese Text*, ed. Ying-hsiung Chou (Hong Kong: The Chinese University Press, 1986), 75–84.

14. In a strict sense, Derrida, who has denounced the signified and indulged in the "clowning" of language, should not be included in this company. His development of themes from Heidegger, however, opens up a counterdiscourse with many echoes of the Taoist and Buddhist projects, hence the phrase "with a twist."

15. See chapters 2 and 3.

16. "Dream-time," a phrase translated from the word *alcheringa*, indicates a realm both outside and inside history, a time linking the legendary, heroic past and the present in a manner that defies conventional categorizations.

17. For T. E. Hulme's project, read the chapter on Hulme in Frank Kermode's *Romantic Image*. Pound's position is clearly stated in his essay "Mediaevalism," and Eliot's in his second essay on Dante.

18. In a sense, Heidegger, rewriting Platonic and Aristotelian terms so as to recover their pre-metaphysical meanings, is very different from Hulme, Pound, and Eliot, whose ideal cultural moments are still invested with layers and layers of institutional codes.

19. William James, *The Will to Believe and Other Essays* (London: Longmans, Green, and Co., 1905), 18–20.

20. The death of the signified was pronounced by Derrida.

21. Almost all the poststructuralists have said a version of this, but I am thinking specifically of Foucault, Said, and Jameson.

22. The translation is mine. This line is from Chapter 32 of Lao-tzu's *Tao-te-ching*.

23. The two long Chinese essays are "The Taoist Theory of Knowledge" and "The Framing of Meaning and Power." Both can be found in my book *History, Hermeneutics, Aesthetics* (Taipei: Tung-tai, 1988). A third related essay, also in the same book, is on the aesthetic-political model of macrocosm-geocosm-microcosm as viewed in seventeenth- and eighteenth-century England: "The Morphology of Aesthetic Consciousness and Perimeter of Meaning in the Example of Pre-Romantic Concept of Nature."

Romanization Conversion Table: Wade-Giles/Pinyin

Ai Ch'ing	Ai Ching
An-hua	Anhua
Ch'an	Chan
Chan Fang-sheng	Zhan Fangsheng
Chang Yen-yüan	Zhang Yanyuan
Chen	Zhen
Chi Chi	Ji Ji
Chi-chu fen-lei Tung-p'o hsien-sheng shi	Jizhu fenlei Dongpo xiansheng shi
Ch'i	Qi
Ch'i-ch'eng-chuan-ho	Qi-cheng-zhuan-he
Chiang Yen	Jiang Yan
Ch'iang-yen	Qiangyan
Chien	Jian
Ch'ien	Qian
Chih Tun	Zhi Dun
Chin	Jin
Ching-chin Tung-p'o Wen-chi shih-lueh	Jingjin Dongpo Wenji shilue
Ching Fang	Jing Fang
Ch'ing-t'an	Chingtan
Ch'u Tz'u	Chu Ci
Ch'ü Yüan	Qu Yuan
Chuang-tzu	Zhuangzi
Chuang-tzu Chi-shih	Zhuangzi Jishi
Chung-kuo hsin-shih-hsuan	Zhongguo Xinshixuan
Chung-kuo hsin-wen-hsueh shih-kao	Zhongguo Xinwenxue shigao
Chung Yung	Zhong Yong
Fan Yun	Fan Yun

Feng-lin	Fenglin
Fu	Fu
Han Shan	Han Shan
Han-hsu	Hanxu
Ho Ch'i-fang	He Qifang
Hu-jih	Huri
Hu Shih	Hu Shi
Hu-t'i yao-pien	Huti yaobian
Huan-chung	Huanzhong
Huang Shih-lin	Huang Shilin
Hun	Hun
Hsi-tz'u	Xici
Hsi-wu	Xiwu
Hsiang-wai	Xiangwai
Hsiao Shen	Xiao Shen
Hsieh	Xie
Hsieh Ling-yun	Xie Lingyun
Hsieh T'iao	Xie Tiao
Hsin	Xin
Hsin-min-chu	Xinminzhu
Hsin-min t'ung-pao	Xinmin tongbao
Hsiung-hun	Xionghun
Hsü	Xu
Hsü Chih-mo	Xu Zhimo
Hsü Kan	Xu Gan
I Ching	Yi Jing
Jen-chien tz'u-hua	Renjian Cihua
K'an	Kan
K'ang Yu-wei	Kang Youwei
Kao Huai-min	Gao Huaimin
Ken	Gen
Kou	Gou
Ku-shih-pien	Gushibian
Kuei Mei	Gui Mei
Kua	Gua
Kuan	Guan
K'un	Kun
K'ung	Kong
Kung-an	Gongan
K'ung Chih-kuei	Kong Zhigui
Kung-yun	Gongyun
Kuo Ch'ing-fan	Guo Qingfan
Kuo Hsi	Guo Xi
Kuo Hsiang	Guo Xiang
Kuo Shao-yu	Guo Shaoyu

Kuo-yü	Guoyu
Lao She	Lao She
Lao-tzu	Laozi
Lei-shu	Leishu
Li	Li
Li Ch'ang-chih	Li Changzhi
Li Ho-lin	Li Helin
Li Ling	Li Ling
Li Po	Li Bo (Bai)
Li-Sao	Lisao
Li Shang-yin	Li Shangyin
Li-shih Ch'uan-shih Mei-hsueh	Lishi Chuanshi Meixue
Li-tai ming-hua-chi	Lidai minghuaji
Lin	Lin
Lin P'u	Lin Pu
Liang Ch'i-ch'ao	Liang Qichao
Liang-han I-hsueh-shih	Lianghan Yixueshi
Liang Tsung-tai	Liang Zongdai
Liang Wu-ti	Liang Wudi
Liu Hsieh	Liu Xie
Liu-shih-nien shih-ko-hsuan	Liushinian shigexuan
Liu Shuo	Liu Shuo
Liu Tsung-yüan	Liu Zongyuan
Lou-hsueh	Louxue
Lou-yün	Louyun
Lu Chi	Lu Ji
Lu Hsün	Lu Xun
Lu-shih	Lushi
Lu Shih-heng wen-chi	Lu Shiheng Wenji
Lun A Q ho t'a-ti pei-chu	Lun A Q he tadi beiju
Ma Chih-yüan	Ma Zhiyuan
Mao Tse-tung	Mao Zedong
Meng	Meng
Meng Hao-jan	Meng Haoran
Ming I	Ming Yi
Nan Kuo Tzu Ch'i	Nan Guo Ziqi
Ni Tsan	Ni Zan
P'ang-t'ung	Pangtong
Pao Chao	Bao Zhao
Pi	Bi
P'i	Pi
Pien Chih-lin	Bian Zhilin
P'u	Pu
Shao Yung	Shao Yong
Shen	Shen

Shen Yo	Shen Yue
Sheng	Sheng
Shih Ching	Shi Jing
Shih-hua	Shihua
Shih-p'in chi-chieh	Shipin Jijie
Shih yu Chen	Shi yu Zhen
Ssu-k'ung T'u	Sikong Tu
Ssu-hsiang	Sixiang
Ssu-ma Piao	Sima Biao
Su p'u	Su pu
Su Tung-p'o	Su Dongpo
Sui-t'u pu-fu	Suitu bufu
Sun	Sun
Sun Cho	Sun Zhuo
Sung	Song
Sung-feng	Songfeng
Ta-chih	Dazhi
Ta Ch'u	Dachu
Ta Chuang	Da Zhuang
Ta Yu	Da You
T'ai	Tai
T'ai Chi	Tai Ji
Tai Chun-jen	Dai Zhunran
Tai Jung-chou	Dai Rongzhou
T'an I	Tan Yi
Tao	Dao
T'ao Ch'ien	Tao Qian
Taoist	Daoist
Tao-te-ching	Daodejing
T'ien	Tian
T'ien-wen	Tianwen
Ting I	Ding Yi
Ts'ai I	Cai Yi
Ts'ai Yüan-p'ei	Cai Yuanpei
Tsang K'o-chia	Zang Kejia
Ts'ang-lang shih-hua chiao-shih	Canglang shihua jiaoshi
Ts'ao Chih	Cao Zhi
Ts'ao Yü	Cao Yu
Tseng Chi-tse	Zeng Jize
Tso-chuan	Zuozhuan
Ts'ui	Cui
Tu Fu	Du Fu
Tu-hua	Duhua
Tu Shen-yen	Du Shenyan

Tui	Dui
Tun	Dun
Tung Chung-shu	Dong Zhongshu
Tzu-jan	Ziran
Wang Chi	Wang Ji
Wang Chih-chien	Wang Zhijian
Wang Hsi-chih	Wang Xizhi
Wang Hsi-yen	Wang Xiyan
Wang Kuo-wei	Wang Guowei
Wang Pi	Wang Bi
Wang Wei	Wang Wei
Wang Yao	Wang Yao
Wei Chi	Wei Ji
Wei Ying-wu	Wei Yingwu
Wen	Wen
Wen-fu	Wenfu
Wen-hsin tiao-lung	Wenxin Diaolong
Wen I-to	Wen Yiduo
Wu	Wu
Wu-chih	Wuzhi
Wu-hsin	Wuxin
Wu-wei	Wuwei
Wu Wang	Wu Wang
Wu-wo	Wuwo
Wu-yen	Wuyan
Wu-yen-tu-hua	Wuyanduhua
Wu-yü	Wuyu
Wu-yü-chieh	Wuyujie
Wu Yün	Wu Yun
Yang T'ing-tzu	Yang Tingzi
Yeh Shao-chun	Ye Shaojun
Yen Ch'eng Tzu-yu	Yancheng Ziyou
Yen Yü	Yan Yu
Yin-chih t'ai-ho	Yinzhi taihe
Yin Chung-kuo ti wen-i fu-hsing	Yin Zhongguodi wenyi fuxing
Yin Chung-wen	Yin Zhongwen
Ying Yang	Ying Yang
Yü Chien-hua	Yu Jianhua
Yü Fan	Yu Fan
Yü Hsin	Yu Xin
Yüeh-fu	Yuefu
Yün-men Wen-yen	Yunmen Wenyan

Index

Compositor: Birdtrack Press
Text: Zapf Calligraphic
Display: Zapf Calligraphic
Printer: Edwards Brothers, Inc.
Binder: Edwards Brothers, Inc.